# The Chicanos
*A History of Mexican Americans*

# The Chicanos

## A History of Mexican Americans

### MATT S. MEIER AND FELICIANO RIVERA

*American Century Series*

**HILL AND WANG**  New York
*A division of Farrar, Straus and Giroux*

*handwritten: Nov 11-20-72*

# CONTENTS

## List of Maps

# Glossary

alambrista   From *alambre*, "wire"; a person who crosses the
         border illegally by (figuratively) climbing a fence
aliancista   A member of the Alianza Federal de Mercedes,
         Reies Tijerina's organization
Anglo   Short for Anglo-American; in the Southwest sometimes
         designating all non-Mexican-descent Americans
arriero   Mexican mule driver
AWOC   Agricultural Workers Organizing Committee, an AFL-
         CIO union
Aztlán   Mythical homeland of the Aztec or Mexica Indians

barrio   District; in the United States, Mexican American quarter of town

¡Basta ya!   Enough!

bracero   From *brazo,* "arm"; a worker, a hired hand, especially a Mexican brought to the United States under labor contract

cabildo   Town council in Spanish colonies

californio   Original Hispanic-Mexican inhabitant of California, or his descendant

caudillo   Strong man; leader, often military

CAWIU   Cannery and Agricultural Workers Industrial Union, Communist-affiliated

Chicano   Truncated form of *Mexicano,* today with overtones of ethnic nationalism and activism

cholo   Pejorative term in California for Mexican immigrant

los científicos   Mexican followers of the positivist philosophy of Auguste Comte; supporters of Porfirio Díaz

Cinco de Mayo   Commemoration of Mexican defeat of the French at Puebla, Mexico, on May 5, 1862

colonia   Small settlement, sometimes part of a town, inhabited by Mexicans

conquistador(es)   Early Spanish conquerors of the New World

contratista   Labor contractor, usually for agricultural work

criollo   Colonial term referring to American-born person of "pure" Spanish parentage

CROM   Confederación Regional Obrera Mexicana, a leading Mexican labor union

CSO   Community Service Organization, founded in latter 1940s

CUCOM   Confederación de Uniones de Campesinos y Obreros Mexicanos

CUOM   Confederación de Uniones Obreras Mexicanas

dorado   Literally "gilded"; refers to Pancho Villa's elite troops, because of their highly decorated uniforms empresario   Land-grantee who was required to bring in a specified number of settlers in order to validate his grant

enganchista   Literally a recruiter; one who recruits farm labor

gabacho   Pejorative term for whites; originally meant French (therefore foreign)

gachupín(es)   Colonial term of derogation used to identify Spaniards

gente de razón   Literally "people of reason"; colonial term referring to members of the upper classes

gringo   Pejorative term for whites; originally from *griego* "Greek" (therefore foreign)

Grito de Dolores   Famous cry of Father Miguel Hidalgo which initiated the Mexican revolution of 1810

hidalgo   A nobleman

Hispano   New Mexican of Hispanic-Mexican origins

LULAC   League of United Latin American Citizens, founded in 1929

machismo   Term used to connote virile manliness; from *macho,* "male"

maderista   Follower or supporter of Francisco Madero during 1910 Mexican revolution

Mande vd., señor   Literally, "Command [me], sir." Often used by Mexicans as a polite response of recognition when spoken to. "At your service."

manito   Truncated form of *hermanito,* "little brother"; slightly pejorative term for Spanish-speaking New Mexican

MAPA   In California, Mexican American Political Association; in Texas, Mexican Americans for Political Action; both organizations formed in the 1960s

mapista   A member or supporter of MAPA

MASA   Mexican American Student Association

MASC   Mexican American Student Confederation

MAYO   Mexican American Youth Organization

MECHA   Movimiento Estudiantil Chicano de Aztlán

mediero   Sharecropper on northern frontier of colonial Mexico

mestizaje   Process of physical blending of Indian and European

mestizo   Literally "mixed"; a person of European and Indian ancestry

mexicano   Usually a person from Mexico; also a person of Mexican descent in the United States Southwest

mojado   Literally "wet"; one who enters the United States illegally, theoretically by swimming the Rio Grande River

mulato   A person of European and African ancestry

NFWA   National Farm Workers Association, founded by César Chávez

Los Niños Héröes   Mexican cadets who resisted American troops at Chapultepec in 1847

nuevo mexicano   Hispanic-Mexican inhabitant of area of New Mexico

pachuquismo   Pejorative term for a "hip" life style within the barrio, usually followed by the young

partido   "Sharecrop" system used in sheep culture on the Mexican frontier

PASO (PASSO)   Political Association of Spanish-Speaking Organizations

patrón   Boss, patron; usually a large landowner

penitente   Member of a fanatical Catholic religious group in New Mexico

peón(es)   Worker, usually tied to the land

pinto   Barrio term for a prison inmate

presidio   Military fort

pueblo   Township, village

ranchero   Owner of a ranch; or related to ranching

rancho   A rural property, often one on which cattle are raised

la raza   Ethnic term for Spanish-speaking people, connoting
a spirit of belonging and a sense of common destiny

La Raza Unida   Political party founded in Texas in 1970

rebozo   A long shawl or muffler worn (usually) by women

rico   Literally a rich person; used in the Southwest to denote
a member of the upper class

santero   Carver of wooden statues of saints

sinarquismo   A right-wing radical political philosophy originating in Mexico with the Unión Nacional Sinarquista

solar(es)   Lot for town house; also town house

surumato   Pejorative term, especially used in New Mexico, for
Mexican; origin uncertain

teatro   Theatre

tejano   Hispanic-Mexican inhabitant of Texas area

tertulia   A social gathering for conversation or entertainment

tio taco   Chicano pejorative version of "Uncle Tom"

TUUL   Trade Union Unity League, Communist-affiliated labor
organization

UFWOC   United Farm Workers Organizing Committee, formed
by merging NFWA and AWOC

UMAS   United Mexican American Students

vaquero   Mexican cowboy

vendido   "Sell-out," one who betrays la raza.

zoot-suiter   Term used by Anglos to describe a person characterized by a certain style of dress and life common in
the 1940s

# Introduction

The first task of a history of the Mexican American is the identification of the leading character—the Mexican American.
This is no easy assignment. The 1930 United States census
listed as Mexican all persons born in Mexico or of parents born
there who were neither Caucasian, Negro, Indian, Chinese, nor
Japanese. The 1940 census substituted "Spanish-speaking" for
"born in Mexico." In the next two censuses the identification
was by Spanish surname rather than language of childhood.
Although none of these techniques of identification is satis-
factory, they do tell us that there are today perhaps seven mil-

lion persons of Mexican ancestry in the United States. More than four million of these are concentrated in the Southwest.

There is no single name for these seven million Americans of Mexican descent. In California they often are referred to as Mexican Americans or "mexicanos," whereas in Texas the common designation is Latin American or "tejano." In New Mexico the descendants of colonists who arrived in the 1600s and 1700s prefer to call themselves "nuevo mexicanos" or "Hispanos." Today many of the younger members of the group, and especially activists, insist on the name "Chicano." The term Chicano, a form of "mexicano" truncated by dropping the first syllable, had a somewhat pejorative connotation in the first half of this century, but it has been taken by many young Americans of Mexican descent as a badge of pride since World War II.

Nearly all Mexican Americans agree that they belong to "la raza," a term connoting not racial but ethnic solidarity, and a sense of common destiny. Unfortunately, this term does not provide a convenient adjective to identify members of the group. Clearly Mexican American is the identification most widely used and accepted today. Used historically, this is the designation that will predominate in this book. But where appropriate and suitable, other terms are also used.

The history of the Mexican American can be conveniently divided into five broad time periods: the Indo-Hispanic period, the Mexican period, a period of cultural conflict during the last half of the nineteenth century, a period of resurgence in the first four decades of the twentieth century, and a period of regeneration from World War II to the present.

The first period covers the development of Indian civilizations in Mexico, their defeat by Spanish conquistadores, the beginnings of *mestizaje,* the blending of Indian and Spanish cultures, colonization of the present-day Southwest of the United States from central Mexico, and finally, the movement of independence from Spain at the beginning of the nineteenth century.

The "grito de Dolores" marks the beginning of the Mexican period in 1810, and political events bring into focus the gulf that existed between the Mexican heartland and the northern frontier. By this time cultures differing in degree from each other but basically related to the mother culture had developed, and continuing isolation led to mounting political differences and unrest. This period culminated in war with the United States, ending with the Treaty of Guadalupe Hidalgo and the loss by Mexico of half her original territory to her expansionist Anglo neighbor to the north.

From 1848 to the end of the nineteenth century, the third time period is characterized by: the effects of Anglo-American migration to the Southwest; investment of capital in mines, railroads, cattle, and agriculture; and the relegation of *la raza* to a minority position of second-class citizenship in what had been its own land.

A rising rate of migration from Mexico introduces the fourth period. As the volcano of revolution in Mexico spewed out its political and social refugees, this migratory movement impelled Mexican Americans to move out of their homeland not only into their traditional places of settlement in the Southwest but also into the agricultural and industrial centers of the Midwest and North. This period also witnessed development of Mexican American organizational efforts and a reversed migratory trend of forced repatriation during the depressed thirties.

World War II begins the contemporary period, marked by continuing migration to the United States; a revival of self-awareness and recognition of the cultural values of the Mexican heritage, especially among Chicano youths; some improvement in the social conditions of la raza; and forceful movements for a greater share in the American way of life through an insistence on education, full civil rights, and equality of economic opportunity.

Today Mexican Americans constitute the second largest and most rapidly growing minority in the United States. Unique in United States history in that they are deeply rooted in a particular section of the country, they constitute the largest minority in the Southwest, that is, the five states of California, Arizona, Colorado, New Mexico, and Texas. They differ most significantly from other immigrant minorities in their proximity to their cultural homeland. They form an ethnic or cultural minority having a high degree of racial, religious, and linguistic visibility in society. The Mexican American is the product of the fusing of Hispanic and Mexican Indian cultures; to a greater or lesser degree he is racially a mixture of Indian and European. Nominally at least, he is Catholic in religion, and to a large degree he has retained his native language, Spanish.

Historically there have been two Anglo-American views of the Mexican American, both inaccurate. One ignored his Indian background and in a romantic fashion viewed him as a Spanish hidalgo, the descendant of the great conquistadores. The other concept was more widespread and sprang from the American frontier experience. This second Anglo-American view ignored the Spanish heritage and saw the Mexican as Indian—therefore characterized as lazy, dirty, and given to drinking and thievery. The Mexican American is often inaccurately stereotyped as an agricultural worker who lives in a rural area or a small town. Although it is true that Mexican Americans form an important part of the farm labor force in the Southwest, today the overwhelming majority is urban.

Another important characteristic of the Mexican American minority is that members are far from forming a homogeneous group. There are, of course, class differences arising out of the occupations Mexican Americans pursue: farming, ranching, business, education, law, medicine, and politics. There are also differences in the varying degree of Caucasian and Indian ancestry, as well as of acculturation and integration into the predominant society. Lastly there are differences that arise out of historical experience.

The historical past of Mexican Americans has created not one, but at least three subcultures: those of the californio, tejano, and nuevo mexicano. These three groups have been affected differently by their economic and social backgrounds in Mexico, their dates of settlement in the Southwest, the geography and natural resources of the settlement area, their degree of interaction with local Indians, and the volume of recent immigration from Mexico. In California alone, there are today at least six distinguishable groups: descendants of early californio families, descendants of emigrés during World War I and the 1920s, *braceros* who came during World War II, descendants of nuevo mexicanos (who consider themselves more Spanish then Mexican), descendants of tejanos who have migrated to the state, and those persons of Mexican descent whose assimilation into the general California community has been so pronounced that they have lost all sense of being part of la raza.

Despite these diversities, Mexican Americans have a basic cultural unity. There has been considerable retention of ethnic traits and customs. Some of these are the Spanish language, pride in their cultural and historical heritage, and retention of and preference for native arts, crafts, and foods. Since World War II, the expansion of Spanish-language radio and television programs has reinforced these cultural elements. The forming of a wide variety of political organizations and ethnic publications has also brought greater unity to the Chicano community in recent years.

In general, the Mexican American community stresses different values from those emphasized in Anglo-American society. The life style of Mexican Americans emphasizes such values as kinship ties and a strong loyalty to the family, individual worth based on honor, respect, and *machismo* (virile manliness). Moreover, Mexican Americans consider that an individual's worth derives more importantly from his being rather than from his achievements.

# The Chicanos

*A History of Mexican Americans*

# one

# The Meeting of Two Worlds

Mexican American history begins with the early story of man in the western hemisphere. Although our knowledge of early human life in the Americas is limited, the evidence of recent research indicates it goes back as much as 50,000 years.

There are various theories about the origin of man in the new world, including a theory that man's original home was in the western hemisphere and that he spread from there to Europe, Asia, and Africa. The prevailing belief of anthropologists and archeologists today, however, is that early American man came from northern Asia. This does not preclude occasional and accidental additions from Europe, Africa, and the South Pacific at various periods of his development. However, most early migrants undoubtedly came by way of the Bering Strait, beginning perhaps 50,000 years ago and continuing over a period of more than 40,000 years.

In various waves these early people slowly spread south along the western and eastern edges of the Rocky Mountains, crossed over the Central American isthmus, and followed the spine of the Andes to the tip of South America. They reached Tierra del Fuego as early as 7,000 B.C., as indicated by archeological finds there. There were, of course, numerous secondary paths of migration from the Rocky Mountains and the Andes into the St. Lawrence River area, the Mississippi Valley, the Caribbean islands, the Amazon basin, and southeastern South America.

At the time of European discovery, there were perhaps twenty-five million Indians in the hemisphere. These people varied greatly in their cultural levels; some were nomadic wanderers, while others, having developed intensive agriculture, had settled and reached high levels of civilization. The influence of this latter group led to the development of a vast arc extending from the Mississippi Valley southward to Chile based on the cultivation of corn. Within this arc developed the three highest civilizations: Maya, Aztec, and Inca.

The regional culture that evolved in the area that is now the southwestern part of the United States was part of this maize arc and had close links with the more advanced peoples of Mexico. Thousands of years before Christ, Indians of the southwest learned corn culture from early civilizations of central Mexico, and later they adopted beans, squash, and other important crops from the same source. About the time of Christ the Hohokam Indians introduced into the area of present-day Arizona irrigation and other cultural innovations from Mexico. The Hohokam culture center at what is now Snaketown, Arizona, became the hub from which their influence spread. Through trading activities their cultural patterns were extended as far west as the California coast. By the time of the arrival of Spanish explorers in the fifteenth century, however, this civilization had disappeared, possibly because of ecological factors, especially soil exhaustion.

About A.D. 500 a new civilization, known as the Pueblo, emerged. This culture, with its highest development in the four-corner area of what are now New Mexico, Arizona, Colorado, and Utah, received strong Mexican influences in cloth-making, pottery, architecture, and government. The Pueblo Indians reached their highest level of development in the period beginning about A.D. 1000. Unlike the Hohokam, large numbers of Pueblo Indians were still living in the Southwest in well-organized societies when the Spaniards arrived.

Far to the east, the mound builders of the Ohio and Mississippi basins also evidently received Mexican influence in their construction of serpent mounds and small pyramid-based temples as well as in pottery-making, agriculture, and other cultural elements. Clearly there was considerable early contact between the area of the southern United States and Mexico.

Relatively little is known about the ancient history of Mexico. Of thousands of archeological sites, only a few have been investigated and only a handful exposed to intensive study. Long before Christ, man began to develop in Mexico a culture of considerable complexity called the Olmec. In Yucatan and Guatemala, the Mayan civilization emerged from this ancient culture, and farther to the north there developed the civilization of the Zapotecs. In the great central plateau rose up the civilizations of the Teotihuacanos, the Toltecs, and the Aztecs. The last, the Aztecs, were also known as the Mexicas, and from this term came the name that eventually was applied to the country and people south of the United States.

Of all these peoples the Mayas were unquestionably the ones who reached the highest level of development. Sometime between 1500 and 1000 B.C., groups from the Olmec culture in the Veracruz-Campeche region migrated southward to modern Guatemala. There, in a relatively hostile tropical environment, they first undertook the formative stage of Mayan civilization around centers like Uaxactún, Palenque, Bonampak, Copán, and Tikal. From about A.D. 200 to about A.D. 1000 there developed in this area what is known as the Classic Period, or the Old Empire, with its main centers in Guatemala and with some late expansion into the Yucatan peninsula.

The Mayas reached levels of civilization not attained by any other aboriginal group. In this early period they developed more than twenty-five religious centers, each the nucleus of an organized city-state. Their cities, linked by an excellent road system, were centers of government, trade, religion, and learning. However, there seems to have been little political relationship between Mayan cities of the Classic Period. Government was based on the clan and tribe; rulers were hereditary and closely allied with the priesthood. Mayan religion was polytheistic and played an important role in daily life. The priestly class had great power, which was perpetuated in part through its control of education. Priests were at the top of a stratified social structure that included nobles, feudal lords, warriors, free men, and slaves.

The culture of the Mayas was shaped by its agricultural base, the cultivation of corn. To a degree, life was communal and cooperative, with the season determining its rhythm as crops were raised in a simple slash-and-burn technique. The principal crops were beans, peppers, tomatoes, squash, cacao, and, of course, corn. Surplus production of corn enabled the Mayas to channel part of their energies into building their great cities and into developing astronomy, mathematics, and other sciences. A thousand years before Europe adopted the Gregorian calendar, the Mayas were using a more precise calendrical system; and their use of the zero also antedated its use in the Old World by a thousand years. This amazing development is recorded in beautiful temples and palaces, with their delicate sculptured hieroglyphic accounts of a great civilization.

This brilliant Mayan civilization reached its height around A.D. 700. Then gradually, over a period of more than a hundred years, the great cities declined, decayed, and finally were abandoned. Why, we do not know. Possibly the causes were ecological—perhaps the complete exhaustion of the cornfields. By the beginning of the eleventh century A.D. the Yucatecan cities, which had been on the fringes of the Mayan region, had become the new centers. At the same time a group of Nahua peoples from the north, the Toltecs, began penetrating the region with their culture and religion. To a considerable degree the Mayas came under the cultural influence of these aggressive invaders, while at the same time the Toltecs borrowed heavily from Mayan accomplishments. This new Mayan era was characterized by an emphasis on militarism and human sacrifice; but at the same time the mild Toltec deity, Quetzalcoatl, the feathered serpent, was accepted as a Mayan god under the name Kulkulcan.

The infusion of Nahua culture resulted in a renaissance of the Mayas in the Yucatan peninsula known as the Late Classic Period, or the New Empire. The first two hundred years of this period were notable for the triple alliance of the leading city-states of Chichén Itzá, Uxmal, and Mayapán, dominated by the first. About the year 1200 this alliance was broken up by the Cocom Mayas of Mayapán, who dominated Yucatan until the mid-fifteenth century. In about 1450 the Yucatan cities overthrew the Mayapán leaders and then fell to warring

among themselves. In the process Mayan civilization disinte-
grated, as roads deteriorated and the great temple complexes
began to succumb to the growth of the jungle. By the time
the Spaniards arrived, there were only vestiges of former
greatness.

To the north, in the high plateau region of central Mexico
a group of Nahua-speaking Indians called the Toltecs separated themselves from their Chichimec clansmen in about the
sixth century A.D. and moved toward higher levels of civilization. Just north of present-day Mexico City they built a
number of cultural centers, especially Tula. In this area they
developed in ensuing centuries a civilization noted for its architecture, stone carving, and metalwork. In religion they became widely known for their worship of the benign plumed
serpent god, Quetzalcoatl. At the height of their power in the
eleventh and twelfth centuries their hegemony extended to
Yucatan and Guatemala in the south. However, in the thir-
teenth century Toltec authority began to decline. At the same
time it was subjected to attacks from more aggressive Nahua
cousins emerging from Chichimeca, especially the Aztecs, also
known as the Mexicas, from which the words Mexico and
Mexican derive.

Coming from a mythical home called Aztlán, the Aztecs
settled near Tula, and when that center fell to advancing
Nahua groups, they moved south into the Valley of Mexico.
In the mid-fourteenth century they reached Lake Texcoco and
settled on an island which became the base of their future
capital, Tenochtitlán (Mexico City today). At first vassals of
one of the local tribes, by 1432 they had advanced to an alliance with the neighboring cities of Texcoco and Tlacopán, and
by the end of the fifteenth century Tenochtitlán had become
the dominant city in central Mexico. In the meantime, the
Aztecs had extended their control south into Oaxaca and

Tehuantepec, east to Veracruz, and west to Guerrero and Nayarit. In 1502 Emperor Montezuma II came to the leadership of the Aztec empire with the immense task of holding together his restless vassals and collecting from them the tribute due to Tenochtitlán. His greatest problem, however, was to arise with the coming of the Spaniards in the early sixteenth century.

From a weak tribal organization the Aztecs gradually developed into a military-oriented state. Like the Mayas, the Aztecs had a highly organized class system. At its head was the emperor; beneath him in this well-defined caste system were priests and other nobles, merchants, free peasants, and slaves. Aztec society was based on corn and other crops common to Middle America, especially cotton, tobacco, beans, squashes, and maguey. Every town had at least one market, and the markets of Tenochtitlán was so extensive and had such a variety of produce for sale as to amaze the Spaniards when they entered the city in 1519. Trade was even more important than among the Mayas; an extensive barter of cotton cloth, featherwork, cacao, jewelry, pottery, and slaves developed. Aztec culture and influence were spread almost as much by trade as by war.

Aztec religion was polytheistic and bloody. One of the principal gods was Huitzilopochtli, who, according to their mythology, had led them from Aztlán to Tenochtitlán. Huitzilopochtli and other deities required a steady stream of sacrificial victims for their temples, which were usually located on top of large, flat-topped pyramids. On special occasions the number of victims reached as many as twenty thousand. This constant human sacrifice was required to postpone the awful day in Aztec theology when the sun would crash and doomsday would envelop the world. By today's standards Aztec religion was fierce and violent.

Aztec culture is considered to be of a somewhat lower order than that of the Mayas. In general it was based on the cultures of the Toltecs, Mixtecs, Zapotecs, and other predecessors and contemporaries. Although they made few cultural contributions of their own, the Aztecs were highly successful in synthesizing elements from the many peoples they conquered. Their special strengths lay in the development of the social, political, and military organization required to administer their large empire of nine million people, living between present-day Guatemala and north central Mexico. They built great cities that were probably the largest cities in the world of their day, with more than a hundred thousand inhabitants each. By the end of the fifteenth century A.D., the Nahua language of these people had become more or less the lingua franca in a wide area that extended southward to Guatemala and eastward and westward to the Gulf and Pacific coasts.

In 1519, the Spanish conquistador Hernán Cortés and about 550 men landed on the Gulf coast of Mexico near present-day Veracruz, and in two and a half years had imposed their rule on the Aztec empire. Fearful of the bearded strangers, Montezuma initially tried to drive them away, first offering rich gifts of gold and silver, then laying ambushes. From their Veracruz base the Spaniards advanced steadily toward Tenochtitlán, alternately negotiating and fighting. Outside the Aztec capital they were met by the emperor and his imposing entourage. Cortés and his men were then invited into Tenochtitlán, the city which was for them both a scene of enchantment and a potential trap.

Completely at the mercy of the thousands of Aztec warriors who surrounded his few hundred men, Cortés seized Montezuma and began ruling the Aztec empire through him, collecting a vast store of gold, silver, and jewels. In the spring of 1520, the threat of a Spanish expedition sent by the governor of Cuba to arrest Cortés for insubordination caused the latter to hurry down to the coast, where he easily seized control of the new force. Returning to Tenochtitlán and finding that his men had aroused the Aztecs to overt defiance by killing a large number of nobles, he decided that it was necessary to withdraw from the city. On the night of June 30, 1520, known as "la noche triste," the Spaniards began their retreat, which quickly became a disaster in which Cortés lost half his force.

But this setback was only temporary. Cortés retreated to Tlaxcala, the home of an independent Nahua tribe living east of Tenochtitlán, and began to build a fleet of ships with which to conquer Tenochtitlán. Leading his small army and his Indian allies into the city in May 1521, Cortés destroyed much of Tenochtitlán in the process of conquering it. The success of Cortés and his men in Mexico was made possible by various advantages possessed by the Spaniards; these included firearms, mastiffs, horses, and a large number of Indian allies, especially the Tlaxcalans.

The rest of Mexico was conquered only gradually. The Spaniards found the Mayas in Yucatan extremely difficult to subdue, and never completely conquered them. Similarly, they made no serious attempt to defeat the Chichimecs to the north. And yet, eventually they took control of all Mexico, Central America, and the southwestern part of the United States.

Wherever they conquered, the Spaniards imposed the Catholic religion and a veneer of European culture on existing societies. Nevertheless, the Indians retained much of their culture and their cultural identity. The conquest by Spain did not eliminate the vitality and creativity of the indigenous Mexicans, as indicated by their important contribution to the immense task of rebuilding destroyed areas and constructing new buildings and towns. This work was carried out primarily by Indian artisans and craftsmen. Evidence of their redirected creativity is still apparent in the older churches of Mexico, especially in ornamentation. Under the supervision of *padres* who followed European architectural models, Indians performed the delicate and artistic work.

Although the Spaniards introduced great changes in religion, government, and technology, they found many elements of the existing Mexican society were well-founded, and they readily adopted those that were compatible with their own. The day-to-day culture of the great mass of the people continued virtually unchanged from the pre-Hispanic times. Moreover, since relatively few Spanish women came to Mexico, from the very beginning of the conquest there was a physical and cultural blending. Spaniards of widely diverse peninsular backgrounds combined with Indians of varying cultures to produce a new culture. This fusion of Indian and Spanish blood produced a new man, the mestizo. In Mexico today, the most important aspect of society is the result of this "mestizaje" process.

The northward expansion of the Spaniards in the latter two-thirds of the sixteenth century furnishes another example of the vitality of the Mexican people. Conquest of the north was carried out with the help of Nahua-speaking Indians, particularly the Tlaxcalans. Indeed, some historians have called this movement the last great Nahuan territorial expansion. Indians and mestizos of the central Mexican plateau accompanied the Spaniards as soldiers and settlers, extending Nahuan culture as far north as present-day New Mexico. A prime example of this pattern is Saltillo in northeastern Mexico, which was established in 1575 with a nucleus of Tlaxcalans. Spaniards used the same pattern of settlement in their colonization efforts throughout the northern frontier, and as a result mestizos and Indians were important in the transformation of this region in the roles of farmers, miners, herdsmen, craftsmen, and servants.

A few held more exalted positions. The wife of the first governor of the province of Nuevo México, Juan de Oñate, was a great-granddaughter of the Aztec emperor Montezuma.

A quick and partial survey of the northern expansion in the sixteenth century will give some idea of the extent and volume of Spanish and Mexican activity in the area. In 1528 Pánfilo de Narváez came from Spain to explore and conquer Florida with an expedition that ended in disaster. Alvar Núñez Cabeza de Vaca, one of a handful of survivors of this ill-fated group, wandered for eight years over much of the southwestern United States and northern Mexico before reaching central Mexico. His reports, which mentioned the fabulous Seven Cities of Gold (Cíbola), inspired other Spanish adventurers to advance into the area. Fray Marcos de Niza in 1539, Francisco Vásquez de Coronado in 1540, and Hernando de Soto in 1541 all explored the southwest, but all failed to find Cíbola or gold. The subsequent discovery of rich silver mines in Michoacán, Zacatecas, San Luis Potosí, and Guanajuato, much closer to Mexico City, diverted Spanish attention from the southwest for the next half century.

After that hiatus, it was not silver but international rivalry that gave the impulse for the permanent settlement of the regions to the north of Mexico. In the late 1570s, Francis Drake, the famed English privateer, sailed through the Strait of Magellan, up the west coast of South and North America, across the Pacific, and on around the world. The Spaniards believed that, instead of circling the globe, Drake had found the long-sought Northwest Passage, or Strait of Anián, thought to lie somewhere north of Mexico. They decided to protect Spanish territorial interests in the strait by settling the region. As a result, Juan de Oñate led a large expedition there in 1598 and founded San Gabriel de los Españoles, today called Chamita, nine years before the English settled Jamestown. In

1609 his successor established Santa Fe de San Francisco about thirty miles to the south as a better center for Spanish activities in Nuevo Mexico—an area much larger than the present-day state of New Mexico, encompassing what are now parts of Arizona, Colorado, Texas, Nebraska, and Oklahoma. From this latter settlement there was a gradual expansion into the Rio Arriba region to the north and the Rio Abajo to the south.

Since Drake had not discovered the Northwest Passage, there was no compelling political need to settle Nuevo México. Mining was the only likely economic basis for developing so isolated a region; however, the small amount of mineral wealth discovered failed to provide sufficient attraction for either the Spanish government or a large number of settlers. A second basis for settlement of the region was Christianization of the Pueblo Indians, and this became an important reason for the colonization of the region.

After a century of settlement, twenty-five missions had been established with some 60,000 to 90,000 Indians of the area congregated in about ninety villages. Santa Fe, the capital of this northern region, had a population of about 1,000, three-fourths of whom were mestizos. Another 1,500 lived in scattered settlements nearby. In addition, a few settlements sprang up between Nuevo México and the mining area of northern Mexico, chiefly at strategic communication points along the upper Rio Grande. One of these settlements, established about 1680, was named Nuestra Señora del Pilar del Paso del Río del Norte. Today it is known as Ciudad Juárez, located across the river from El Paso, Texas.

In 1680 colonization efforts in the northern region suffered a severe setback. After a century of Christianization the Pueblo Indians, resentful of exploitation and dubious about the benefits of civilization, rose up in revolt under the leadership of Popé, a famous medicine man. After carefully plotting the

Sonoma

San José

Monterey

M

QUIVIRA

Missouri R.

Arkansas R.

OLD SPANISH TRAIL

Colorado R.

SANTA FE TRAIL

Santa Barbara

E

CÍBOLA

Taos

Santa Fe

Los Angeles

San Diego

Socorro

Albuquerque

Red R.

Gila R.

Tucson

PIMERÍA
ALTA

Pecos R.

Brazos R.

Sabine R.

Nacogdoches

TEXAS

BAJA CALIFORNIA

El Paso

San Antonio

Bahía

Chihuahua

Nueces R.

Rio Grande

PACIFIC

OCEAN

I

Monterrey

GULF

Torreón

Saltillo

OF

Culiacán

MEXICO

Zacatecas

San Luis
Potosí

Guanajuato

Veracruz

Mexico City

**COLONIAL NEW SPAIN**

0    Scale of Miles    500

slaughter of their oppressors, Popé and his followers in early August of 1680 launched an attack on all Spanish settlements in the region, massacring men, women and children. Only Santa Fe was able to withstand the ferocity of the initial attack. Soon, however, the Spaniards were forced to abandon all of northern Nuevo México and to retreat down the Rio Grande to the El Paso region.

In the ensuing decade several efforts were made to reconquer the area of the upper Rio Grande in order that the old settlements might be rebuilt. Finally, in 1692, the newly appointed governor, Diego de Vargas, was successful in retaking Santa Fe. Popé having died in 1690, the Indian pueblos soon began to submit to Spanish authority. Nevertheless, Spanish control of the pueblos was reëstablished only after Vargas and his soldiers had bested the Indians in a number of encounters during the decade of the nineties. In addition to reëstablishing their former settlements, the Spaniards founded Albuquerque in 1706. However, continued attacks by Navajos, Apaches, and Comanches, who surrounded the Pueblo region, made expansion in Nuevo México difficult, and the colony grew slowly.

In the early 1700s a new threat appeared in the form of French traders from the Illinois country and Louisiana who began to penetrate Nuevo México in an effort to open trade relations with Spaniards and Indians. This French economic thrust quickly became a matter of great concern to Spanish officials, who responded to it by expanding the mission system and encouraging new settlement. Efforts to attract Spanish-Mexican settlers to the region were unsuccessful, however, and at the end of the eighteenth century it had fewer than 8,000 Mexican settlers in fourteen towns and villages. Thus Nuevo México remained an isolated province, having little contact with the heartland of Mexico.

The area that is now the state of Arizona developed even more slowly than that of present-day New Mexico because the same conditions and problems existed, but in an accentuated form. The presence of more aggressive Indians and of few semi-sedentary ones, the failure to develop a mining industry, and a lack of good agricultural land and water held back Spanish expansion there. Spanish colonization was principally the result of Father Eusebio Kino's missionary work, especially among the Pima Indians. His efforts were capped in the early 1700s by the founding of the mission of San Javier del Bac, near present-day Tucson, and Tumacacori to the south. In the second half of the eighteenth century, the continued threat of Indian raids, principally by Apaches, the incursion of French traders and the discovery of some mines all contributed to the push and pull of migration and settlement in Arizona. Although a general pacification of the Indians had been achieved by the beginning of the nineteenth century, still there were fewer than 2,000 settlers in Arizona. The great majority of them were mestizos and mulatos, living in a handful of pueblos in the extreme southern region, near the present border.

The settlement of the areas that have come to be the states of Texas and California had a different history, resulting from the threats of foreign powers to establish themselves in these regions. In Texas, initial interest in settlement came as a result of the La Salle expedition down the Mississippi River in 1582 and his later efforts to establish a French colony at its mouth. Continued French interest in the area led to increased Spanish military and mission activity. In 1690 two missions were established on the Neches River, and in the following year the area of Texas was made a province. Subsequently six additional missions and a presidio were founded. Finally, with the establishment of the mission, presidio, and pueblo of San Antonio de Béxar in 1718, Spanish settlement of the area became a reality.

Expansion of settlements and missions within the Texas area continued to aggravate the conflict between Spaniards and Frenchmen until Spain acquired Louisiana from France in 1763. From that time until 1800, when Louisiana was ceded back to France, the Texas area developed slowly. At the beginning of the nineteenth century the Mexican population of Texas was about 3,500, with approximately half of the settlers located in San Antonio. The remainder lived in the two settlements of La Bahía, southeast near the Gulf coast, and Nacogdoches, northeast near the Louisiana boundary.

Whereas the threat of French expansion encouraged Mexican settlement in Texas, it was the potential threat of both Russian and English interests that spurred Spanish efforts to settle California. In the 1760s reports that the Russians were advancing southward from Alaska reached the Spanish court. These reports, coupled with English activity on the Pacific Coast, aroused Spanish fears so that they took steps immediately to counter these threats.

José de Gálvez was sent to Mexico as special representative of the Spanish crown to begin colonization of California. The initial thrust was the expedition by Junípero Serra and Gaspar de Portolá from Baja California. Father Serra was given the responsibility of establishing missions—a work he began by establishing the mission of San Diego de Alcalá in 1769. Governor Portolá of Baja California, as leader of the expedition, founded the Presidio of Monterey in the following year. By 1823 a string of twenty-one new missions had been added to the existing mission system of Baja California. In addition, three presidios and three towns were established between Baja California and San Francisco Bay.

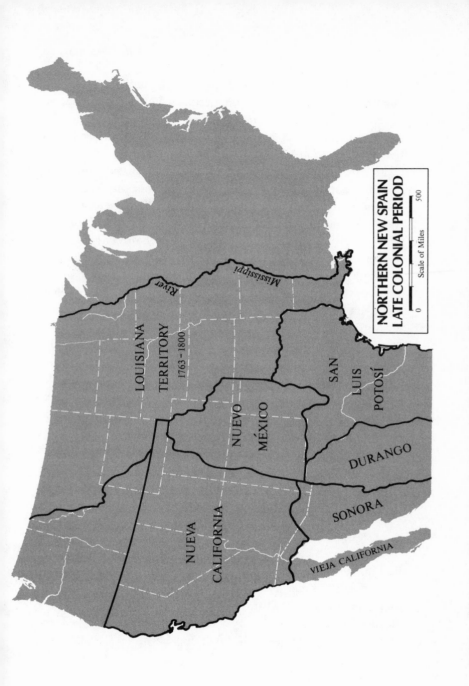

NORTHERN NEW SPAIN
LATE COLONIAL PERIOD

Scale of Miles

0                    500

Mississippi River

LOUISIANA
TERRITORY
1763-1800

SAN
LUIS
POTOSÍ

NUEVO
MÉXICO

DURANGO

NUEVA
CALIFORNIA

SONORA

VIEJA CALIFORNIA

In summary, the initial European exploration and development of the Southwest were undertaken by the Spaniards between 1530 and 1800. Major areas of settlement were in what are now the states of New Mexico, Texas, and California. The two centuries that separate the beginnings of New Mexico and California were years of cultural and racial development in both the Southwest and in Mexico. Because of cultural evolution in Mexico, the people who settled Los Angeles in 1781 were different in cultural and ethnic make-up from those who had established Santa Fe in 1607. In New Mexico and Arizona the Spaniards and Mexicans added to their cultural diversity by adapting and building on the more developed local Indian cultures. In California and Texas the level of Indian development did not encourage cultural borrowing by the Spaniards nor rapid Spanish exploitation of the regions.

In addition, dissimilar geographic and economic conditions in the Southwest accentuated differences as time went on and determined the direction in which the separated areas developed. In Arizona and New Mexico, settlement patterns evolved around mining and missionary activities. In Texas and California colonization was initiated by Spain to hold back rival colonial powers. The economy of the first two areas was based partly on mining; this meant that it was an export economy with associated activities. In the latter two areas subsistence ranching and agriculture developed and became the economic mainstay.

These settlements of the Southwest have given birth to a romantic myth that the early settlers were Spanish dons and flashing-eyed señoritas. The historical record indicates, however, that the majority of settlers were mestizos, Mexican Indians, and mulatos. Historically, frontier regions have never attracted members of the upper classes in any number, and this area was no exception. The government in Mexico City recruited colonists for the northern frontier from among the lower classes with promises of land and other inducements. As a result, this northern frontier offered attractive opportunities to the lower economic classes of Mexico, as it still does today.

# two

# Revolution and Chaos

In the last quarter of the eighteenth century and the first quarter of the nineteenth, revolutions swept the western world. The first of these began in 1775 as a war of independence for Britain's colonies in North America. The French Revolution broke out in 1789, and two decades later Spain's colonies in America revolted. This series of events had a profound impact on the later history of California, New Mexico, and Texas. Mexicans were directly involved in two of these revolts—the one in the English colonies in 1775 and the one in Mexico in 1810.

When American revolutionary leaders sought foreign help,

they logically turned for aid to England's traditional and ancient rivals, France and Spain. Both responded favorably. Spain was principally involved in Florida and the region of the Mississippi Valley. Bernardo de Gálvez, governor of Louisiana, sold munitions to the American rebels and allowed them to cross Spanish Louisiana and to use the port facilities at New Orleans. He also led a large body of militiamen in a successful campaign against the English along the Mississippi River, capturing Natchez and a number of other river ports. By preventing England from gaining control of the Mississippi, the governor greatly aided the American revolutionaries in their struggle against England. Some of Gálvez's militiamen in the Mississippi campaign were Mexicans, and the bulk of his funds and supplies came from Mexico. More important, the success of the American revolution set an example that Mexican revolutionaries later attempted to follow.

There were, however, other more fundamental and long-term social and economic bases for the Mexican revolution of 1810. From the very beginning of colonization in Mexico there had developed a series of Indian rebellions against their Spanish masters. These uprisings were varied in their manifestations; some were simple riots, some were rebellions, and some were outright revolutions. Most were aimed at improving the conditions of the lower levels of society, namely the Indians.

In the sixteenth century the outstanding Indian uprising against Spanish control was the Mixton war of 1541–1542. Brutal treatment by early Spanish conquerors of the Indian tribes of Michoacán, Jalisco, Nayarit, and Sinaloa caused them to rise up in a ferocious revolt of extermination led by the Zacatecas Indians. So threatening was their attack that the Spaniards, vastly outnumbered and fearing extinction, were forced to bring forces from as far away as Guatemala. Only after a brutal campaign led by Viceroy Antonio de Mendoza himself was this uprising suppressed. The final battle, fought in the Mixton hills north of the city of Guadalajara, resulted in the dispersion of the Indian rebels. This incident, the most critical and dangerous to the Spaniards during the entire colonial period, resulted in the elimination or enslavement of most of the rebellious Indians.

The seventeenth century was marked by numerous Indian rebellions motivated largely by hunger, a condition felt particularly strongly by the Indians, whose population had already been decimated by disease and exploitation. The most notable of these revolts took place in 1624, when Indians, alleging food shortages, burned the government headquarters in Mexico City. In 1692 another significant attack against the Spaniards led to the burning of the viceroyal palace by Indians who shouted, "Death to the Spaniards who are eating our corn."

Hunger and exploitation by the Spaniards caused the Indians of Nuevo León to try to expel the hated gachupines from their lands early in the eighteenth century. After a long four-year campaign the revolt was finally suppressed, only to break out anew a few years later. Far to the south the entire Yucatan peninsula erupted in racial conflict between Mayan Indians and their Spanish rulers in 1761. In this war Jacinto Canek developed a scorched earth policy while leading the Mayan Indians against both mestizos and Spaniards.

The best-organized rebellion against Spanish domination took place in 1802 in the provinces of Tepic and Nayarit. This movement, organized and led by an Indian known as "el Indio Mariano," attempted to restore the empire of Montezuma II. After a prolonged struggle this revolt was suppressed when Indio Mariano was captured and executed.

However, the end of Spanish colonialism came not from a racially oriented movement led by Indians but from continuing conflict between criollos ( American-born persons of pure European or *criollo* parents) and peninsular-born Spaniards. In the first decade of the 1800s, rising political and economic antagonism between criollos and the Spanish crown led to the development of secret revolutionary groups. The activities of Father Miguel Hidalgo, pastor in the small village of Dolores and a member of one of these groups, led to the outbreak of Mexico's revolution for independence. On September 16, 1810, at his little parish church, Father Hidalgo uttered the now famous "grito de Dolores": "Long live our lady of Guadalupe, down with bad government, down with the Spaniards."

The motivation of the revolt that ensued was overwhelmingly political and economic rather than social or racial. Indians formed the bulk of the early revolutionary forces, while mestizos provided much of the leadership. During this period the mestizo emerged for the first time as a dynamic social force which was to have tremendous impact on the future of Mexico.

Led by Father Hidalgo, 50,000 Indians and mestizos quickly united under the banner of the Virgin of Guadalupe. Sweeping south toward Mexico City by way of Celaya, Querétaro, and Guanajuato, Hidalgo's undisciplined army soon arrived within sight of Mexico City, the center of Spanish colonial power. Although the capture of the city was almost certain, Hidalgo hesitated outside the capital and soon withdrew his forces toward Guadalajara. This unexplained action on his part was the turning point in this initial phase of the struggle for independence. Soon abandoned by most of his followers and eventually betrayed by one of his own officers, Hidalgo was captured and executed in 1811.

At this point the standard of revolution was picked up by Father José María Morelos, a mestizo from Morelia. Morelos had a military and political capacity which Hidalgo notably lacked. He trained his revolutionary troops and called a congress, which declared Mexican independence in November

1813. A subsequent constitution issued at Apatzingán committed the Mexican revolt to a social and political egalitarianism which Morelos had already initiated. Under Morelos the Mexican revolution achieved its widest geographical extent, but his social objectives repelled many criollos. With his support declining and royalist forces on the increase, Morelos was captured in 1815, tried, and executed.

The death of Morelos left the revolutionary leadership divided, and after 1815 activity was reduced to occasional guerrilla warfare carried on by small and isolated groups of partisans fighting in Mexico's mountains. By the end of the decade the 1810 revolutionary movement was almost completely suppressed, and the conservative Spanish government of Fernando VII seemed in almost complete control.

Events in Europe soon changed this situation, however. In 1820 a revolt in the Spanish port of Cadiz initiated a revolutionary movement which forced the king to accept the liberal constitution that had been drafted previously by the Spanish *cortes* (parliament) in 1812. In Mexico, conservative elements felt that the new constitution and liberal government in Spain threatened their privileged position. Their response was a conservative counterrevolution headed by a Mexican royalist officer, Agustín de Iturbide. With his forces, Iturbide joined the guerrilla remnants of the earlier Hidalgo movement and with them declared Mexico independent in 1821. A year later, Iturbide was inaugurated as Agustín I, Emperor of Mexico. His failure to retain the support of the many political factions, however, especially the liberals, quickly led to his downfall. In March 1823, he was deposed by a revolutionary republican coup initiated by a young officer, Antonio López de Santa Anna.

This politically minded soldier was to play a very important role in the next half-century of Mexican history as a chief protagonist in the Texas secessionist movement of 1836, in the war with the United States, and later in the Gadsden Purchase. His influence in Mexican history makes him the leading figure in the early national period.

After the deposition of Agustín I, the leaders of the new political movement, among whom Santa Anna was one of the most prominent, then called a constituent assembly which drew up a federalist constitution. This 1824 constitution gave virtual autonomy to the states of the new Mexican republic, and, despite considerable internal strife over the issue of federalism versus centralism, it remained in effect until 1835. Mounting reaction to extreme federalism then led to a revolt which overthrew the government and brought to power López de Santa Anna, who quickly called a convention to organize a strongly centralized government in 1836. Installation of this new government caused widespread reaction throughout the country, however. Opposition to this new centralism led to militant action, especially in the northern regions that were later to become a part of the United States.

For a better understanding of the historical development of this northern region of Mexico during the period from 1810 to 1836, it is necessary to see how political events in central Mexico affected various parts of the area. The 1810 revolution in central Mexico was the first major political issue to confront the californios (Mexican citizens of the province of California) in the nineteenth century. Although they knew about the revolution, they remained largely unconcerned with the ideology of the independence movement. Indeed, insecurity resulting from the fact of recent colonization and great isolation made californios hesitant to break with Spain and risk their future on the unpredictable outcome of the independence movement. This attitude tended to reinforce the sympathies of the inhabitants for the Spanish crown and was especially prevalent among government officials, including the clergy. Besides, many californios asked themselves whether an independent Mexico would be able to protect a remote, isolated California from possible attacks by foreign powers or Indians. For these basic reasons, californios were little involved in the revolution.

Nevertheless, the fact that supply ships no longer brought basic necessities and luxuries from Mexico made the californios indirectly aware of the 1810 revolt for independence. The inconvenience caused by the disruption of trade with Mexico was minimized by the existence of mission manufacturing coupled with an expanding foreign commerce. Boston merchants, English shippers, and the Russians at Fort Ross supplied most of the goods that were not produced locally.

The only event that really involved californios in the revolution was the arrival of the Argentine privateer Hippolyte Bouchard with his two ships, the *Argentina* and the *Santa Rosa*. Bouchard briefly put California under the blue and white Argentine revolutionary flag in 1818, when he landed at Monterey and urged the citizens to rise up against the Spaniards. Finding little acceptance for his idea of revolt against Spain, he ravaged the town, burning the presidio and the homes of all Spaniards. The privateers then sailed south to Santa Barbara and San Juan Capistrano, where they engaged in minor skirmishes with local californios, who were informed and prepared for their arrival. Unsuccessful in his effort to solicit support, Bouchard sailed off to South America.

Politically, California was virtually independent of Mexico, political events taking place there meant little to the californios. When they learned of the success of Emperor Agustín I in 1822, California Governor Pablo Vicente Solá called a town meeting at Monterey to consider California's relationship to the new government. Discussion indicated only one possible course of action, and thus the governor and troops swore allegiance to the new imperial Mexican government on April 11. A few months later, a representative from Mexico City successfully engineered the election of a criollo, Luis Argüello, as the first Mexican governor of the province.

When, early in 1823, Iturbide's empire was replaced by a republic, Governor Argüello pledged California's support. A year later the Constitution of 1824 arrived in Monterey and was quickly ratified by the californios. Despite this rapid political change and the acceptance of the new constitution, California's social structure and way of life went on relatively undisturbed. With the development of greater economic and political stability in the latter 1820s there was an increase in migration from Mexico to California.

At the same time, a rapid rise in anti-clericalism after independence, government hope for revenue to be generated from the transfer of mission lands, interest of the landowners in increasing their property holdings, and expectations of californios that they would obtain Indian laborers from the missions led to important changes in Mexican California. In the 1830s the California missions were secularized by orders from the central government, and a struggle for control of mission property immediately ensued. Political unrest mounted rapidly when Santa Anna forcibly instituted the Constitution of 1836. This centralist constitution increased political instability both in central Mexico and in the northern frontier areas, where conflict with the United States was already brewing, caused by the increasing Anglo-American penetration of the provinces, which was beginning to affect their social and political structures.

Like California, Nuevo México also remained aloof from events in old Mexico during the period 1810 to 1836, generally receiving little help or leadership from the central government. The suppression of Apache raids in the late 1700s had led to the revival of migration from Mexico, which resulted in the expansion of ranching, farming, and mining in the region. Mining development was especially important, because it lessened isolation of the region at the beginning of the nineteenth century through the expansion of trade with the important trading and mining center of Chihuahua to the south.

The curbing of Indian raids led to renewed interest in the development of mining in this isolated area. Some placer gold was discovered, but copper was the most important mineral mined in the region. The discovery of copper ore at Santa Rita in the southwestern part of Nuevo México led to extensive mining operations.

Large amounts of copper were produced and sent to the mint in Mexico City by mule caravan. As a consequence, the traditional trade route between Santa Fe and Chihuahua gained renewed importance. At the same time, routes from Santa Fe to what was then the United States frontier were being explored by fur trappers. However, the Spanish and later Mexican governments discouraged contacts with the United States, because they feared encroachment upon their territories.

The revolt from Spain in 1810 and the establishment of an independent government hardly affected most of the Mexican settlers of Nuevo México. Primarily concerned with the problems of daily living, they remained politically inactive and largely loyal to Spain. However, their security was diminished by the transfer of frontier garrisons to central Mexico during the revolution, which left the northern provinces vulnerable to renewed Indian raiding. As Indian attacks increased, mission activity declined, and settlers living in the more isolated areas fled or were killed. Eventually missions, ranches, farms, and mines were abandoned as missionaries and settlers moved to safer locations, particularly to larger centers such as Santa

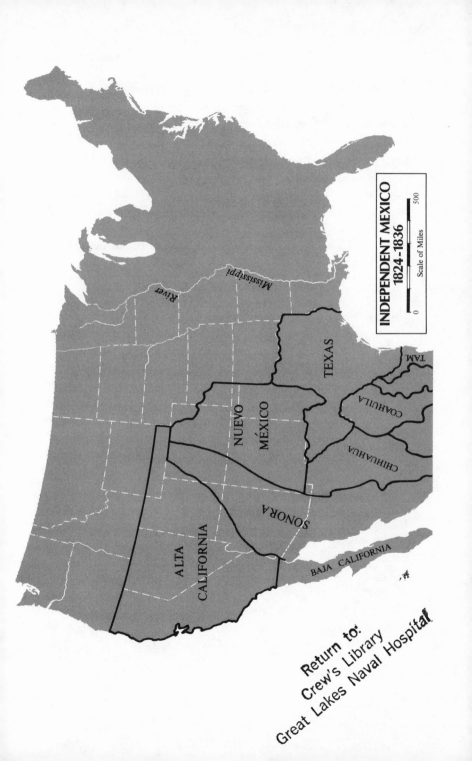

INDEPENDENT MEXICO
1824-1836

0    500
Scale of Miles

TEXAS

TAM

COAHUILA

CHIHUAHUA

NUEVO MÉXICO

SONORA

ALTA CALIFORNIA

BAJA CALIFORNIA

Mississippi

River

Fe. Some returned to old Mexico because problems of labor, transportation, isolation, and security became too great. The missions were further affected when, in the late 1820s, the Mexican government expelled all Spaniards, including Spanish missionaries, from its territories.

In 1822 the isolation of northern Nuevo México was temporarily reduced as a result of the blazing of the Santa Fe trail by William Becknell. The resultant trade between the Missouri frontier and the Santa Fe region led to a minor economic revolution and a revival and expansion of the New Mexican frontier. Nuevo México was now able to obtain low-priced consumer goods from Saint Louis more easily than from the nearest Mexican trade center, Chihuahua. The trade with the United States also provided a relatively easy outlet for New Mexican products.

Anglo-American traders who followed Becknell's lead settled around Santa Fe and became Mexican citizens. Some, like Charles Bent and James Magoffin, married into Mexican families, thereby becoming an intimate part of local society. Others antagonized the New Mexicans with their racial arrogance, sneering disparagement of the Catholic religion, and crude, boorish manners. Mexican officials had well-founded suspicions about the loyalty of these new citizens and feared that this group of traders was only the vanguard of a much larger migration. Thus, as in California and Texas, Nuevo México began to develop an Anglo faction whose loyalties to Mexico were questionable and whose religious and social heritage was incompatible with Mexican culture.

Meanwhile governmental changes in Mexico City began to affect the political and social structure of this northern region. The 1824 constitution organized Nuevo México (present-day New Mexico and Arizona) as a territory with Santa Fe as its capital. The new territory had a population of more than

20,000, most of whom were mestizos; approximately 8,000 were Indians. The majority lived in small communities in north central New Mexico. In the Arizona area only Tucson and Tubac had a sizable Mexican population.

Between Mexican independence in 1821 and the war with the United States in 1846, there was considerable migration from Mexico into the valley of the upper Rio Grande, particularly in the area between Socorro and El Paso. During this period the area north of Socorro developed an important cattle- and sheep-ranching economy. In addition to stock raising, mining attracted settlers to the region, especially after the discovery of gold in the Sierra del Oro between Santa Fe and Albuquerque in the late 1820s. One of the most important mines in this region was the Ortiz mine, which by the early 1830s was producing about $20,000 in gold yearly and by the end of the Mexican period had produced more than $3,000,000.

This discovery of gold in Nuevo México led the Mexican government to take a renewed and greater interest in the area because of its dire need for revenue. In the mid-thirties Santa Anna's centralist attempt to impose tighter controls over the region was resisted by the New Mexicans. In 1835 the centralizing efforts of the newly appointed governor, Albino Pérez, sent from Mexico City, led to a New Mexican revolt. One of the instigators of this revolt was the former governor, Manuel Armijo, a wealthy merchant and politician involved in military intrigue. After Governor Pérez was captured and killed by the rebels, Armijo switched sides and suppressed the revolt, and took over the reins of government. Subsequently confirmed as governor, he remained in this critical position until the war with the United States. His close relationships with Anglo-American traders and land speculators antagonized many Mexican settlers and created conditions which facilitated American expansionist activities in New Mexico.

Of the three provinces in the northern frontier, Texas was unquestionably most affected by the political events occurring in central Mexico between 1810 and the 1830s. Preceding the 1810 revolution, Mexican interest in Texas had languished, because the transfer of adjacent Louisiana from France to Spain in 1763 ended the expansionist threat from its former owner. This security, however, was short-lived because of the development of a new menace to Mexican control of the enlarged Texas region.

The east Texas plains with their large herds of wild horses and cattle, descendent from those escaping from early Spanish expeditions beginning with Francisco de Coronado in 1540, had begun to attract Anglo-American horse traders by the last decade of the eighteenth century. Some Americans also became active in trading with Mexicans and Indians of the area, while others began to acquire land grants and engage in ranching. A few had far more elaborate goals. With the backing of Spanish officials, Aaron Burr and General James Wilkinson developed a scheme for seizing the area and establishing an empire for themselves. The location of Texas far from the center of power in Mexico and close to the United States made it highly vulnerable to political unrest and filibustering by both Mexicans and Americans. After the Louisiana Purchase in 1803, which extended American dominion over the trans-Mississippi West, this activity became even more pronounced.

Although the 1810 Mexican revolt against Spain initially had little effect on Texan loyalties to Spain, the unique position of this frontier region caused it to become a center of intrigue. After the death of Father Hidalgo, one of his followers, José Bernardo Gutiérrez, fled from Mexico and took refuge in New Orleans. In this port city he plotted with Augustus Magee, a former United States Army Officer under Wilkinson, to free Texas from Spanish control. As a result of these intrigues, the Gutiérrez-Magee expedition of about 200 men invaded Texas in 1812 and captured Nacogdoches, Goliad, and San Antonio. Dissension quickly developed among the invaders, however, enabling Spanish government forces to recapture San Antonio. As a result, Gutiérrez and some of his men fled back across the border into American Louisiana.

Subsequent filibustering activities in Texas were frustrated by the United States government, which did not want to antagonize Spain while negotiating a treaty for the acquisition of Spanish Florida. Late in 1819, news reached the Louisiana frontier that the United States had bought Florida through the Adams-Onís Treaty. By this treaty the United States gave up its claims to parts of eastern Texas, thereby establishing a clearly defined boundary between Louisiana and Texas. This compromise led to jingoistic protest meetings among the aggressive, land-hungry frontiersmen of the old American Southwest. One of these meetings at Natchez, Mississippi, led to the organization of another filibustering expedition into Texas by James Long with the help of José Bernardo Gutiérrez. Long and his men crossed the Sabine River boundary between Louisiana and Texas, seized Nacogdoches, and declared a republic, with Long as president. Moving southwestward, Long and his men captured Goliad in October 1821 and declared their activities to be part of the Mexican revolution for independence. Long's success was short-lived, for his army was defeated; he was captured, taken to Mexico City, and later executed. Gutiérrez, however, subsequently became the first governor of the Mexican state of Tamaulipas, across the Rio Grande from Texas. Although this military escapade ended in failure, American interest in and penetration of Texas continued.

After 1821 much of the area between the Nueces River and the Rio Grande was parceled out in land grants by the newly independent government in Mexico City. These land grants resulted in a rapid movement of Mexican settlers into the area. Coupled with this northward colonization was an even more rapid movement of Anglo-Americans into the region east and north of the Nueces. This immigration set the stage for the eventual acquisition of the entire Southwest by the United States.

The achievement of Mexican independence had a limited but lasting impact on the northern provincial tier of Mexico. The changes of government in Mexico City affected the social, economic, and political structure of the Mexican frontier. Legislatures and other elements of local government were established; Indians and mestizos were given full citizenship. New republican and egalitarian ideals influenced some leaders, but many found the old authoritarian ways hard to give up. Wealthy landowners (patrones) continued to dominate the government and the economy, and refused to relinquish their positions of power.

Mexican independence did bring some social and economic improvements to the area. Increased interest in education led to founding of a few schools in major settlements of the three regions. This was a frontier region where traditionally formal education was not a matter of widespread concern. The introduction of printing presses into California and Nuevo México stimulated new interest in the printed word, although the chief product of these presses was religious materials, since the church dominated education.

This period also brought economic development to the three regions that were to become part of the United States. In California, expansion of the hide and tallow trade led to increased ranching activity, which became the economic mainstay during the 1820s. In Texas, stock raising and cotton cultivation became more important as the demand for cattle and textiles increased. In Nuevo México, the Santa Fe trade brought about a most important change in the economy during this period. New trade routes were also developed, the most important being the Old Spanish Trail from Santa Fe to Los Angeles, pioneered in 1829 by Antonio Armijo. As a result of expanded trade activities, there was increased social and political contact with Americans, some of whom settled in the region. Many of these immigrants added to the existing unrest through their dissatisfaction with Mexican control. By the 1830s the entire Southwest and California were on the threshold of a new era.

# three

# Man and Land
# on the Frontier

The thrust of Spanish expansion into the northern frontier region of New Spain and subsequent settlement there were based on economic, religious, and political motives. A typical pattern for this movement emerged. First came the initial conquest or occupation of the region, usually motivated by the hope of economic gain, privately financed, and having the indispensable crown approval. Second came the Christianization of local Indians, undertaken by one of the various missionary orders; the most prominent of these in the Southwest was that of the Franciscans. A third element in this process of settlement was securing the region, a task undertaken by the mili-

tary, who established small garrisons, usually near missions
and pueblos. Soldiers stationed in these frontier garrisons were
often persuaded to remain after their terms of service had ex-
pired by grants of land. In this way the population was increased, the defense of the province bolstered, and there grew
up around the missions and garrisons settlements which later
attracted a small artisan and merchant class.

The societies that developed along Mexico's northern frontier in these isolated clusters differed not only from the parent
society in Mexico but also from one another. There were, of
course, many institutions, customs, activities, occupations, and
attitudes with common elements. There were also regional differences deriving from varied origins, histories, adaptations to
the geography of the frontier, and other factors. Perhaps best
known of these regional cultures is the society which developed in California in the Spanish and Mexican periods.

The initial interest in colonizing California arose from the
threat of possible foreign encroachment, the rumor of Russian
advance from Alaska down the Pacific Coast. Alta California
was founded as a mission colony, an extension of the Baja
California missions, administered by the Franciscans, who were
accompanied by some soldiers, government officials, and a few
colonists. The development of a mission system in Alta California was accompanied by the parallel establishment of a few
presidios and pueblos. As a result of the zeal of the missionaries
and the work of the Indians, by the 1830s, the missions had
become central to the economy and society of Mexican California.

The missions were self-contained economic units and included substantial numbers of Indians, who performed all
necessary agricultural and manufacturing labor. Their self-sufficiency was based on their extensive herds of cattle, flocks of
sheep, orchards, vineyards, and workshops. The province was

well on its way to becoming economically as well as politically independent from the center of government in Mexico City. Self-sufficiency was indeed necessary for the californios; they could not depend on supplies from Mexico because lines of communication, both by land and by sea, were long and uncertain. Blessed with the best climate and natural resources of all the Spanish borderlands, California became the most prosperous province in northern New Spain.

There were two main elements in the social and economic life of California, the mission and the rancho, both highly dependent on the ready availability of labor and land. As in central Mexico, the missions were granted sufficient land to carry out the many tasks of Christianization; in addition to these mission grants, land was also allotted to private individuals. During the period of Spanish control, which ended in 1822, about thirty private land grants were awarded in California, principally for services rendered to the crown. These grants remained relatively undeveloped during the Spanish period and were used for subsistence agriculture and small-scale ranching. When independent Mexico supplanted Spain, most of these grants were confirmed by the new government.

After independence the granting of land in California was rapidly accelerated. In the Mexican period between 1822 and 1846 several hundred land grants were awarded by officials in both California and Mexico City. Some of these grants went to frontier soldiers upon termination of service, as was the case with Rancho Entre Napa awarded to Nicolás Higuera, a soldier of the San Francisco presidio; others went to recently arrived Americans like William Hartnell, who received title to Rancho Patrocinio Alisal near Monterey, and William Dana, who obtained Rancho Nipomo in San Luis Obispo. In the Los Angeles area, Abel Stearns acquired several ranchos; among them were Alamitos and Laguna, which covered over 200 square miles.

During the 1830s there was a great expansion of the rancho economy in California. By 1830 some ranchos had become self-contained units and began to compete with the missions for economic domination. In this conflict the ranchero's chief criticism of the missions was that they controlled the main source of labor, the Indian. Secularization of the missions by the Mexican government in the 1830s solved this labor problem. The appropriation and sale of mission properties both enlarged rancho holdings and made available the labor necessary for their continued expansion. The justification for secularization was that it would benefit the California Indian by making him master of his destiny, the missionary by freeing him for work on new frontiers, and the Mexican government by providing a new source of taxation. However, rancheros were the chief beneficiaries. Mission lands and buildings, as well as other mission resources, were leased, sold, or granted by the governor to influential rancheros at their petition. Ultimately most of the mission lands ended up in private hands, and many of the mission Indians settled on ranchos and continued the familiar work patterns of their former mission life.

From the beginning of settlement, the ranchos, like the missions, provided most of the daily needs of their owners and workers. They raised sheep and hogs, and cultivated grapes, fruit, wheat, and other grains. Cattle-raising became increasingly important, and by the beginning of the Mexican period it had become the largest single industry. The incentive for expansion in cattle-raising came from the increased demand for the production of tallow and hides. By the end of the Mexican period a few of the larger and more successful ranchos had become self-sustaining units similar to the haciendas of northern Mexico.

Typically, a rancho consisted of a number of simple, flat-roofed adobe buildings with hard-packed earthen floors. In these buildings the routine household tasks—cooking, washing, and candle, soap, cloth and wine making—were performed. A nearby garden supplied squash, beans, chilies, and other vegetables; cattle and sheep furnished meat for the table and leather which was made into various articles of clothing, boots, harnesses, and saddles. Tallow and grease supplied the basic raw materials for candles and soap, and the wool was spun and woven into cloth and blankets.

Owners of the larger ranchos usually maintained a town residence as well. At the end of the Mexican period there were perhaps 10,000 californios, of which 800 were ranch owners. Oliver Larkin, first American consul at Monterey, estimated that about 50 of these men wielded the political and economic power of the province.

Although the availability of good land promoted more extensive development of ranch life in California than elsewhere in the Southwest, old Spanish urban traditions led to the creation of some towns as well. Three towns were established by law—San José, Los Angeles, and Villa Branciforte, the last-named located near present-day Santa Cruz; other settlements grew up around forts and missions—Santa Barbara, San Diego, San Francisco, and Monterey, for example. In the southern half of the province, Nuestra Señora de Los Angeles de la Portiúncula became the economic and social center, while in the north, Monterey held a similar position.

In these early California settlements, the typical pattern of Spanish American town organization prevailed. Daily life revolved around the plaza, a park-like square which formed the center of town. On one side of the plaza stood the church. Opposite the church was the town government building, known as the cabildo, and on the remaining two sides local rancheros built their town houses on lots referred to as solares.

From the plaza a few dusty, rutted lanes led out of town, used primarily by horsemen and heavy two-wheeled carts.

During the Spanish period the homes on the solares were usually one-story adobe structures, with two or three small rooms. The interior walls were whitewashed, and in the corners there were small shrines to the Virgin and other saints. Most of the furniture, hardware, crockery, and utensils were produced locally, usually on the rancho or at one of the missions. As the rancheros became more affluent, their homes were enlarged and better furnished. Some household goods were also brought from Mexico during the Spanish period; later on, the furnishings were supplied by the Boston trade, while luxuries like silverware were imported from England.

On the California rancho, as throughout the Southwest, the extended family pattern was the norm. A typical household included parents, children, grandchildren, in-laws, other relatives, occasionally orphans, and Indian servants all living together. The head of the household filled the role of patriarch and demanded unquestioning obedience from his children. His authority was recognized and respected by the subordinate members of the family regardless of their ages. The conditions of frontier life reinforced this pattern of family cohesiveness.

Another characteristic of colonial California society that arose partly out of its frontier nature was its open hospitality, especially to travelers. Ranch owners supplied lodging and food for the occasional traveler because they were happy to have company and news from beyond the local area. Indeed, californios were often prodigal in their generosity, providing not only free lodging, meals, and riding animals to their guests, but sometimes also money for their needs.

Within the californio society there was much class stratification, yet social mobility was greater than in other parts of

Mexico. The more rigid and feudal patterns of *patrón* and *peón* never developed in California as in New Mexico, though there was a caste system. The californios were divided into three classes. At the top were "la gente de razón," landowners who constituted roughly 10 percent of the population. Members of this group held the important social, economic, and political positions and maintained tight control of their privileged status by marrying predominantly within their class.

The second group constituted the majority of the population —the artisans, small landowners, vaqueros, herders, soldiers, some servants, and immigrant colonists. During the Mexican period the term "cholo" was widely used for members of this class. Composed mostly of mestizos and mulatos, they were generally illiterate as well as poor. At the bottom of the social ladder was the Indian, who endured a condition of wardship under the supervision of the padres. Exploited by the mission system, the Indian after secularization was reduced to a more desperate state—peonage.

These class distinctions were reinforced by differences in the quality and composition of dress. The ranchero's work clothes were practical, but his festive clothes were luxurious and of high quality. He wore a pair of deerskin shoes, studded with silver or sometimes gold; and his breeches were of satin, velvet, or leather, often decorated with rows of silver buttons. A wide-brimmed, flat-topped sombrero protected him from the elements. To complete his outfit he wore a silk or velvet vest, a wide satin sash, and a leather or embroidered dark cloth jacket.

The rancher's wife was somewhat more sedate in her dress. A typical outfit consisted of a full, dark-colored dress over many petticoats, fine linen undergarments and silk stockings from England, and satin or velvet shoes made in Mexico. A colorful rebozo of striped silk or fine cashmere from Mexico completed the costume of the well-dressed californiana, but on special occasions she might also wear a beautiful lace mantilla imported from Manila. The quality of the rebozo and mantilla gave an indication of the social position of the wearer.

The dress of members of the lower classes reflected their inferior position in society. Basically clothes worn by the humbler members of society tended to be of lower quality than that of the upper classes—less ornate, more utilitarian, and usually of home manufacture. Shirt, trousers, sandals, a sombrero, and a vest or serape, formed the traditional dress for the male; women wore homespun skirts and blouses and carried cotton rebozos draped over their shoulders.

Typical of an isolated frontier area, the entertainment of the californios was a natural outgrowth of their daily activities. Much social intercourse centered on the church; weddings, christenings, and wakes were occasions for seeing friends and catching up on local gossip. Considerable sociability was also generated by the celebration of individual and town patron saints' days. An essential part of cattle-raising, the roundup or rodeo was another important occasion for socializing. These activities were often followed by days of festivities which included dancing, horse-racing, bullfights, cockfights, bull and bear fights, and rooster pulls. Picnics and informal evening parties, called tertulias, were common and provided opportunities for card games, reciting poetry, and singing. Among men gambling was a popular and widespread activity, in which all social classes indulged. Hunting was a favorite sport, and a peculiarly californio variant was the hunting of grizzly bears with horse and lasso. Other forms of entertainment were provided by occasional theatrical performances and the rare appearance of traveling circuses.

As can be seen, Mexican frontier life during this period was a combination of hard work and an occasional fiesta, typical of most frontier folk societies. Anglo-Americans traveling or residing in this area during the early nineteenth century failed to recognize and understand the positive aspects of Mexican society. Consequently they often viewed the Mexican as backward and were critical of his life style.

With their own cultural heritage characterized by the Protestant ethic and a spirit of rugged individualism, Anglos considered anyone who did not adhere to these concepts as foreign and inferior. They associated the Anglo way of life with virtue and godliness, and rejected any other cultural styles. Early Anglo-American accounts of the Hispanic-Mexican Southwest frequently revealed condescending attitudes of self-righteousness and disdain for Mexicans. These views held by early writers have been transmitted and perpetuated in books which have been hailed as literary or historical masterpieces and are still widely used in American schools.

Typical examples of such writing were Zebulon Pike's report on his expedition, Richard Henry Dana's *Two Years Before the Mast,* and William Perkins' *Journal of a Forty-Niner in Sonora.* All these people had their prejudices, and most of their readers, interested in bolstering their own egos, accepted the same attitudes.

Obviously a negative characterization of Mexicans in literature led to a negative stereotype in real life. The end result was the rapid creation of a fullblown image of Mexicans as lazy, ignorant, cruel, drunken, violent, dirty, priest-ridden, and superstitious. What began as hearsay soon became folklore, was later reinforced in early half-dime novels, and finally became legitimized as part of our western heritage.

In reaction to this negative view, there developed at the end of the century a school of writers who embellished and romanticized the Hispanic-Mexican experience in California. This school was characterized by the writings of authors such as Gertrude Atherton, Helen Hunt Jackson, Joaquín Miller, and Charles F. Lummis. The reality of early California society lies between these two views.

Although basically Hispanic-Mexican, a style of life different from that of the californios developed on the central and northeastern frontier of Mexico for a variety of reasons. In New Mexico frequent Indian attacks led to a preference for town living. Towns served as an effective means of protection; each home was almost a fortress with barred windows, heavy doors, and adobe walls two or three feet thick built around a central patio which contained a well. In time of danger the stock was brought into this patio for protection. Each household included storerooms with provisions for the long sieges, which were not unusual during the early period of settlement.

Settlers in New Mexico engaged in subsistence agriculture with some form of irrigated farming providing a delicate accommodation to local conditions of soil, temperature, and water. Following both medieval Spanish and local Pueblo Indian patterns, New Mexicans went out each day from the village to the fields where they cultivated corn, beans, wheat, and varieties of chili. The missionaries introduced fruit raising and the cultivation of cotton—two important contributions to the agricultural economy. Most New Mexican farm holdings were located along rivers, especially the upper Rio Grande and its tributaries. These rivers provided water for two widely used agricultural techniques in colonial New Mexico, irrigation and flood plain farming.

In addition to basic crops, farmers raised sheep and cattle which they pastured on land held in common by the villagers. Because there was no outside market for beef, hides, or tallow, cattle-raising was of minor importance in New Mexico throughout the colonial period. Sheepherding began to compete with farming in the late 1700s, and after the turn of the century became the most important economic activity. As the demand for sheep increased and trade routes became more secure, large numbers of sheep were driven southward to the important center of Chihuahua.

In Texas subsistence agriculture was also the initial activity of the settlers. Besides the usual staple crops of the north Mexican frontier, some sugar cane was cultivated. However, because of the thousands of wild cattle that roamed the Texas plains, cattle-raising soon became more important than agriculture. By the early eighteenth century the area of Texas had become an important source of Mexican longhorns, which were rounded up and driven southward across the Rio Grande into the neighboring province of Tamaulipas. After the Treaty of Paris in 1763, the new and expanding Anglo frontier in Louisiana created a market, for which cattle were driven eastward to Louisiana. Moreover, expansion of the Caribbean sugar industry in the 1700s brought about an additional demand for Texas cattle to feed the enlarged plantation labor force. Paralleling the increased demand for Texas cattle was a rising world market for cotton. Thus the economy of Mexican Texas from 1821 to 1836 focused on cattle and cotton; American cotton growers were attracted to the area, increasing the Anglo intrusion into Texas.

Isolated from one another as well as from central Mexico, towns in New Mexico and Texas became self-sufficient units. Most of their social and economic activities were patterned after models of Old Mexico. In New Mexico the town market place became an economic center where surplus produce of subsistence farmers was sold or exchanged. Here also dried beef, wild turkey, and venison might be exchanged for leather goods, blankets, or pottery, and mutton, beef, pork, cheese, fruits, sage, herbs, chilies, and many other vegetables were sometimes obtainable. Some New Mexican towns developed a small but important craftsman and artisan class. Scrap iron was melted down by smiths to manufacture pots and hardware, and New Mexico became known for its weavers and santeros (carvers of wooden statues of saints). Examples of the santero's anonymous art can still be seen in rural churches of northern New Mexico and southern Colorado.

As settlement of the northern frontier expanded and life became somewhat more secure, transportation routes opened and trade assumed an increasingly important role. The arriero was the truck driver of the period, driving his string of heavily laden burros from Chihuahua, the terminal point for the early New Mexican trade, to Santa Fe and Taos. Some of the bulkier goods were carried in heavy two-wheeled carts called carretas. However, luxury items such as chocolate, silk shawls, and rebozos made up most of the trade goods from Mexico. In return for this merchandise the nuevo mexicanos sent fur, hides, coarse woolen blankets, and sheep down the long trail to Chihuahua. In a good year as many as 400,000 sheep might be driven down the Rio Grande, across at El Paso, and on to Chihuahua 600 miles away.

The expansion of the Louisiana frontier in the late 1700s led to a blossoming of trade in the Texas area during the Mexican period. At this time there was much contraband trade in both New Mexico and in Texas, but especially in the latter. Because of the long and largely unsettled Texas coast and the presence of many adventurers of different nationalities, there was widespread evasion of the customs laws of Mexico.

An especially important aspect of the trade expansion during the Mexican period was the organization of an annual autumn trade fair at Taos in northern New Mexico. Chihuahua merchants, who dominated the New Mexican trade, were a significant part of the fair, but this bustling economic and social event was attended by settlers from all over New Mexico, as well as by Pueblo and even plains Indians. After 1800 American and French mountain men also began to attend this exciting affair at which there was brisk trading of livestock, horses, furs, cloth, hides, hardware, silver, and liquor.

Each spring Taos merchants prepared to host a motley assortment of richly dressed Chihuahua traders, serious-visaged Indians, and mountain men, some with their brightly dressed Indian wives. The Indians and trappers exchanged their year's catch of beaver pelts and other furs for necessities of life, bright cloth for their squaws, gewgaws, and alcohol. The fair was a combination of market and saloon, permeated with a colorful and festive spirit. After days of intensive trade, gambling, prodigal living, alcoholic indulgence, and general debauchery this yearly commercial and social event wound down to a unremorseful end, and the various participants returned to their daily routine of life for another year.

After 1821 Santa Fe became the dominant trade center in northern New Mexico because of its proximity to the Anglo-American frontier, its importance as a local distribution center, and the size of its population. This expanding trade brought a vanguard of American interests and closer economic ties with the United States. As a consequence, American and New Mexican traders soon dominated the local economy, the provincial government became heavily dependent on income generated by customs duties, and the merchant and artisan class enjoyed the benefits of a rising standard of living. The relationship of this prosperity to the Santa Fe trade and the economic alliance of American traders facilitated later Anglo-American conquest.

Long before trade expanded in New Mexico, an isolated village culture had become firmly entrenched by the end of the seventeenth century. Because of its long historical development, New Mexican society had a considerably greater degree of social stratification than California. From the beginning of Hispanic-Mexican occupation and colonization, cohabitation and intermarriage between settlers and local Pueblo Indians occurred and the mestizos soon became the largest racial element in New Mexico.

Mestizos and Indians, who made up the lower class of New Mexico and Texas, lived in circumstances ranging from very humble to impoverished. Mestizos, most of whom were peones or sharecroppers, called medieros, existed just above the subsistence level of the Indians. The Indians were the poorest of the poor, exploited by the upper classes, including government officials who ironically were supposed to protect them. Some Indians were ill-used to the point of enslavement, especially in New Mexico, where black slavery was virtually unknown. In Texas, the growth of a cotton economy led to greater use of Negro slaves, especially after the beginning of Anglo-American settlement.

In New Mexico, a distinct, semi-feudal social pattern evolved. In this patriarchal structure a wealthy few known as patrones ruled over the peones in a despotism that was usually relatively benevolent. This ruling oligarchy of about twenty closely interrelated families generally considered itself to be of criollo origins, descendants of early frontier pioneers. Besides the patrón, the missionary and the parish priest held top positions of leadership and often disputed the rulings of the governor himself. By the Mexican period, the Church in New Mexico, as in Texas and California, had become a powerful force that dominated the daily lives of the settlers.

The life style of the nuevo mexicano and tejano, like that of the californio, was derived from Hispanic and Mexican cultural traditions. In New Mexico the Pueblo Indian culture was important in shaping both the economy and society. Indian techniques of agriculture, especially those of irrigation, were necessary for the subsistence economy of New Mexico, while many Pueblo religious rituals became part of Christian practice. The intellectual aspects of this society were adversely affected by the exiling of all Spanish missionaries along with all other Spaniards early in the Mexican era.

Formal school-oriented education was never a major concern on the northern Hispanic-Mexican frontier from Texas to California—an attitude common to most frontier areas. However, missionaries and priests ordinarily provided a basic education for the children of the more prominent Indian and colonist families. Late in the colonial period and in the Mexican era a few public schools were organized in Texas, New Mexico, and California, but they usually lasted only a short time because of the shortage of teachers. At the beginning of the nineteenth century Governor Elguézabal of Texas issued a compulsory school attendance law for children up to age twelve, but it could not be enforced. New Mexico, an older, more stable area, experienced some intellectual development; leading New Mexican families sometimes sent their sons to Mexico and even to Europe to study, especially to study for the priesthood.

Reading material became somewhat more available to New Mexicans toward the end of the Mexican period when a printing press was shipped to Santa Fe. In the summer of 1834 the first New Mexican paper, *El Crepúsculo de la Libertad,* was published with this press by Antonio Barreiro. Later the press was purchased and moved to Taos where it was used to print school manuals and religious works by Father Antonio José Martínez. Father Martínez played a prominent role in the early American period, especially during the American takeover. He is generally believed to have had a passive part in the Taos revolt to oust the Americans, but seems on other occasions to have counseled an attitude of accepting the inevitability of Anglo control. Having earlier served in the local Mexican legislature, he was also elected to the American territorial legislature of New Mexico and became its first president. When Jean Batiste Lamy was appointed bishop, a quarrel quickly developed between him and Fr. Martínez; as a result the Taos priest broke with the Catholic hierarchy and headed a schismatic church until his death in 1867.

The most important single factor affecting the development of institutions and attitudes in all of the regions of the northern Mexican frontier was unquestionably the cluster pattern of settlements and their isolation from central Mexico and from each other. This isolation adversely affected the whole range of human activities from society to government, and with the political instability of the government in the Mexican capital, led to the greatest and most dramatic change in the history of the northern frontier—the loss of the area to the United States.

# four

## The Clash
## with Manifest Destiny

Chaos marked the first half-century of Mexican history as federalists and centralists struggled with each other for political power and domination of the country. Launched by President Guadalupe Victoria in 1824, the First Republic was federalist in organization. However, federalism ran counter to Mexico's colonial experience and at best meant local autonomy, at worst, anarchy. Plagued by lack of unity and poor leadership, the federalists proved incapable of governing the country effectively. Passage of extreme liberal legislation such as secularization of the missions, suppression of the clerical University of Mexico, government control of church appointments, and reduction in the powers of the church and army courts in the early 1830s led to widespread antagonism and mounting political unrest, especially among wealthy criollos and the clergy. This spreading tension eventually resulted in a successful centrist revolt in 1834.

This change in government brought to power Antonio López de Santa Anna, a rising young political and military leader who was to dominate Mexican politics for the next quarter-century. The sometimes morose, sometimes charming caudillo now proceeded to put into effect his ideas of centralist government. When he initiated steps to draft a unitary constitution, an immediate reaction resulted and quickly spread around the periphery of the Mexican republic.

On the entire perimeter of Mexico—in Yucatan, California, New Mexico, and Texas—opposition to centralism led to militant action as local leaders refused to accept the domination of Mexico City. Yucatan declared its independence and submitted to central control only after a long struggle ending in 1843. In Texas reaction to the new government was more violent and was successful largely because of the overwhelming number of Anglo-American colonists. Least affected by these events were California and New Mexico, areas that continued to be isolated and largely unconcerned with Mexican politics. Nevertheless, centralism was to play an important part in the early steps toward the subsequent loss of this entire northern area to the United States.

California government was first affected by the centralist movement in Mexico City when Mariano Chico, an insignificant Mexican congressman, was appointed the new governor in a political pay-off for his support of centralism. By his arbitrary actions Chico soon became hated and despised by the californios and was forced to return to Mexico early in 1836. At this point, Juan B. Alvarado, a leading young californio, led a successful revolt against the provisional governor who succeeded Chico. The Alvarado government declared California independent until Mexico agreed to reinstate the federalist constitution of 1824. This independent californio government lasted until 1840, when Manuel Micheltorena, the new centralist appointee, arrived from Mexico City. Micheltorena's attempt to enforce centralism was Mexico's last effort to control California, exemplifying Mexico's tenuous hold on the province.

At first mild unrest was also experienced in New Mexico when the centralists imposed their political reforms there. However, in 1835, Albino Pérez, the centralist governor, was overthrown and killed. Then the former governor Manuel Armijo manuevered himself into the provisional governorship, and subsequently obtained confirmation from Mexico City. Armijo then dominated New Mexican politics until the outbreak of hostilities between the United States and Mexico.

The eastern border province of Texas was also the scene of a revolt against Mexican centralism. Here, however, the political circumstances were different and so was the outcome. The Texas uprising was not only an expression of reaction to denial of local political control, but also a result of Anglo convictions about manifest destiny. It was the response to the preceding half-century of Texan history, a history of neglect by Mexico and poor judgment in allowing Anglo settlement.

Manifest Destiny was a peculiarly Anglo-American version of the chosen race theory. Early in the nineteenth century Americans began to believe that their country was destined by divine providence to control and settle the area from the eastern seaboard to the Pacific Ocean. More extreme exponents of Manifest Destiny spoke of the Arctic Circle to the north and Tierra del Fuego in the south as the only logical limits to the inevitability of such Yankee expansion. As it turned out, the country to suffer most from Manifest Destiny was Mexico, since half of its territory lay between the American frontier and the Pacific Ocean.

During the half-century dating from the Spanish acquisition of the Louisiana territory in 1763, the security of Texas ceased to be a major concern of the Spanish government. One result of this territorial change was the withdrawal of troops from the Texas region and a concurrent increase in Indian depredations. As a result of this more active Indian hostility, many missions and settlements were abandoned, leading to a decline in Hispanic-Mexican population. By the end of the eighteenth century, of the twenty-seven missions established in Texas, only six were still functioning, and the civilian population was reduced to 3,500.

After the United States purchased the Louisiana territory in 1803, there was some Spanish migration from that area into Texas. Despite government efforts to encourage immigration, the population continued to decline and this trend became even more pronounced after the 1810 revolution in Mexico. By the end of the decade, the provincial governor was asking for settlers from central Mexico to augment the 2,000 inhabitants who so weakly held the vast region. This request was made in vain. Population decline and the fear of possible encroachment by France, England, and the United States help explain why both the Spanish and Mexican governments encouraged Mexican and foreign colonization in the area. Unfortunately for Mexico, this attempted solution to the serious problem of underpopulation ultimately led to the loss of Texas.

In the meantime horse and cattle traders on the western frontier and southern cotton farmers were becoming deeply interested in Texas. In 1821 the Spanish government gave to

Moses Austin of Potosi, Missouri, an *empresario* land grant, under which he was to receive free land for bringing a specified number of settlers into Texas. Austin, a Catholic and former Spanish subject who still held a Spanish passport, died before he could carry out his project to bring in 300 Spanish families from Florida.

Two years later his son Stephen received a similar grant from the newly independent Mexican government. Thus an influx of Anglo-Americans began, and eventually twenty *empresario* grants were awarded to other United States citizens, mostly by the state of Chihuahua-Texas. Stephen Austin chose his immigrants with care and was scrupulous in carrying out the terms of his agreement with the Mexican government. These terms included the requirement that all settlers be of good moral character, that they either be or become Catholics, and that they swear an oath of loyalty to Mexico. Most *empresarios,* however, failed to respect or complete the terms of their grants, while their settlers generally ignored all Mexican institutions and regulations and developed their own social patterns. When the Mexican government tried to compel one of the Americans, Haden Edwards, to abide by the provisions of his grant in 1826, there was a minor crisis known as the Fredonia Revolt. This separatist movement, which broke out at Nacagdoches, was supported by many recent American arrivals. However, Austin and his colonists refused to support this revolt and helped the Mexican authorities to suppress it.

By 1830 there were about 25,000 Americans in Texas, compared with about 4,000 Spanish-speaking Mexicans. Many of the Americans in Texas were illegal aliens who had migrated from the slaveholding South and set themselves up as cotton farmers. Contemptuous of Mexican culture, government officials, and laws, they made little effort to become acculturated. Mexico therefore became concerned about the large number of legal and illegal aliens in Texas and tried to stem the tide of migrants.

Alarmed at the efforts of the American minister, Joel R. Poinsett, to purchase Texas, and encouraged by the British *chargé d'affaires,* Henry George Ward, President Guadalupe Victoria sent General Manuel Mier y Terán to study the Texas situation in detail. Mier y Terán eventually recommended that the government take vigorous measures in Texas before it was too late. In 1829, President Vicente Guerrero, implementing Mier y Terán's recommendations, abolished slavery in Mexico by executive decree. This blow was aimed at Texas, the only Mexican area in which slavery was still important. Threatened economically by this decree law, Anglo and Mexican Texans protested vigorously, and so the decree was suspended in Texas. However, the following year the Mexican congress enacted legislation severely curtailing Anglo-American immigration into Texas and completely prohibited the importation of slaves. At the same time the Mexican government began to strongly encourage European immigration to offset the sizable Anglo population already in Texas. Another law established customhouses and presidios along the Texas-United States frontier, and soldiers were dispatched to Texas to enforce Mexican laws, especially customs regulations.

Customs collection became the most abrasive issue between the Anglo colonists and the government, leading to strong anti-customs sentiments. At San Antonio de Béjar, Stephen Austin led a movement to seek legal redress and was successful in obtaining some concessions from Mier y Terán. Other colonists took a more radical approach. Some activists made guerrilla attacks on customhouses and presidios, and in 1832 fighting broke out between Mexican troops who supported centralism and those who favored federalism. That same year Texas held a convention to discuss relations with the central government. Seeking repeal of the 1830 legislation and separation of Texas from Coahuila, it sent Austin to Mexico City to petition for these changes. Austin found little sympathy for the Texas viewpoint and was jailed after he sent a letter to the Texas colonists urging them to form an independent state government. Finally he was released and returned to Texas. The change in Mexico from a federalist to a centralist government in 1834 added fuel to the fire, and on November 7 the Texans declared conditional independence, siding with Mexican federalists in demanding a return to the 1824 Constitution.

In response to this move, President Santa Anna sent 4,000 federal troops under his brother-in-law, General Martín Cos, to Texas early in 1835. After establishing his headquarters at the Alamo in San Antonio, Cos was soundly defeated by a group of federalist rebels and forced to withdraw southward to Mexico. The following year President Santa Anna assumed personal command of the army in the field, determined to avenge this defeat. Recruiting and organizing a conscript army as he marched north to Texas, he proclaimed a policy of no quarter. Santa Anna's subsequent actions must be viewed in proper historical perspective. Directed by the Mexican Congress to suppress the seditious revolt in Texas, he rightfully considered the Texans to be traitors and rebels and set out to smother the flames of rebellion.

Meanwhile, a Texas convention of Anglos and Mexicans declared by a two to one vote that it wanted reinstatement of the Mexican Constitution of 1824 and it appointed Sam Houston as commander of all forces. Political difficulties within the provisional government led to a second convention at Washington-on-the-Brazos, during which fifty-nine Texas delegates unanimously declared complete independence on March 2,

1836. A few days later they elected David Burnett as provisional president and Lorenzo de Zavala, an exiled Mexican liberal, as vice-president, and they reappointed Houston to head the army.

The first major encounter between the soldiers of the new republic and the forces of Santa Anna took place in San Antonio at the former Franciscan mission known as the Alamo. Here 187 Texans, led by William Travis, including Mexican Texans under the leadership of Captain Juan Seguín and fighting under a Mexican flag, were wiped out. A month later the Mexican army repeated this Alamo victory by slaughtering 450 Texas rebels at Goliad. However, Santa Anna's victories were short-lived. Hundreds of Mexicans lost their lives, and the battles generated a fierce resistance on the part of the rebels. On April 21 the overconfident Santa Anna and his army were routed at San Jacinto by Sam Houston, and Santa Anna himself was taken prisoner. This Texan victory led to the Treaty of Velasco by which Santa Anna agreed to Texan independence in exchange for his freedom. Needless to say, the Mexican government repudiated this arrangement, but it was unable to force the Texans to resubmit to Mexican authority. By 1840 the Texans had succeeded in obtaining recognition of their government from the United States, France, and Great Britain.

Having achieved de facto independence from Mexico, Texas pressed for annexation to the United States; however, annexation became a problem, for America was trying to maintain a balance between the admission of slave and free states. As the intensity of the slave conflict grew and the abolitionist movement gained support, Texans devoted less and less effort to annexation. Attainment of economic and political stability in some other fashion became their prime concern. To achieve national viability some Texans suggested expanding the republic to the Pacific, while others preferred to annex the New Mexico area.

In 1841 a Santa Fe expedition was organized by the Texas president, Mirabeau Buonaparte Lamar to try to persuade the New Mexicans to separate from Mexico and become part of the Texas Republic. If this move failed, Texans were willing to settle for a share in the lucrative Santa Fe trade, as documents carried by the leaders of the expedition indicated.

In June 1841, some 300 Anglo and Mexican Texans, organized into five military companies led by General Hugh Mc-Leod, left Austin for Santa Fe with twenty-one wagons and about $200,000 worth of trade goods. On the way they encountered hostile Indians, raging prairie fires, and blistering heat, and they also lost their way, thereby adding more miles to their 600-mile journey. The ill-fated and poorly managed expedition split into two groups, believing that this would speed their journey; when they finally reached New Mexico, they were suffering intensely from hunger, thirst, and exhaustion. Here the naïve members allowed themselves to be disarmed by a ruse and were taken as prisoners by Governor Armijo without a shot being fired. At Santa Fe some of the Texans were executed and the remainder were sent by foot on a long death march to prison in Mexico City. The survivors were eventually released after strong American and British protests. This unsuccessful attempt to annex New Mexico and the brutal treatment of the prisoners of course contributed to the antagonism between republican Texans and nuevo mexicanos.

Meanwhile, the United States and Mexico were moving toward a war for which neither country was prepared. In Texas domestic conflicts between Anglo-Texans and tejanos coupled with raids on both sides of the border by both Mexi-

MEXICAN
CESSION
1848

Colorado R.

1836
to
1850
CLAIMED
BY
TEXAS
and
NEW
MEXICO

GADSDEN
PURCHASE
1853

Rio Grande

Red R.

Brazos R.

TEXAS
REPUBLIC
1836

Nueces R.

CLAIMED
BY
TEXAS
AND MEXICO
1836–1848

**TEXAS CLAIMS AND
MEXICAN WAR RESULTS**

0          Scale of Miles          500

cans and Texans intensified mutual antagonisms. Because of financial difficulties, Mexico was unable to pay its acknowledged debts to America, and the latter's repeated efforts to buy part or all of the Southwest was viewed with great alarm in Mexico. At the same time new American claims against Mexico arising from border difficulties and mistreatment of American citizens kept feelings on both sides at a fever pitch.

The climax finally came in March 1845, when the United States annexed Texas, an event which Mexico had previously warned could lead to war. Mexico immediately broke diplomatic ties with the United States, and their relations entered a new phase of crisis. In August, President James Polk sent John Slidell to Mexico with instructions to negotiate the purchase of California and New Mexico and to discuss settlement of the disputed Texas-Mexican boundary. However, the Mexican government refused to discuss these matters with Slidell because of the intense anti-American feeling in Mexico arising from the annexation of Texas. Finally, Slidell was forced to leave Mexico by a new anti-American government, installed by a coup brought on by the apparent willingness of the former administration to negotiate with the American envoy for the sale of Texas.

Failing in his attempt to acquire the territory by negotiation, Polk sent General Zachary Taylor to the Nueces River area in Texas in hope that a military clash with Mexico might lead to war and bring about the acquisition of the entire Southwest. Polk made these moves in response to widespread American expansionist attitudes, and armed hostilities did break out between the United States and Mexico.

In May 1846, as a result of a clash between American and Mexican troops in the disputed triangle of land between the Nueces and Rio Grande rivers, the United States declared war on Mexico. Ordered to carry the war into the heart of Mexico,

General Taylor crossed the Rio Grande and occupied Matamoros; from there he moved west to capture Monterrey without difficulty in September. The following February, at Buena
Vista, near Saltillo, Chihuahua, there was a hard-fought, in-
decisive battle between Taylor's troops and Mexican soldiers
under Santa Anna. The fatigued and starving Mexican recruits
fought valiantly against the better-trained and well-armed
Americans; however, Santa Anna, unaware of Taylor's plan to
withdraw to Monterrey, disengaged his forces and returned to
Mexico City. Taylor claimed a victory.

Meanwhile, New Mexico was taken without a fight. Anglo
traders in Santa Fe had convinced many Mexican businessmen
that the province would be better off under the United States
than under the unstable and ineffective Mexican government.
There is some indication that Governor Armijo himself may
have been bribed by the Americans. In any event, after organizing a large body of militia, he decided not to oppose the
invading army of seventeen hundred Americans under Colonel
Stephen Kearny. Instead, Armijo suddenly disbanded his larger
force and departed for Chihuahua. Armijo's change in plan was
perhaps influenced by Kearny's earlier assurances to the New
Mexicans that he came as a protector rather than a conqueror.
When he entered Santa Fe in mid-August, acting Governor
Juan B. Vigil and some twenty leading nuevo mexicanos
greeted him and the American troops warmly and promised
that all New Mexicans would be loyal to the United States.
In response to this warm reception, Colonel Kearny assured
them that the United States government would respect the
property and religious rights of all who showed peaceful intent.
Then, while the townsmen and Kearny toasted each other with
wine and brandy, the American flag was raised over the governor's palace. Two days later a group of Pueblo chiefs came to
Santa Fe and declared their allegiance to the United States,

stating that their traditional beliefs foretold that one day they would be redeemed from Spanish injustice and oppression by men from the east.

After completing the formalities of imposing military control over New Mexico, Kearny ordered a framework drafted for the establishment of a new American government in the Southwest. Known as the Kearny Code, this instrument was based on American and Mexican state laws and included provisions for the appointment of government officials. Despite Polk's orders to retain the existing New Mexican political power structure, Kearny generally ignored the leading nuevo mexicanos in organizing the new government. He appointed Charles Bent—an American merchant, landowner, and leader of the pro-American faction in New Mexico—to be acting governor. From the existing Spanish-speaking political structure, Donaciano Vigil was appointed secretary of the territory, Antonio J. Otero was named one of three territorial court judges, and many minor Mexican officials, after taking an oath of allegiance to the United States, were kept in office.

With New Mexico presumably secure, the ambitious Kearny set out for California late in September 1846 to aid in the conquest of that area. Shortly after leaving Santa Fe he met Kit Carson, who informed him that the Bear Flag Revolt had occurred and that California was already under Anglo control. Upon arriving in southern California, however, Kearny found the californios in full revolt and his dragoons opposed by a small force under the local Mexican commander, Andrés Pico. Severely defeated by Pico's lancers and wounded himself in the battle of San Pascual, east of San Diego, Kearny was forced to seek help from Commodore Robert Stockton, who had arrived earlier on the California coast as commander of the Pacific Squadron. With the support of Stockton's forces, Kearny finally reached the security of San Diego on December 12, 1846.

To understand the California experience during the war between Mexico and the United States better, it is necessary to review some of the history that led to hostilities in California. Prior to 1846 California underwent a socio-political experience similar to those of Texas and New Mexico. Like those areas, California had received an influx of Anglo-American immigrants. Those who came in the 1820s and 1830s tended to become an integral part of California society. Many married into californio families, became Mexican citizens, acquired land grants, and a few even held public office. Anglos who arrived in the early forties by way of the Oregon Trail were of a different type, however. Many came with their families, had no intention of becoming Mexican citizens, and deliberately settled in areas remote from Mexican control. They came as the vanguard of American expansionism known as Manifest Destiny.

Accelerated American immigration, coupled with californio dissatisfaction with the Mexican centralist government, led to a rebellion which broke out in northern California just before the war between Mexico and the United States began. This uprising, known as the Bear Flag Revolt because of its banner depicting a bear, quickly became a part of the Mexican War. Initially spearheaded by a group of uncouth adventurers, this revolt established the basis for Anglo conquest of California. John Charles Frémont, a United States Army captain who was in the province on a reconnaissance expedition for the United States government, quickly assumed command of the revolt. When official word came that Mexico and the United States were at war, the bear flag was replaced by the stars and stripes.

Soon thereafter, the arrival of the Pacific Squadron, at first under the command of Commodore John Sloat and later under Robert Stockton, readily secured American control of the entire area. Poor leadership of the American occupation forces in Los Angeles led, however, to a californio revolt in September 1846, and to the only serious fighting that took place in the Southwest.

Stockton quickly antagonized the californios, both by establishing a large number of tactless and restrictive controls and by placing Captain Archibald Gillespie in command of southern California. Gillespie, insensitive to the local life style and feelings, issued further unnecessary and irksome regulations, which caused the southern californios to launch a successful attack against his forces. Eventually, however, by the combined efforts of Gillespie, Stockton, Kearny, and Frémont, the southern California revolt was ended, and American control was reëstablished through negotiation of the Treaty of Cahuenga with the californios in January 1847. This treaty terminated hostilities in California, independently of the government in Mexico City.

Far to the south, in central Mexico, Santa Anna and a newly organized army battled General Winfield Scott, who had landed near Veracruz with 10,000 men. The war went badly for Mexico. She was severely divided by internal strife, her leaders were mistrustful of each other, and the majority of Mexicans were demoralized and unclear as to the objectives of the struggle. Some Mexican states even refused to provide troops for defense against the invaders; the army was made up principally of poorly motivated, ill-trained Indian conscripts.

Partly as a result of these factors, within six months the American forces advanced from Veracruz to Mexico City, reaching the valley of Mexico by mid-August 1847. At Chapultepec Hill, just outside the capital, one hundred young

Mexican military cadets, motivated by patriotism, showed how well Mexican troops could fight. However, the bravery of these "Niños Héröes" was in vain. They were unable to turn back the United States invasion, and on September 14 the American army successfully occupied the Mexican capital. With the conquest of Mexico completed, the only step remaining in President Polk's program was to write a treaty of peace.

Earlier in 1847 Polk had sent his personal representative, Nicholas Trist, to Mexico to negotiate a treaty which would achieve his expansionist goals. Because of personal antagonism between Trist and General Scott, however, the president ordered Trist recalled. Trist ignored the order and continued his negotiations with the provisional Mexican government. Finally, on February 2, 1848, agreement was reached and the treaty signed in the village of Guadalupe Hidalgo.

Despite Polk's irritation with his representative's insubordination, this treaty achieved the president's territorial objectives, and so he submitted it to the Senate. In the United States Senate, Article IX of the treaty, dealing with the political rights and eventual citizenship of the inhabitants, was replaced with a similar but shorter article taken from the Louisiana Purchase treaty, and Article X, which the Senate felt would have raised problems of land ownership in Texas, was completely excised. However, when the amended treaty was discussed with the Mexican representatives in May, written assurances were given that titles to all kinds of personal and real properties existing in the ceded territories would be recognized and protected; moreover, all civil, political, and religious guarantees specified in the original Article IX would be retained. These assurances are known as the Protocol and were made after the amended treaty was ratified by the Mexican Congress at Querétaro on May 21, 1848. Four days later, with the exchange of ratifications, the treaty went into effect.

By the Treaty of Guadalupe Hidalgo, the United States acquired the territory that now forms the states of Arizona, California, Nevada, New Mexico, Utah, and half of Colorado, and received clear title to Texas with the southern boundary that had been previously claimed. Mexico lost more than one million square miles and was paid $15 million in partial compensation. Although Mexico lost approximately 50 percent of her national territory, she lost less than 1 percent of her population. Nearly all 80,000 Mexican citizens living in the ceded territory eventually became citizens of the United States; about 2,000 moved southwest across the new political border in order to retain their Mexican citizenship.

The chief provisions of the Treaty of Guadalupe Hidalgo that relate to Mexican Americans are those concerning citizenship and property. Mexicans living in the ceded area had a year in which to decide whether they wanted to retain Mexican citizenship or to become citizens of the United States. Those still living in the area at the end of the prescribed time who had not specifically declared their intentions to remain Mexican citizens were presumed to desire United States citizenship.

Article IX of the treaty guaranteed that these former Mexican citizens would receive the protection of the United States government in the exercise of their civil and political rights. It also specifically provided that they would have the right to worship freely and that their property rights would be protected. Ironically, no mention was made in the treaty concerning the political and civil rights of local Indians, who had been given citizenship under Mexican law.

A second important provision dealt with real and personal property of Mexicans, whether or not they resided within the bounds of the area. It stipulated that such owners would retain full title to all property, with rights of disposal and inheritance, and it guaranteed full protection of these rights by the United States government. Item Two of the Protocol which accompanied the treaty specified that valid Spanish and Mexican land grants would be recognized by the United States and that the United States would accept as legitimate all property titles recognized under Mexican law.

By this treaty the United States gained not only an immense new territory but also a large group of new citizens. Although they were left in their same geographic and cultural setting, these new United States citizens were now exposed to unfamiliar legal, political, and social institutions. Guaranteed full freedom of religion, they remained Catholic, but they were soon inundated by a flood of Anglo-Saxon Protestants. Guaranteed full protection of property rights, they soon became enmeshed in a web of confusing Anglo-Saxon laws which required proof of ownership unfamiliar to them.

Accustomed to Anglo-Saxon legal forms, careful surveys, and complete documentation, the American newcomers were appalled at the Mexican system of property laws, with its lack of survey, indeterminate boundaries, and frequent failure to register grants. The Americans, having traditions of preëmption and occupancy rights, sought out vacant lands, where they proceeded to establish homesteads, making improvements on them as basis for ownership. In complete disregard of Mexican legal traditions, they often settled on the most desirable agricultural lands, usually near rivers. Some loudly argued that conquest gave them the right to oust Mexican grantees and to open land to Anglo settlers in the pattern of the midwestern American frontier.

Conflict was unavoidable as Anglo-American and Mexican societies met. The Treaty of Guadalupe Hidalgo tried to solve the problems of the change of citizenship, but many difficulties inevitably arose from the differing cultural viewpoints. Anglo-

American views of the frontier heavily stressed the role of the individual, who was expected to use it for his personal benefit. On the other hand, the Spanish-Mexican view tended to subordinate the individual's welfare to that of the community. Although the treaty provided guarantees of individual rights to former Mexican citizens, it failed to take into consideration their rights as a distinct cultural entity.

The Mexican War was merely an incident in a malignant conflict of cultures that arose some years before and survived long after the ratification of the Treaty of Guadalupe Hidalgo. Within the framework of this ancient conflict it is possible to discover the roots of the conflict that permeates the relationships between Anglo and Mexican American in the Southwest. With their own cultural background, Anglos have failed to respond adequately to the major events in a pattern of conflict which has prevailed from Brownsville, Texas, to San Francisco. Many Anglos have simply discounted Mexican Americans as beings who lack industry, live for mañana, sit on their haunches all day in the sun, come alive at fiestas, and delight in gambling and dancing all night to the strains of wild and exotic music.

Neither the Anglo nor the Mexican was prepared or willing to understand and respect the other's heritage and culture. The aggressive, land-hungry Anglo, not appreciating the unique Mexican life style, looked upon Mexicans as lazy, deceitful, foreign, and incapable of assimilation. Finally, years of misunderstanding and conflict between the two groups led to a situation in which the Mexican American found his lands gone, his religion seriously challenged, and himself a citizen of a country whose language, laws, and social customs he did not understand. Domination by an ever-increasing Anglo majority, with its negative attitudes toward Mexican Americans, did not permit significant acculturation. Thus, despite treaty guarantees of property rights and equality of citizenship, bitterness and conflict grew between the Anglos and the Mexican Americans during the latter half of the nineteenth century. The depth of this animosity becomes apparent in the relations between the two communities in the period following the Treaty of Guadalupe Hidalgo.

# five

# Roots of the Poison

Never before had the United States at the stroke of a pen taken into its borders so many people of another culture as it did at the end of the Mexican War. The Treaty of Guadalupe Hidalgo, which terminated hostilities, pledged to these new citizens the protection of United States laws for their religion, property, and political liberty. Absent from the treaty, however, were provisions for protection of their social institutions. Historically, the acculturation process for newcomers to the United States was facilitated by the American school system. Acculturation was not a goal in the early days of the American West; there frontier conditions and institutions, in-

cluding schools, had not developed objectives of cultural assimilation.

Following the war the Southwest remained much as it had
been under Mexican rule. There was little immediate change
in traditional Mexican cultural patterns, except in eastern
Texas and northern California, where an immediate and massive influx of Anglo-Americans brought on sudden and far-
reaching changes. In California the gold rushes of 1849 and
later years quickly altered the language and society in the
northern half of the region, while Mexican ways persisted in
the southern half until the 1880s. Then large-scale Anglo immigration brought about a massive dilution of the life style of
the southern californio as well.

The discovery of gold in the northern foothills in 1848 had
an immediate and sweeping impact on California's economy.
It brought prosperity—even wealth—to some californios, but
it also brought rapid and overwhelming Anglo penetration
and domination to the area. Californios rushed from town
and rancho to the diggings, and some had great success in the
gold fields. In the foothills they were joined by other gold-
hungry adventurers, including several thousand Mexicans from
Sonora, who introduced such innovative mining techniques as
panning and drywash separation of gold. Resentment engendered by the mining success of these Sonorans was one of
the first factors in the increasing antagonism between Anglos
and Mexicans in California. The hostility between the two
groups was based initially on attitudes formed during the
Texas independence movement and the Mexican War. By 1849
competition for the better mine sites rekindled and intensified
existing animosities and eventually led to open conflict in the
gold fields.

In this highly competitive and potentially inflammable situation, californios and Mexicans soon became the focus of dis-

crimination. Posters appeared in mining areas warning that foreigners had no right to be in the mines and threatening violence if they remained. Californios found that they were unable to convince 80,000 suspicious or hostile Anglos that they, too, were Amercian citizens. The presence of 8,000 Mexicans, 5,000 Chileans and Peruvians, and numerous French, Germans, and Irish further complicated the issue of the californio's American citizenship. The Anglo, uninterested in distinguishing between californios and Spanish-speaking foreigners, lumped them all together under the denigrating term "greaser."

This pattern of Anglo exclusion, based on economic, nationalistic, and racist attitudes, quickly moved from suspicion to threats, violence, restrictive legislation, litigation, and back to violence. In the spring and summer of 1849, Anglo vigilante groups, arguing that mineral wealth was peculiarly reserved for Americans, expelled many of the Spanish-speaking miners from the northern mines. Meeting at San José, the first California Assembly, by a vote of 22 to 2, supported this view by asking the United States Congress to bar all foreigners and californios from working in the mines. The following May, a Foreign Miners' Tax Law, aimed primarily at Sonorans and californios, was passed by the state legislature, but it was neither uniformly enforced nor uniformly accepted. Because of the loose compliance with this law, Mexicans and other Spanish-speaking miners were terrorized by vigilante groups and their property often destroyed. Sonora, a California foothill mining town established by Mexicans, was put to the torch by two thousand rioting Anglo miners. Shooting at every Mexican in sight, they continued to harass the townspeople for days. Scores were murdered or lynched, causing most of the Spanish-speaking people to flee farther south. The Spanish-speaking were blamed for subsequent highway robberies and violent deaths, which led to further vigilante action. Although this persecution of Mexicans and other Spanish-speaking miners had widespread popular support, the injustice repelled some Anglos, who dared to speak out against it. Early in 1851 the tax law was repealed. While it was in effect, however, it had eliminated most of the Spanish-speaking miners and greatly reduced immigration into California from foreign countries.

The discovery of gold and the influx of 100,000 people into California in 1849 created other problems as well, most notably the critical need for adequate civilian government. Seeking a solution to this problem, General Bennett Riley, the military governor, called a constitutional convention to meet at Monterey in June 1849. Of the 48 delegates elected to this convention, eight were Spanish-speaking californios. They participated actively in committees and in writing the constitution; one of them, Mariano Vallejo, was elected a member of the first California senate the following year.

Being particularly concerned with civil rights and land titles, this handful of Spanish-speaking delegates was successful at the constitutional convention in securing some legal protection for themselves and their fellow californios. By working in committees and addressing the delegates on issues important to them, they molded parts of the constitution having to do with voter qualification and taxation. A major contribution to the constitution was their successful thwarting of a move to limit the vote to whites. Among their other victories was securing a unanimous vote in favor of the proposal that the legislature print all laws in Spanish as well as in English. They also obtained the right to local election of tax assessors as a protection against possible discriminatory taxation of their lands. The 1849 Constitution is the only major state document in which the legal heritage of the californios was represented and which they helped shape. When the constitution was completed, they were reasonably well pleased with the results and joined in the widespread celebration of the work. In later years Hispanic-Mexican legal tradition formed the basis for California's communal property- and water-rights legislation (which differed markedly from Anglo-Saxon practice) and the state's mineral rights and mining practice (for which there was little precedent in Anglo-Saxon law).

While the 1849 Constitution was being written, in the northern half of the state forces were at work that would have a far-reaching effect on the economic position of most californios. Close on the heels of the hordes of miners came Anglo squatters, who established themselves on rancho property and began fencing off certain parts for their own use. With the exhaustion of placer gold, many miners turned to other pursuits such as farming, and squatting on the lands of the californios became increasingly common.

After the gold rush, the history of land in California is often a story of greed, corruption, and robbery. Most of the good land was held by californios under titles from the Mexican and Spanish governments, and the Treaty of Guadalupe Hidalgo explicitly guaranteed Mexican Americans free enjoyment of their property. However, pressure from increasing numbers of immigrants motivated political leaders to seek a solution to the squatter problem by questioning the validity of land titles and then seeking legal means to vacate as many of them as possible. Thus, the United States Congress was persuaded by California congressmen to pass the Land Act of 1851, the alleged purpose of which was to clarify land titles. The act required all grantees to appear before a Board of Land Commissions within a fixed period and to prove their titles.

Many serious and justifiable complaints against the implementation of the 1851 law and against the attitudes and actions of the board were made by the californios. Much of this criticism grew out of ambiguities directly resulting from the Land Act itself. The act gave an ever increasing number of squatters hope and support for their illegal actions. Each new wave of squatters added to the conviction of the righteousness of their cause and to their fierce determination. Even renters who had previously accepted californio ownership now refused to make further payments until their landlord's title was validated. At the same time, efforts were made to pass legislation making grant lands available to squatters. In 1856, after the board had completed its task, a law was passed converting all unconfirmed grant acreage into public domain. However, the law was declared unconstitutional by the state supreme court the following year. Additional californio resentment against the board arose from its unfamiliarity with Mexican and Spanish traditions of land usage. Under the Spanish system, land ownership was largely determined by length of occupancy and use, and exact boundaries were of less importance. However, the board insisted on complete fulfillment of grant conditions, and showed a general disposition to decide cases on technicalities rather than on broad issues of justice.

The board met from January 1852 to March 1856, when it finally adjourned. Californio grantees appeared before it with their Anglo lawyers, their grant papers, maps, statements of long possession, and other evidence of ownership. In the long run the results of the hearings were a disaster for the californios. Of 813 claims, 521 were initially confirmed, 19 were discontinued, and 273 rejected. Of the 273 rejected, 132 were appealed, and in 98 cases the board's ruling was reversed. Of the 521 claims approved by the board, 417 were appealed by government attorneys, who, however, won only 5 reversals. Cases were appealed as many as six times. Government attorneys clearly showed excessive zeal in trying to prove a maximum number of California land grants fraudulent.

The process of validating land grants was long and arduous. To establish clear title took an average of about 17 years, during which time the owner's control of his land was limited. About three-fourths of the California grants were eventually confirmed, but the process proved extremely expensive for most grantees. In order to pay the heavy costs of lawsuits and appeals, many landowners had to borrow, using their land as collateral. Even when they won clear title, they were still often eventually forced to sell part of their cattle or landholdings to pay lawyers' fees and court costs. For some rancheros confirmation did not assure security of title; some continued to be harassed and persecuted by persistent and determined Anglos. For example, one notable family, the Berryesas, were molested and badgered by premeditated acts of violence that brought many of its members to insanity or death. As the result of intimidation, outright robbery, forced sales, litigation, and treacherous lawyers, land ownership in California had undergone drastic changes by 1856.

Pueblo and mission land grants posed additional problems. Not until the 1880s were these worked out. The early California historian, Hubert H. Bancroft, considered the federal government's treatment of the California land claims problem so bad as to be indefensible.

Illegal squatter activity was only one form of lawlessness that affected the californio as a result of the gold rush. In addition, the presence of large numbers of adventurers, outcasts, and other social misfits from many lands and the lack of adequate law enforcement led to considerable violence; thievery, robberies, and murders were common throughout the gold-mining period. Because of the stereotype most Anglos had of Mexicans, the latter provided convenient scapegoats for these crimes. There were, of course, cattle thieves and bandits among Mexicans, just as there were among Anglos. However, much so-called Mexican "bandit activity" was in part a response to widespread persecution and violence perpetrated against the Mexican community by Anglos. The response of some individual Mexicans led to great notoriety. Joaquín Murieta is perhaps the best-known (if partly legendary) californio bandit-hero; he was credited with terrorizing much of Calaveras County in 1852–1853. His activities and those of other highwaymen, such as Juan Flores and Three-Fingered Jack García, led to retaliation against all Mexicans. Indeed, many innocent Mexican Americans suffered as the result of legal and extralegal efforts to reduce crime and banditry in California. To accuse a Mexican of stealing was tantamount to finding him guilty and sometimes led to his sudden death.

There were many Joaquíns so accused, but Californians tended to blend them all into one image and credited Joaquín Murieta with every crime committed in the state. According to the legend that quickly grew, Murieta was a peaceful Mexican miner whose claim was jumped by gold-hungry Anglos, who whipped him, hanged his brother, and raped his wife. Enraged by these wanton acts, Murieta dedicated his life from then on to avenging his family honor by bringing death and destruction to all "gringos."

As more and more travelers insisted that they had been robbed by him, his reputation grew by leaps and bounds. Despite a certain Robin Hood aura that grew around him, the California legislature created early in 1853 a special ranger force under Captain Harry Love to hunt him down. A $1,000 reward was also posted. After chasing alleged Joaquíns all over the southern mining region for several months, in July Love's rangers killed two Mexicans, one of whom was identified by many as Joaquín Murieta. However, there was some dispute of this fact, and the details of Murieta's life and death continue to be debated.

Anti-Mexican hostility and antagonism in California was not limited to the mining region. By the mid-1850s, Anglo prejudice against Mexican Americans, especially toward those of marked Indian appearance, became wide-spread throughout the state. In Los Angeles the Spanish language newspaper, *El Clamor Público*, championed the rights of Mexican Americans, describing their persecution and criticizing the unequal application of Anglo-American law. However, no relief was forthcoming. Some californios even considered emigration as a solution to their many problems, and a few tried it, but most preferred to remain in California, hoping that the situation would become better.

In the 1850s a number of factors in southern California eased the adjustment of Mexican Americans to the new conditions of American control. A limited number of Anglo settlers were attracted to this area because of the lack of gold and the scarcity of water. In addition, a steady influx of Mexicans from Sonora into southern California kept the Spanish-speaking people a majority there until the 1870s. This majority position helped to smooth the course of political transition. During this period californios filled important positions in the government of Los Angeles city and county; Juan Sepúlveda was a Los Angeles *alcalde,* and Antonio Coronel became Los Angeles' first superintendent of schools and later held other high offices. Many others held government positions of lesser importance at many levels. The Spanish-speaking were dominated, however, by Anglos in both business and government in the south, as well as in the north.

Another factor that eased the position of the Mexican Americans during the transition to the new regime in the southern counties was the economic prosperity of the 1850s. These counties were pastoral and agricultural, and during this period they supplied large numbers of cattle at greatly inflated prices to the readily accessible market created by the gold rush. The bonanza income from cattle sales enabled many southern California rancheros to enjoy a high standard of living.

However, the Texas and Sonora cattle drives in the late 1850s, combined with the California drought of the early 1860s, put a quick end to the California cattle boom. Cattle which had sold for $5 a head before 1849 and as much as $100 during the height of the gold rush were selling for less than $1 a head in the spring of 1864. Many rancheros, heavily in debt as the result of extravagant living, lost their lands to creditors or experienced foreclosures because they could not pay their taxes.

One beneficial effect of the end of this cattle boom, however, was that it led to diversification in agriculture, with a shift to sheep-raising and the cultivation of grapes, citrus, corn, wheat, and other crops. Southern California's sheep industry especially expanded as the Union Army's need for wool soared during the Civil War.

The American Civil War found Mexican Americans, like other Americans, divided in their sympathies. Because there were many Confederate sympathizers in California (especially in the south), the United States was concerned about the loyalty of its recently acquired citizens. The overwhelming majority were loyal to the Union, however, and some Mexican Americans served in the Union forces. The most notable group was a battalion of 450 californio cavalrymen, led by Captain Salvador Vallejo. Patrolling the Mexican border and fighting Apaches, these troops helped to frustrate Confederate plans to seize control of New Mexico.

The Civil War also had a political impact on the Mexican American. Since many Democrats had come to be looked on as traitors, it brought great success for the Republican Party, to which most Mexican Americans belonged at that time. As a result, a larger number of californios were elected to political office in the years during and after the war.

Cultural and historic ties with Mexico and the sustained movement of Mexicans into California during the second half of the nineteenth century continued to have an impact. Mexican civil strife in the late 1850s known as the War of Reform and the subsequent French intervention in the 1860s aroused the renewed interest of californios in what was happening in Mexico.

As a result of the Mexican government's suspension of payment on all foreign debts in 1861, France invaded Mexico early the following year. A combination of the ambition of Napoleon III to establish a second French empire and conservative Mexican interest in reëstablishing a monarchy brought the Archduke Maximilian of Austria to Mexico as its emperor in 1864. In this critical situation Benito Juárez, the great Mexican leader, fought desperately against the combined forces of Mexican monarchists and French imperialism. Initially thwarted at the city of Pueblo on May 5, 1862 (Cinco de Mayo), the reinforced French forces pushed on to Mexico City and finally drove the Juárez government to the northern frontier of Mexico.

Benito Juárez, the man who fought the French so doggedly, was a full-blooded Zapotec from the city of Oaxaca. Born of a poor Indian family and orphaned at the age of four, he was raised by an uncle; he first studied for the priesthood but then switched to law. He was a quiet and reserved person who developed a reputation for honesty and efficiency in government. Elected governor of Oaxaca in 1847, he quickly rose to national prominence as one of the outstanding young liberals and became leader of the resistance against the French in the 1860s.

Driven to desperate measures by French successes, President Juárez sent General Placidio Vega to California to seek financial aid and volunteers. His activities brought some results; Mexican patriotic and benevolent societies mushroomed, $200,000 was raised to fight the French, and both californio and Anglo volunteers enlisted. However, few actually ever reached Mexico.

After Juárez successfully drove out the French invaders, activities of Mexican patriotic societies in the American Southwest continued. Mexican Californians felt a much greater sense of identification with their mother country than ever before. The annual celebration of two Mexican national holidays, Cinco de Mayo and the Grito de Dolores, is one indication of this new attitude after the 1860s. Another factor in this change was the continuing immigration of Sonorans who gave evidence of stronger bonds of patriotism and affection for their mother country than did many of the californios. As Sonorans became a major group in the Spanish-speaking community, there was a blurring and a breaking down of distinctions between Mexicans and californios. These immigrants, with their patriotic zeal, reinforced the cultural patterns of the earlier Mexican society and initiated a new phase in California's Mexican American culture.

A new era for the Mexican Americans of southern California began in the 1870s with the advent of the transcontinental railroads. In 1876 the Southern Pacific Railroad reached Los Angeles, and in 1887 the Santa Fe became connected with the East by purchasing short existing lines and building the necessary links. These two railroad lines brought into the southern half of the state large numbers of Anglo-Americans, who engulfed the Mexican culture there. These new immigrants bought family farms from old landed Mexican American families and sections of ranchos for raising oranges or grapes. They rented rancho lands to run sheep in large numbers. They also established their own churches, schools, and other cultural institutions.

Because of these changes, Mexican Americans quickly found themselves in an entirely new social, economic, and political situation. By 1880 this new Anglo immigration had reduced the Mexican Americans to about 25 percent of the total southern California population, and ten years later they formed only 10 percent. In the economy new conditions led to modifications of Mexican American occupational patterns. A small Mexican American middle class developed, made up largely of doctors, jewelers, clerks, and harness-makers. This middle class lived widely dispersed throughout Los Angeles, and although not totally accepted by Anglo society, it lived considerably better than the rest of the Mexican population. A majority of Mexicans lived in a colonia known as Sonoratown, south and east of Los Angeles plaza, and worked in such low-paying jobs as farmers, day laborers, seamstresses, butchers, barbers, etc. Unlike their emerging middle class comrades, they had only limited opportunities for upward social mobility and continued to be victims of wide-spread prejudice, discrimination, and mistreatment.

Further changes in employment patterns were also brought about by new mining developments in northern California. The expansion of the New Almaden quicksilver mine near San José created an economic opportunity which attracted some 1,500 Mexican Americans to that region. Others moved into gold-mining areas, where they performed most of the common labor and semi-skilled work. This movement of work-

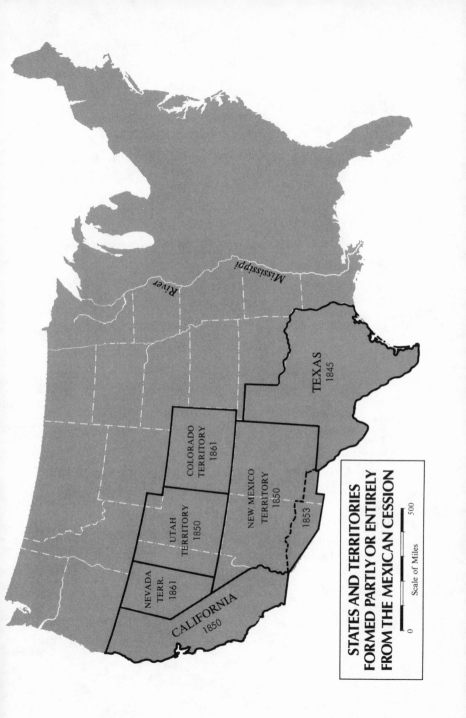

**NEVADA TERR.** 1861

**UTAH TERRITORY** 1850

**COLORADO TERRITORY** 1861

**CALIFORNIA** 1850

**NEW MEXICO TERRITORY** 1850

1853

**TEXAS** 1845

*Mississippi River*

## STATES AND TERRITORIES FORMED PARTLY OR ENTIRELY FROM THE MEXICAN CESSION

Scale of Miles

0        500

ers to the northern part of the state created an economic vacuum by depleting the Mexican labor pool in Los Angeles. This temporary shortage was quickly remedied by renewed immigration from Mexico. As a result of this influx there were as many Mexicans as californios in the state by the turn of the century, and a full blending of their related cultures seemed to be taking place. At the same time, much of the californio upper class was absorbed more completely into the dominant Anglo-American culture than previously. Because of these economic and social changes, by 1900 the culture of the californios, built up for over a century, became almost extinct, swallowed on the one hand by the flood of Anglos and on the other by the waves of immigrants fleeing economic injustice, social turmoil, political repression, and racial discrimination— all rampant in Mexico at this time. A new period was beginning for the Mexican American in California.

The history of the Mexican American in Texas in the second half of the nineteenth century differed in many respects from that of the californio. It was in Texas that the initial clash of Mexican and Anglo cultures took place—a clash which led to the bitterest antagonism between Anglos and Mexicans in all the Southwest. The prevailing racial attitudes and economic values of Anglos in Texas set the pattern of relationships between the two peoples. Since more than 80 percent of early Anglo migrants to Texas came from the deep South, racial attitudes toward black people were readily transferred to Mexicans. From the very beginning, these racial feelings were the single most important ingredient in Anglo-Mexican relations. Because of their distinctive culture, Mexican Americans were considered innately inferior and an obstacle to a progressive economy and society. The resulting hostility was intensified by the fact that many Mexican Americans in Texas were quite proud of being tejanos and considered themselves superior, not only to more recently arrived Mexicans but also to Anglo-Americans. As a result of these attitudes on the part of both tejanos and Anglos, the word Mexican early took on a pejorative connotation in Texas.

After Texas became independent in 1836, a floodtide of Anglo immigration into the area quickly reduced the tejanos to a small percentage of the population. By 1840 they constituted 10 percent of the total population, and by 1860 they were reduced to only 6 percent. Border areas, however, remained heavily Mexican in population and continued to attract a steady migration from Mexico. During this period the new international boundary set by the Treaty of Guadalupe Hidalgo was ignored by all, facilitating this constant flow of immigrants to southern Texas.

Social interaction between the upper strata of Anglos and tejanos resulted in a considerable amount of intermarriage between these two groups, leading to a degree of acculturation in the period immediately following Texas independence. Nevertheless, discrimination was wide-spread, especially against the poorer class of Mexicans who were not only considered racially inferior but also accused of helping runaway slaves escape across the border into Mexico. Border banditry involving Anglos, Mexican Americans, and Mexicans, especially in the heavily Mexican area between the Nueces River and the Rio Grande, aggravated the bad relations among these three groups.

The Cart War conflict of 1857 was one example of these bad relations. From colonial times Mexicans had been extremely able teamsters and had organized a successful trade in carrying goods between the Texas coast and San Antonio. Because they hauled at cheaper rates than their Anglo competitors, they became the focus of the latter's anger. This bitterness finally led the Anglo teamsters to begin attacking Mexican freight trains, stealing their goods, burning their carts, and even murdering their drivers. After the Mexican minister to the United States complained about these outrages, federal troops were sent into southern Texas. Their presence and Anglo vigilante action against some of the guilty Anglo teamsters brought the Cart War to a quick end.

At the close of the 1850s Juan Nepomuceno Cortina, who was later to become governor of the northeastern Mexican state of Tamaulipas, excited the popular imagination by his banditlike actions, much as had Joaquín Murieta. After an uneventful early life as a member of a border ranchero family, Cortina first came to the public notice in 1859, when he shot a Texas marshal while rescuing a peón whom the lawman was brutally mistreating. Then, early on the morning of September 28, 1859, Cortina and a band of about 100 followers burst into Brownsville, shouting "Viva Cortina! Mueran los gringos!" In short order they had taken over the town; they killed three Americans accused of mistreating Mexicans, attempted to raise the Mexican flag, and finally left. From his hideout Cortina issued a statement that he would continue to fight for the emancipation of his fellow Mexicans. The citizens of Brownsville appealed for American troop protection. When they failed to receive it, they obtained help from the Mexican army, which chased Cortina across the Rio Grande into Mexico. Subsequent clashes between Cortina and American forces resulted in victory for Cortina, who became a great hero to Mexicans on both sides of the river. Apparently genuinely interested in redressing wrongs committed against Mexicans, Cortina attracted strong support when he proposed the creation of a Mexican organization to achieve this end. His temporary success was at last brought to an end in December, however, by the arrival of additional American troops, who chased him deep into Mexico. However, Cortina's success and fame continued on the southern side of the Rio Grande; as governor of Tamaulipas and brigadier general in the Mexican army, he continued to support forays into Texas until the 1890s.

The enmity between Anglo and Mexican was also in evidence during the Civil War. After Lincoln had been inaugurated as president in March 1861, a Texas convention voted (109 to 2) to join the Confederate States of America. There is little to indicate that most Mexican Americans concurred in this, however. During the war years many of them became Union supporters and harassed Anglo-Confederate Texans by "liberating" their cotton, cattle, horses, and other property. After Lee's surrender, swarms of unpaid and destitute Confederate veterans ranged the Texas countryside; robbery, thievery, and violence became wide-spread, with Mexicans often the targets of this outlaw activity.

A running border war in western Texas developed from a series of events which also had their beginnings during the Civil War. In 1862 Mexicans living in the El Paso area began to take salt for both their personal and commercial use from the Guadalupe salt lakes located about 100 miles east of the city. In 1866 Samuel Maverick of San Antonio claimed a large portion of the salt lakes and began to monopolize the salt beds. The lakes quickly became a political issue between Maverick and El Paso Mexicans. For the next ten years the issue took many complex turns, largely as a result of the efforts of two Mexicanized Italians, Father Antonio Borajo and Luis Cardis, to gain control of the lakes for their own benefit by influencing and manipulating the vote of the local Mexican population.

In 1877 a Democratic politician, Charles Howard, took over the salt lake area not already held by Maverick and posted notices that henceforth a fee would be charged for taking salt.

Trouble began when Howard had two Mexicans arrested for allegedly planning to take salt from his property. Violence erupted when Howard shot Cardis; in retaliation Mexicans, encouraged by Father Borajo, killed Howard and two other Anglos and inflicted considerable property damage in El Paso. Racial feelings and violence ran at a high pitch as adventurers came into the area to get into the fight. Officials on both sides of the Rio Grande seemed uninterested in suppressing robbery and murder as the violence continued. Finally, after six months of bloody warfare, relative peace was restored with the arrival of American troops and a United States Army investigating commission. In the end everyone had to pay to take salt from the Guadalupe lakes.

In the period after the Civil War, the western frontier became a refuge for many social outcasts and misfits, the refuse of western mining booms, and former Confederate soldiers, all of whom kept the entire area in a state of insecurity. Extensive violence continued in the Southwest between Anglo and Mexican communities, encouraged by bandits from both sides of the border. Along the Rio Grande there were many callous killings by American and Mexican gangs, who found the border region a safe haven, uncontrolled by either the United States or Mexican governments. Mexicans and Mexican Americans unfairly received most of the blame for these brutal crimes. Captain L. H. McNelly, first head of the Texas Rangers, indicated at the time that responsibility for such criminal acts was not one-sided, and he expressed the fear that Mexicans might rise up in armed protest against their suffering. By the mid-1870s the attacks had become so widespread that both Mexicans and Anglos moved from their ranches and farms into towns for safety. Some Mexicans even moved across the Rio Grande into Mexico. Indeed, many small Mexican border towns of today were established by groups fleeing violence and persecution during that period. In 1875 bandits made a raid on Nuecestown (now Corpus Christi) in which both Anglos and Mexicans were robbed, shot, and their stores and houses burned out. Indiscriminate retaliation by Anglo posses against Mexican suspects was brutal and murderous. However, by the end of the decade, the border conflict was greatly reduced, largely as a result of Porfirio Díaz' ascent to political power in Mexico. The Díaz administration was able to extend the control of the central government to the northern border region, and, by collaborating with the United States Army, it brought the beginnings of law and order to the region.

In Texas history the period after the Civil War was characterized by a number of economic developments that affected the Mexican American markedly. The first of these was the great Texas cattle boom of the 1870s and 1880s, which was given impetus by improved transportation and by increased American and world demand for beef. This boom provided employment for many Mexican American vaqueros on cattle and grazing lands originally owned by Mexicans. Before the Civil War, Texas had experienced less of a problem with questions of land ownership than had California. Few individual land grants had been made during the Spanish period, and *empresario* grants (such as the one given to Moses Austin and implemented by his son Stephen) awarded during the Mexican period were usually clearly defined and led to few problems of disputed ownership. Some grants had been invalidated during the Mexican period, and many later claims, mostly made by Anglos, were declared fraudulent by the Republic of Texas. As a result of the cattle boom after the Civil War, however, the loss of land by tejanos to Anglos was accelerated. In many cases these lands were acquired by forced sales for nonpayment of taxes, with Anglo speculators often obtaining tejano lands at only a few cents per acre. In one such sale in 1877 a 3,027-acre parcel in Hidalgo County went for $15.00.

A second economic development affecting Mexican Americans in Texas during this period was the growth of the sheep industry. As railroads opened new markets for Texas wool, sheep-raising spread rapidly in the 1870s, especially in the heavily Mexican region of south Texas. In some areas sheep took on greater economic importance than cattle. This growth was made possible in part by Mexican labor and expertise in raising sheep.

A third factor was a great increase in cotton-growing, which began in the mid-1880s. The expansion of cotton acreage, which was based principally on Mexican labor, led to a steadily growing stream of migrants from Mexico in the 1890s. The movement of workers north from Mexico, coupled with an increased flow of poor white migrants from the old South, who brought with them their overt color prejudice, renewed and increased the existing racial antagonisms in the area. Racial conflict became an accepted part of the social order, and it became intensified throughout Texas, especially along the border where the concentration of Mexicans was heaviest.

Despite these problems, a degree of acculturation had occurred in Texas and elsewhere in the Southwest by the beginning of the twentieth century. According to one Mexican American authority, George I. Sánchez, Anglo culture might have assimilated the Mexican at this time, had the American people and government been thoughtfully aware of the basis of conflict in the differences between the two cultures. But little or no thought was given to the social, economic, and political well-being of Mexican Americans at this time, because of racial attitudes based on color and the unwillingness of the majority culture to accept them as equals. Then came the Mexican revolution of 1910, which unleashed an immigrant flood that expanded and exacerbated the existing Anglo-Mexican cultural conflict.

# six

# The Conflict of Cultures in New Mexico

New Mexican history between 1848 and 1912, the year it achieved statehood, is characterized by much the same conflict arising from the clash of two distinct cultures as marked the other states of the Southwest. From the very beginning of the American period many New Mexican landowners and merchants, often referred to as "ricos," welcomed Anglo take-over and control. Naturally this group was readily accepted by the new Anglo social and political hierarchy. During the period of territorial status, New Mexico was dominated by a small group of Anglo and Hispano politicians and businessmen, although the area continued to have a predominantly Hispano population. Conflict was intensified because most Spanish-speaking New Mexicans, except some of the rico class, found it difficult to understand and accept American concepts of government, taxation, and land tenure based on Anglo-Saxon legal norms. The dimensions of this conflict were enlarged by the make-up of Anglo migration into the New Mexican Territory after 1848. Predominantly middle class, these new settlers found it difficult to adjust to the nuevo mexicano class system with ricos at the top, peones at the bottom, and no middle class between. Economic, political and social discord resulting from the failure of Anglo immigrants to understand Mexican culture and resistance of nuevo mexicanos to Anglo institutions made mutual understanding virtually impossible, resulting in prolonged and acrimonious struggle in New Mexico.

After 1848 New Mexicans suffered the usual indignities of military conquest, but without the additional economic, social, and political problems brought on by a gold rush, as in California, or the proximity to the American South, as in Texas. Moreover, New Mexico contained many more Mexicans than California or Texas, and their history in the area went back to the sixteenth century. In the many small villages along the upper Rio Grande, Hispanic-Mexican culture was deeply rooted, and a distinct regional subculture with local Indian elements had become well established. This unique Hispanic-Mexican life style was able to persist, because of the area's physical and cultural isolation and the small amount of Anglo immigration in the first quarter-century of American control. Despite these two factors, the 60,000 nuevo mexicanos could not fight off Anglo encroachment indefinitely.

The roots of the conflict originated in 1846 with the conquest of New Mexico by General Kearny, who brought little to the area except the United States flag and the Kearny Code. Anglo conquest had little immediate effect on Mexican culture; however, when the United States formally took over the region, most of its residents acceded to American rule. This acceptance was facilitated by the feeling of many that they were more Spanish than Mexican and thus owed little loyalty to the distant and ineffective Mexican government. Nevertheless, beneath the surface of this seemingly untroubled conquest, there existed a deep undercurrent of bitterness and anger on the part of some, who felt they had been betrayed by Governor Armijo. Other New Mexicans, especially those residing near the new border between Mexico and the United States had historically maintained strong loyalties toward the mother country. More than two thousand of these, demonstrating their loyalty to Mexico, moved across the border rather than accept American rule. Ironically, many of this group found themselves back in the United States when this area was acquired by the Gadsden Purchase in 1853.

The majority of the upper class remained in New Mexico after 1848 and readily accepted the United States government; however, for political and economic reasons some of the rico class opposed the Americans. Among the most prominent of these were Colonel Diego Archuleta and Father Antonio José Martínez, two important long-time leaders in the New Mexican community. Spurred by rumors that land would be confiscated and that the clergy would lose its privileges under American rule, these two men plotted with the Taos Indians to oust all Americans from New Mexico. In December 1846, Territorial Secretary Vigil heard about a plan to assassinate the governor and other leading Americans. Colonel Sterling Price arrested some of the conspirators in the ill-fated plot; however, Archuleta and others fled to Mexico. Because of his great power and influence in New Mexico, Father Martínez escaped punishment.

With the suppression of this Mexican and Indian plot and

the arrest of the ringleaders, Americans thought that all danger was past. This sense of security was destroyed, however, when on January 19, 1847, Governor Charles Bent was brutally assassinated and scalped at Taos pueblo. His killing rekindled the flames of nativist revolt, and in the ensuing violence many homes were sacked and fifteen or twenty prominent landowners, all either pro-American or Anglo, were killed. Before the military was able to suppress the rebellion completely in the summer, some 200 Indians and Mexicans had been killed or seriously wounded. The ringleaders of this revolt were later convicted in a trial of dubious legality and fifteen of them were sentenced to death. The hanging of these leaders for the crime of treason against a government which they did not accept deeply shook the entire New Mexican region and left a long heritage of ill will and bitterness between Anglos and nuevo mexicanos.

Despite the bitterness felt by the Spanish-speaking population as the result of the Taos suppression, they soon became more amenable to American rule, as Texas once again threatened their existence as a political unit. Many distinctly remembered the Texan invasion of New Mexico in 1841 and viewed a renewed aggressive mood in Texas with considerable apprehension. In 1848 the Texas legislature passed a law which attempted to incorporate the eastern half of New Mexico as a Texas county. Claiming that her western boundary extended to the Rio Grande, much of which runs through the middle of the present state of New Mexico, Texas sent officials under Judge Spruce Baird to organize the area politically. However, Baird was frustrated by New Mexican opposition and finally gave up his effort and returned to Texas in July 1849.

Refusing to recognize Texas' boundary claims but recognizing the seriousness of the Texas threat, New Mexicans called a state constitutional convention early in 1850. This convention, made up overwhelmingly of upper-class landed Hispanos, drew up a constitution which included the prohibition of slavery in New Mexico. At this juncture the issue of New Mexican statehood became enmeshed in the controversy going on in the United States about the slavery issue, which was temporarily solved by the Compromise of 1850. After considerable debate in Congress, New Mexico was made a territory rather than a state. In the subsequently elected territorial legislature, Hispanos played a prominent role. For example, Miguel Otero, a member of a leading nuevo mexicano family, and Father Antonio Martínez became outstanding leaders during the 1850s.

The slavery issue, which had local as well as national implications, became a divisive factor. Many patrones were attracted to pro-slavery views because of their accepting peonage as an economic institution. Other New Mexicans turned toward secessionist politics as a reaction against the Union because of the initial failure to achieve statehood. The principal leader of this faction was Miguel Otero, whose influence on the territorial legislature led to the enactment of a slave code in 1859. Later, however, when the Civil War broke out, Otero was reluctant to take sides, as were many nuevo mexicanos.

In spite of open solicitation by Confederate sympathizers for Mexican American support, most New Mexicans remained at least passively loyal to the Union, only dimly aware of the basis for the Civil War. Many viewed Confederate troops advancing into New Mexico from Texas, a part of the Confederacy, as simply a repeat of the 1841 Texan invasion. Traditional fear of Texans caused about half of the Mexican population of the Mesilla Valley to flee across the border into Mexico during the war years. That their fear was not entirely without foundation is shown by the fact that some prominent pro-Union leaders like José M. Gallegos and Facundo Pino were placed under arrest when Confederate forces invaded New Mexico. Other Hispanos served ably in the militia, and by 1865 about 5,000 nuevo mexicanos had volunteered for service in the Union army.

The first Confederate invasion of New Mexico occurred in mid-1861, when a small force moved northward from El Paso and secured the southern half of the territory for the South. A second and larger force, under the command of General Henry Sibley, advanced up the Rio Grande early in 1862 and succeeded in occupying Albuquerque and Santa Fe. From Fort Union, the last Union stronghold, the Northern forces sent out an expedition to intercept the Confederates. At Glorieta Pass, southeast of Santa Fe, a Union force commanded by Colonel Manuel Chávez destroyed the Confederate supply base, bringing about the defeat of the Southern force and eventually forcing it to retreat back to Texas. The Confederate withdrawal caused embarrassment and difficulties for the small pro-Southern faction in New Mexico, which included the former Mexican governor and his brother, Manuel and Rafael Armijo. New Mexicans sympathetic to the South suffered financial losses as a result of the Confederate expulsion. The Armijo brothers, for example, lost advances of about $200,000 made to the Confederate army, and in 1864 their ranches, store, flour mill, and other property were confiscated by the Union forces.

Conflict between nuevo mexicanos and Anglos increased after the Civil War, brought about by widespread lawlessness in New Mexico and throughout the western frontier area. Conditions became worse than in the unsettled fifties as desperadoes and escaped convicts from the more settled parts of the West sought refuge in the New Mexico region. Adding to this lawlessness were bands of Sonoran outlaws who ravaged the more isolated portions of the territory from time to time. As a direct result of this turmoil a circular pattern of provocation and retribution developed between Americans and Mexicans. Periods of discrimination often drove Mexican Americans as well as Mexicans south of the border. Contributing further to this atmosphere of instability and racial violence was the continuing disorder and agitation resulting from Indian warfare, widespread range wars of Anglo cattlemen and Mexican sheepherders, and the bloody conflict between cattlemen and homesteaders.

The famous cattlemen's range war, known as the Lincoln County War, was part of this frontier instability. In 1878 Lincoln County, in south-central New Mexico, became the scene of a bloody feud between rival cattle organizations in which the notorious Billy the Kid played an important role as a gunman. Mexicans were caught in the middle of this strife since they formed a substantial part of the vaquero class. In an attempt to bring order to the violence-ridden territory, President Rutherford B. Hayes appointed General Lew Wallace as governor. Wallace, by offering amnesty to all involved, finally achieved a degree of peace in the area. The fighting finally came to an end when Sheriff Pat Garrett ambushed Billy the Kid in July 1881.

This era of New Mexican lawlessness produced its share of Mexican American folk heroes—one of them the almost unbelievable figure of Elfego Baca. During a campaign for sheriff in the 1880s, Baca arrested a rampaging Texas cowboy and, in the ensuing fracas, shot a Texan. A mob of Texans then decided to "arrest" Elfego for murder, and for the following thirty-six hours he fought off eighty Texans, wounding several and killing four. He finally surrendered on promise of a fair trial and was subsequently acquitted. Later Elfego Baca became sheriff of Socorro County and remained an important leader in New Mexico to the end of the century.

Another legendary New Mexican figure, a contemporary of Elfego Baca but a completely different sort, was Sostenes L'Archeveque, who was born in Santa Fe of Mexican-French parentage. L'Archeveque went on a killing rampage when his father was murdered by Anglos, and within a short time he had shot to death more than twenty Anglo Americans in retaliation for his father's murder. However, his very success as an avenger became his undoing when his own people, fearing retaliation by Anglos for L'Archeveque's killings, ambushed and killed him.

The advent of the transcontinental railroads in the late 1870s added a new element to the relations between Anglos and Mexican Americans. Harbingers of the changing economy in the United States, railroads opened new economic opportunities for Anglos with capital, especially attracting those with speculative as well as entrepreneurial attitudes. Economic change in New Mexico began to take place through the development of extensive empires in timber, cattle, minerals, and cotton. A heavy demand for labor resulted, especially in the mining and railroad industries, and workers were attracted from northern Mexico, from as far south as the state of Zacatecas. Besides providing greatly needed · labor, Mexican migrants served to reinvigorate New Mexican culture with transfusions from the mother civilization in Mexico.

In the seventies improved transportation, pacification of the Apaches and Comanches, expanding population, and other factors created a cattle boom in New Mexico and led to large-scale Anglo cattle operations, which created heavy demands for land. Since most of the better agricultural and pasture land was in the hands of nuevo mexicanos, the greatly increased demand for grazing land led to Anglo acquisition of both village and private lands by any means—purchase, chicanery, or violence. Many Mexican Americans along the upper Rio Grande gave up subsistence farming because of these pressures and moved east into the New Mexican grasslands, where they quickly shifted to sheep-raising. This movement was accelerated by expansion of the partido (share) system of sheep-raising. The New Mexican sheep industry spread rapidly and reached its peak just after the turn of the century.

Unlike in Texas and California, the influx of Anglo Americans into New Mexico in its early years was not so great as to cause irreconcilable damage to relations between Anglos and Mexican Americans. In the mid-eighties, however, after the collapse of the cattle boom, hundreds of Anglo farmers began settling in the eastern grasslands region. This movement of people produced additional and even keener competition with Hispanos for land.

This rivalry for desirable lands was accentuated as the result of a congressional act of 1891 which set aside large tracts of land in New Mexico as national forests. Restrictions on grazing within these areas were detrimental to the interests of nuevo mexicanos, forcing them to reduce their sheep and goat herds, economic mainstays in many northern New Mexican villages. These restrictions, in turn, seriously affected the manufacture of woolen cloth, thereby causing a depression in one of New Mexico's basic home industries.

Increased Anglo-American influx in the eighties and nineties modified the economic, political, and social climate of New Mexico. The area began to undergo a change from a rural to a commercial and industrial economy as newcomers, ignoring the Mexican attitude of man living in harmony with the land, introduced a concept of changing the environment to meet his needs. Mexican Americans, hard put to adjust to these new conditions and to middle-class Anglo attitudes, rejected many ingredients of change such as competition, education, taxation, and individual political rights. Overwhelmed and bewildered by this domination, many nuevo mexicanos withdrew from contact with Anglos to the security of their own cultural group. This withdrawal was made easier by the persistence of a strong folk culture in New Mexico which lent itself to this neo-isolationism.

Another response to Anglo take-over of New Mexican lands was vigilante action by Hispano organizations like La Mano Negra and Las Gorras Blancas. Terrorist bands formed in the 1880s sabotaged the property of Anglo homesteaders, ranchers, and even railroads as these three groups fenced off lands and inhibited the free movement of nuevo mexicano sheepherders and their flocks. Railroads and ranchers suffered especially severely at the hands of these vigilantes. In 1889, the Atchison, Topeka and Santa Fe Railroad had 9,000 ties cut in half during one night by about 300 masked men; the following year nine miles of barbed wire fence was destroyed in a single night. By the early 1890s the Gorras Blancas had become a convenient name to cover all kinds of lawlessness, from personal feuds to organized cattle stealing and banditry. Finally Governor L. Bradford Prince of New Mexico issued a proclamation calling on the Gorras Blancas to disband and threatened to call out the militia and, if necessary, federal troops. This action, plus the reaction of Anglo and Mexican Americans alike to the excesses of these bands, led to the decline and eventual end of the Gorras Blancas.

In the late 1840s, Anglos began acquiring land from Hispano grantees who were either moving to old Mexico or in desperate need of cash. During this early period land transfer was usually based on mutual respect and agreement and there was little conflict over land titles. Confirmation of titles was readily accepted by all in the 1850s and 1860s when a few dozen land grants were confirmed by Congress upon recommendation of the United States Surveyor General for New Mexico. In the following two decades more grant titles were confirmed, and by 1886, out of a total of 205 private land claims filed, 141 had been approved.

Economic changes of the seventies and eighties, however, began to exert heavy pressures on the supply of land. Local and territorial politicians used their power to obtain large amounts of land for themselves and their friends. A notorious alliance of Anglo politicians and some twenty rico families, known as the Santa Fe Ring, enabled its members to acquire large tracts of land, much of it by devious means. The Ring at times used political and legal cunning to force grants to be put up for auction, so that Ring members could purchase them cheaply. It was also able to influence court decisions and legislative action. Thus, a group of unscrupulous lawyers, corrupt politicians, venal government officials, greedy bankers, and land-hungry nuevo mexicanos conspired to take over millions of acres of New Mexico. In the process, many nuevo mexicanos were dispossessed of lands which their families had owned for generations and were deprived of their traditional means of livelihood.

By 1880 pressures from advancing railroads, increasing Anglo immigration, and delay in congressional confirmation of land grants, made a rapid solution of the land issue imperative to Anglos. These influences forced Congress to act, and so, in 1891, it created the Court of Private Land Claims for New Mexico, Colorado, and Arizona. Because of a chain of historical accidents, proving title in New Mexico was extremely difficult. Early land grant records were destroyed during the 1680 Pueblo Indian revolt; then, in 1846, additional records were removed by Mexican troops retreating from the area. Adding to this loss of records was the sale of much of the Santa Fe archives for waste paper in 1869 and 1870 and the burning of the capitol in 1892. Moreover, many New Mexican grants dated from the seventeenth and eighteenth centuries and were therefore complicated by divisions and transfers. Many titles could not be proved in court, though undoubtedly valid. On the other hand, there was much fraud and attempted fabrication of titles. By 1904 the court had completed its assigned task; out of 301 petitions it had confirmed 75 land grant titles. Many nuevo mexicano grantees were unjustly deprived of their lands, often within the letter of the law. Even those whose titles were confirmed had to part with large segments of their grants to pay lawyers' fees. A Santa Fe lawyer and political leader of the Ring, Thomas B. Catron, in 1894 owned about two million acres and was part-owner or attorney for an additional four million. Eventually Anglos came to own four-fifths of the grants.

In New Mexico, mining, though a less devisive matter between Mexicans and Anglo-Americans than land ownership, still generated a degree of conflict. During the Spanish colonial period small-scale gold mining had developed in north-central New Mexico, and from the beginning it was based on Mexican-Hispanic labor and technology. When new gold deposits were discovered northwest and northeast of Taos after the Civil War, a small gold rush took place in 1867 which brought in many Anglo-Americans. Later in the century important new gold discoveries were made in the north-central part of New Mexico in the vicinity of Elizabethtown. After the Civil War some old abandoned silver mines were re-opened, and in the 1870s new silver discoveries were made in the Silver City and Socorro areas. In the following decade a number of rich silver strikes were made in neighboring Sierra

County around Kingston. Toward the end of the century, coal mining began to become important when deposits in the area of Ratón, Gallup, and Santa Fe in northern New Mexico were developed. In all of this mining activity Mexicans played an extremely important part, supplying techniques, skills, and the bulk of the labor. In addition, they worked old placers and the tailings of copper mines, sometimes making fair wages by panning old ore dumps.

However, the mining future of New Mexico lay not so much with precious metals as with copper. In southwestern New Mexico the Santa Rita copper mines, after being closed down because of Apache hostilities, reopened in the 1870s when the area became somewhat secure. Skilled Mexican miners brought from Ciudad Juárez early in the decade developed other copper deposits at Clifton, just across the New Mexican territorial line in Arizona. These gold, silver, coal, and copper mines employed many Mexicans from both sides of the border. Although some mining towns were considered Anglo camps, all had a high percentage of immigrant Mexican workers, and in many mining camps they constituted a majority. Nevertheless, a discriminatory dual wage system developed that favored Anglo miners by paying them at a higher rate than Mexican workers for the same type of work. Besides suffering from discriminatory wage practices, Mexican miners were restricted largely to menial and dangerous work, and they lived in segregated areas.

Mining expansion in the seventies created a greater need for machinery and supplies, which in turn made freighting one of the largest industries in New Mexico. Before the advent of the railroads, heavy equipment was shipped from European and eastern seaboard ports by way of Cape Horn to Guaymas on Mexico's west coast and from there to New

Mexico, while food and other provisions were freighted from Sonora. Machinery, equipment, and supplies were transported overland by Mexican arrieros, who operated long wagon trains between New Mexico and northwest Mexican ports. Men like Jesús Carranza, E. Arriola, and José M. Castañeda became successful teamster-operators, and one of them, Esteban Ochoa, became an outstanding leader in the freighting business and merchandising and later was mayor of Tucson. Carting remained an important adjunct of mining until railroads replaced this early, slower form of transportation.

Railroad construction and operation in the west had great impact on the history of the Mexican American in New Mexico. It caused freighters to reduce the numbers of their teams, and eventually it forced many of them out of business, causing arrieros to be laid off in increasing numbers. Although railroads brought about the decline of the carting industry, leading to the displacement of many arrieros, at the same time they provided thousands of new jobs. Construction of railroads in the southwest was based heavily on Mexican labor. The subsequent economic transformation that this new transportation system made possible affected the traditional mode of life in New Mexico. Although most nuevo mexicanos continued to maintain their village culture, by the end of the nineteenth century a new life style was noticeable among the younger villagers. This new way of life was characterized by the use of many middle-class Anglo symbols of progress, such as sewing machines, iron stoves, phonographs, canned foods, and all sorts of factory-made goods. Acceptance of these symbols of Anglo technological values clearly indicated that Hispanic-Mexican cultural patterns were breaking down at this time and a trend toward an amalgamation with Anglo society was taking place. Another indication of this can be seen in the inroads that Protestant missionaries were beginning to make in this overwhelmingly Catholic society during the latter decades of the nineteenth century.

Unlike the California and Texas experience, in New Mexico religion became an arena of conflict for Mexican Americans. The expulsion of all Spanish clergy during the Mexican period left only fourteen Catholic priests in the territory at mid-century. Church influence had dropped to an all time low when in 1851 Jean Baptiste Lamy was appointed vicar apostolic of the Arizona-New Mexico region by the Vatican. Bishop Lamy was given the task of reforming and reorganizing the isolated and corrupted New Mexican church. A man of great dedication and drive, but unfamiliar with Hispanic-Mexican culture, the new bishop soon became involved in a quarrel over tithing with Father Antonio Martínez, self-appointed leader of the New Mexican clergy. This disagreement with Father Martínez' position that giving to the church be voluntary escalated into a long feud between older Hispano clergy and the European clergy that Bishop Lamy had brought into New Mexico. In reaction to reforms initiated by Bishop Lamy, Father Martínez resigned as pastor of his Taos parish and in defiance of the bishop continued to minister to his parishioners independent of the hierarchy. This defiant action caused Bishop Lamy to suspend Father Martínez as a priest. The latter ignored the suspension and the outraged bishop reacted by excommunicating him. In the end, the conflict separated not only the local clergy and Bishop Lamy but also nuevo mexicanos and what they considered a foreign church. In spite of this conflict Father Martínez remained an important religious and political leader until his death in 1867, at which time his schism died with him.

Another issue of church conflict involved the fanatical religious organization whose members were known as penitentes.

These were laymen who had assisted clergymen in religious matters from the beginning of the New Mexican settlement. During the Mexican period this lay organization became far more important as its members took over the religious functions of priests who died or were forced into exile by the liberal government because they were Spaniards. After the war between Mexico and the United States, attempts by Bishop Lamy and the new church hierarchy to gain control of the organization led to increased secrecy within the brotherhood. The suppression of many penitente activities led to a decline in its religious functions and forced the organization into political activities, in which its influence was put to the service of the Republican Party. Continued attempts on the part of the hierarchy to bring the penitentes under control caused a bitter struggle which ended in the official disbanding of the organization by the church in 1889 and excommunication of its members. Turning to secrecy because of this action and the curiosity of Anglo tourists, the brotherhood carried on its religious activities on a reduced scale. As a fraternal organization, however, the penitentes continued to play an important political and cultural role in rural New Mexico until World War I. Although today their power has declined, they still retain some religious and social influence in New Mexico and southern Colorado.

In the second half of the nineteenth century local penitente organizations formed one important base which the New Mexican patrones used to maintain their political power. A second important element sustaining their power was peonage. Although outlawed by Congress in 1867, vestiges of this colonial institution continued to play an important role in New Mexican politics. Patrones, by controlling their workers through economic pressures and by delivering their votes to Anglo politicians, were able to share in the fruits of political power.

In territorial politics a few ricos coöperated with Anglos to dominate elections and governments. With their education and their acquaintance with Anglo institutions, patrones found politics a natural outlet for their leadership qualities. The Otero family affords an excellent example of the political strength of the patrón system and its effects on New Mexican society. Prominent in Santa Fe politics for half a century, this family produced several noteworthy political leaders.

Miguel Antonio Otero was elected to the United States House of Representatives for three terms in the 1850s, after having previously served as secretary to the territorial governor. During the Civil War he founded the important business house of Otero, Sellar, and Company, and later he was a director of the famous Maxwell Land Grant Company and vice president of the Atchison, Topeka, and Santa Fe Railroad. His son, Miguel II, became the first nuevo mexicano to be named territorial governor of New Mexico, being appointed by President William McKinley in 1897 and serving till 1906. By organizing the Mexican American voters and obtaining control of some federal appointments in the state he developed a strong political machine and greatly enhanced the power of the governor. His long tenure in office was the result of his efficient and well-organized administration. Another member of the family, Manuel B. Otero, was candidate for the governorship early in the twentieth century.

The long territorial status was another factor that helped the patrón to retain power in New Mexican politics and society. The absence of a merit system in the territorial government enabled the winning party to control political jobs from highest to lowest levels. Fortunately for nuevo mexicanos, territorial status meant greater federal control and a weaker Anglo power base in New Mexico. The first attempt to exchange territorial status for statehood failed because of the slavery issue; later attempts in the latter half of the nineteenth century ended in failure because of racial discrimination, religious bigotry, and political prejudices in Congress. Finally, in 1912, after a long and bitter struggle, New Mexico was admitted as the forty-seventh state; this long-overdue action came about because of national rather than local political realities.

A congressional decision in 1910 that New Mexico and Arizona would be admitted as separate states led to a constitutional convention at Santa Fe. At this convention Hispano delegates, who constituted one-third of the total membership of 100, made a strong and ultimately successful effort to make the Hispanic heritage part of the document they drew up. The constitution includes provisions for the legal equality of Spanish and English and reiterates the guarantees of the Treaty of Guadalupe Hidalgo. Recognizing the bilingual nature of New Mexican society and its Hispanic and Mexican heritage, Article VIII requires the legislature to provide training to provide teachers equally capable of teaching in Spanish and English. This provision has never been implemented.

As the movement for statehood reached its climax, cultural changes were taking place which added new dimensions to existing conflicts in New Mexican society. One aspect of this change was a tendency of nuevo mexicanos to disassociate themselves from the heavy influx of Mexican migrants who began arriving at the end of the century. Considering themselves superior to the immigrant Mexicans and feeling their socio-economic position threatened by this new group, nuevo mexicanos denied having anything in common with the recent arrivals. This attitude of superiority was buttressed by their calling themselves Hispanos or Spanish Americans rather than Mexicans, thereby attempting to refute their Mexican heritage. They often referred to immigrants from Old Mexico as "surumatos," a pejorative term which many nuevo mexicanos use even today when referring to Mexican immigrants. Another aspect of this change was the tendency of Hispanos toward acculturation with Anglo society, which reduced somewhat the conflict between the two cultures. This pattern of change and acculturation was suddenly interrupted at the beginning of the twentieth century by a cataclysmic event in Mexico which caused thousands of Mexicans to flee across the border into the United States. This event, which greatly altered the circumstances of the older Mexican American population of the Southwest, was the Mexican Revolution of 1910.

# seven

# North from Mexico

Anyone traveling from Mexico into the United States in 1848 would have found it difficult to know when he had crossed the frontier unless border guards and signs marked the boundary. The culture on both sides of this border reflected an undistinguishable continuity in society and economy. Throughout most of the second half of the nineteenth century, economic and social interaction between the American Southwest and adjacent regions of northern Mexico remained relatively undisturbed. As communication and transportation in northern Mexico improved toward the end of the century, events taking place in the central region began to have greater impact on Mexican Americans. At the same time, political and economic developments in the Southwest began to affect the course of Mexican history. At the end of the nineteenth century and in the first two decades of the twentieth, this expanded interrelationship became particularly important to Mexican Americans in the Southwest as immigration reinforced their culture and restructured their society.

These changes were in part brought on by the refugee flow from Mexico across the border into the Southwest, particularly the Texas area, as revolutionary leaders and their followers fled across the border to escape capture by government forces. One of the early exiles to this area, whose later political career greatly affected the history of both Mexico and the Southwest, was Porfirio Díaz. As a young mestizo officer he rose to prominence during the war against the French as one of Benito Juárez' most successful generals, but he later broke with his commander-in-chief. In the presidential elections of 1867 and 1871 he ran against Juárez and lost both times; at the second loss he accused Juárez of fraud. After Juárez' death in 1872 and the inauguration of his successor, Sebastián Lerdo de Tejado, Díaz made another bid for power. In 1876, while in Texas, he organized a successful plot to overthrow the Mexican government. Believing that Mexico needed a strong caudillo to give the country greater stability, Díaz led a revolt, seized control of the government, and proclaimed himself president. From his assumption of the presidency in 1876 to his overthrow in 1911, he was the master of Mexico, controlling both the government and the economy, the development of which he made his prime concern. Political stabilization and domestic tranquility encouraged foreign investors to take advantage of railroad subsidies, of government support of mining and oil development, and of Díaz' liberal policy with federal lands. Additional property became available to large landowners, mostly foreign speculators, as the result of new legislation which brought about the break-up of Indian communal lands. While the rich got richer, the Mexican poor got poorer. During this period wages remained stable, but the cost of living greatly increased. Left landless, many small Mexican landowners were forced into peonage; at the same time debt peonage rose to new heights, while domestic and foreign investors in Mexico prospered.

These economic policies of the Díaz government were promoted by a group of positivists, followers of the French philosopher, Auguste Comte. Known in Mexican history as "los científicos," these Comtians planned and worked for a modern, scientific Mexico, which would take its rightful place among the nations of the world. They accepted the widely held contemporary scientific theory that certain races were inferior as the result of heredity and environment and believed that Indians and Indian culture were inferior and therefore not a sound base on which to build a modern Mexico. On this premise, los científicos set out to Europeanize Mexico and its Indian population in order to achieve progress. Partly as a result of these ideas, Yaquis and other Indians were brutally hounded, and many were sold into virtual slavery to large landowners. By the beginning of the twentieth century, Mexico had become known as the stepmother of Mexicans and the mother of foreigners, as European and American businesses extended their economic and political control over Mexico.

During the 1910 centennial celebration of independence from Spain, the government prohibited darker-skinned Mexicans from working in those Mexico City hotels where foreign visitors stayed and excluded them from much of the downtown area. Both foreign and domestic companies were allowed to practice economic discrimination based on race and color. For example, American railroad and mining companies in northern

Mexico maintained a dual-wage system, in which Mexican workers were paid a substantially lower rate than their American counterparts in all work categories and were restricted to the lowest-paying jobs. Such economic and social injustices contributed to forces which eventually led to the downfall of Díaz and the revolution of 1910.

Before the revolution, as more and more land came under the control of a limited number of hacienda owners, the scarcity of land for rural Mexicans increased class conflict. To compound this land monopoly problem, Mexico's population increased from 9,400,000 in 1877 to 15,200,000 in 1910, largely as a result of a dramatic lowering of the mortality rate. At the same time, the standard of living of the Mexican peón, working for less than twenty cents per day, became even worse than before. These factors encouraged Mexicans, principally those from the central and eastern border states, to move out of their native country and into the United States Southwest.

By the time of the revolution, Mexico had constructed 15,000 miles of railroad, built almost exclusively for the export of minerals; five railroads connected the mines of Chihuahua, Sonora, Nuevo León, Zacatecas, Durango, and San Luis Potosí with the United States border. Peones and miners of northern Mexico had supplied most of the labor for building these railroads and as they were completed, many Mexican laborers abandoned Mexico for a new way of life in the United States. In the Southwest they worked for American railroads and mining companies. Some of them subsequently returned to Mexico, carrying back new social and political ideas engendered by their experiences in the United States. Some had been involved in the rapidly developing American labor movement and its early efforts to secure social and economic gains for workers. The American labor union experience of those returning to their homeland led to demands for similar improvements in Mexico.

As workers in Mexico began to voice complaints about Díaz' social and economic policies, many anarcho-syndicalists, who espoused the belief that all government is a form of oppression and that the product of all labor should be use, not profit, came to the forefront as leaders in social and labor reform. Under this new and militant leadership, a liberal party was founded in 1900. Many of its leaders, driven out of the country because of their socialist philosophy and radical tactics, emigrated to Mexican American communities in the Southwest.

In 1904 Ricardo and Enrique Flores Magón, Antonio Villarreal, and Juan Sarabia, important leaders of the liberal political movement, fled to Texas when they were persecuted by the Díaz government. They settled in San Antonio, where they began to publish a newspaper called *Regeneración,* in which they criticized Díaz as the cause of Mexico's ills. The following year the Flores Magón brothers and other Mexican liberals moved to Saint Louis, where they continued to publish *Regeneración* and organized the Mexican Liberal Party in exile, dedicated to the removal of Díaz from power. Díaz' influence was so great that Mexican government agents followed the Flores Magón brothers into the Midwest with the implicit sanction of the United States. Persistent harassment by Díaz compelled the brothers to flee the country, first to Toronto, then to Quebec. Finally, in September 1906, they returned to the United States and settled in El Paso. Using that city as a base for their revolutionary activities, they continued to appeal to both Mexicans and Mexican Americans for help and were moderately successful. To attract Mexican Americans to their cause, they promised land in Mexico in return for financial and political support.

Meanwhile, the two brothers, along with other Mexican political exiles, began organizing Mexican and Mexican American workers into labor unions and encouraging the union leadership to move toward greater political activism. For example, an important leader in this reform movement, Praxedis Guerrero, organized the Obreros Libres (Free Workers) in southeastern Arizona at Morenci, a copper-mining town with a predominantly Mexican labor force. To the south of Morenci, during this same time, Enríquez Bermúdez was publishing *El Centenario* at the border town of Douglas. This newspaper and other revolutionary propaganda were circulated among Mexican workers in the Arizona copper mines, as well as across the border in Mexican mining towns.

Soon the activities of these Mexican political exiles began to be felt in both the Southwest and across the border in Sonora and Coahuila. In September 1906, rebellions organized by the exiles at Douglas, El Paso, and other frontier towns broke out, but were suppressed. Leaders of these ill-fated attempts who were apprehended were jailed; however, some avoided arrest by fleeing to the sanctuary of other Mexican American communities. Among those who managed to escape was Ricardo Flores Magón, who fled to Los Angeles, where he and other leaders found support among Los Angeles Mexican Americans. In Los Angeles a group under his leadership began publishing a newspaper known as *Revolución* and continued to work for the overthrow of the Díaz dictatorship by denouncing the regime. Disseminating revolutionary pamphlets, organizing anti-Díaz cells, holding meetings, and raising funds for their activities, this movement made an important contribution to the eventual downfall of Díaz' regime. Groups of Mexican exiles and Mexican Americans were already organized to fight in Mexico against Porfirio Díaz when the revolution broke out in 1910.

The event which finally precipitated Díaz' downfall was the political campaign waged by Francisco Madero against him in the 1910 presidential elections. Because Madero dared to challenge his dictatorial control, Díaz had him thrown in jail at San Luis Potosí. Released from prison after the elections, Madero fled north, seeking refuge in the Mexican American community in San Antonio, Texas. In San Antonio, Madero, recognizing it would take more than political rhetoric to overthrow Díaz, began plotting with other exiles and Mexican Americans to invade Mexico.

At the western end of the border the Flores Magón brothers had been preparing for the moment, and when the Madero revolt began, they crossed over into Chihuahua with about 100 men, including some Mexican Americans. Quickly disillusioned with Madero because he had no revolutionary aims other than reëstablishing free elections, the brothers soon returned to the United States and set up their headquarters in Los Angeles, from which city they organized a second invasion, this time into Baja California. They were successful in capturing Tijuana and Mexicali but were later forced to withdraw back across the United States border into California. In Los Angeles they again went to work to initiate another revolution in Mexico.

Meanwhile, more vigorous leadership by Pancho Villa, Venustiano Carranza, and other followers of Madero (maderistas) in the north enabled the revolutionary movement quickly to sweep southward. As a result, in 1911 Díaz, senile and abandoned by most of his supporters, was forced to resign and to go into European exile. In the elections that were quickly held, Madero won overwhelmingly and assumed the presidency. Everyone thought the revolution over; however, it had only begun.

In the south the revolutionary leader, Emiliano Zapata, disappointed because Madero had failed to restore lands to the

Indians, called his followers to arms and renewed the killing of hacendados and the burning of haciendas. Other less revolutionary leaders followed his example in opposing Madero. Early in 1913 a counterrevolutionary plot against Madero led by Bernardo Reyes, an old Porfirian general, and assisted by the American ambassador, Henry Lane Wilson, resulted in bloody fighting in the center of Mexico City. Madero's betrayal and subsequent assassination on orders from his own general, Victoriano Huerta, were symbolic of the bloodstained years to follow.

General Huerta quickly took over control of the government. However, his tenure as president was short, since one revolutionary leader after another denounced him as a bloody tyrant and "pronounced" against his government. In the north, Venustiano Carranza, governor of Coahuila, initiated a movement against Huerta and was quickly followed in this by Francisco ("Pancho") Villa, who denounced Huerta and led his fearsome dorado cavalry in an orgy of shooting and looting in support of Carranza. On Mexico's west coast Alvaro Obregón's terrifying Yaqui troops also moved against Huerta, and in Morelos, Emiliano Zapata's bloody revolutionary record soon earned him the name "Attila of the South." Within seventeen months, Huerta suffered complete defeat and went into exile, first to Jamaica, then England, then Spain, and finally, in March 1915, to New York City.

From there, he entrained for San Francisco in June, but he surreptitiously left the train in New Mexico, where he was quietly detained by Justice Department deputies for questioning. He was later released on bond. Reports of pro-Huerta plotting in the colonias of Galveston, San Antonio, and Eagle Pass quickly followed. Refugee Mexican officers who visited Huerta at this time were harassed by American officials in an effort to discourage counterrevolutionary activity. Later in the year, when he was jailed again, a fear developed that the Mexican colonia in El Paso might try to free him. However, this concern proved unfounded, and Huerta remained in American custody. Huerta, who had a history of alcoholism, began to drink heavily at this time, causing his health to deteriorate rapidly. As a result of his excessive dissipation, he died early in January 1916, after an unsuccessful gall bladder operation.

Meanwhile, conflict among various revolutionary leaders for domination of the movement continued. Contending armies looted, burned, raped, and committed other atrocities throughout Mexico in the name of the revolution as they fought for power. Finally, in May 1920, this gory phase of revolution came to an end with the assassination of Carranza and the rise of Obregón to power.

The 1910 revolution, a period of great violence and confusion in Mexican history, directly affected the Southwest. An estimated one million Mexicans lost their lives in the decade of fighting, and a large-scale displacement of people took place. Thousands fled from the countryside into the larger cities of Mexico, while at the same time other thousands fled from the central portions of Mexico northward to the United States. No one knows precisely how many Mexicans were involved in this great exodus; one estimate holds that more than one million Mexicans crossed over into the United States between 1910 and 1920.

In addition to thousands of ordinary peasants uprooted by the revolution, many soldiers and supporters of revolutionary leaders like Villa, Obregón, Carranza, and Zapata immigrated into the United States. Also included in this mass movement were supporters of the government in power. Because many fled political persecution, this wave of migrants came from more varied backgrounds than those of any other Mexican migrations before or since; included in this group was a large percentage of women, children, and older people. These displaced people greatly increased the population of Mexican American towns and barrios. Despite plans to the contrary, most of them never returned to Mexico, as they found acceptance and cultural security in the familiar milieu of the Mexican American communities in which they settled. Those who later did return found that Mexico had changed and that they had as well. Consequently, many returnees eventually came back to the United States.

In this wave of Mexican immigrants brought on by the revolution were some who managed to escape with enough capital to go into business for themselves in the Southwest. This increased substantially the size of the Spanish-speaking middle class along the border by 1920. However, most refugees from the revolution were peones without financial resources, and these people were forced to accept menial agricultural and industrial work in order to survive. Accommodation to life in the United States was relatively easy for many Mexican refugees, since they changed only their geographic location, not their way of life.

When the revolution freed the peón from the hacienda, it not only overthrew the peonage system which historically had tied him to the land but also physically displaced him. At the same time that the revolution was uprooting thousands of peones, the demand for workers in the Southwest was rapidly increasing, making the northward move economically attractive.

The demand for labor in the Southwest came about because of a number of coinciding factors during this period. Between 1870 and 1900, the total farm acreage in the West had tripled, and lands under irrigation had increased dramatically from 60,000 to 1,446,000 acres. At the beginning of the twentieth century, sugar-beet acreage in California and Colorado expanded rapidly as a result of protective sugar rates established by the Dingley Tariff in 1897. Five years later, the expansion of lands under irrigation, promoted by the Reclamation Act of 1902, began to open up much of the Southwest to the cultivation of cotton. When the Roosevelt Dam was completed, thousands of previously untilled acres in Arizona became available for farming, and soon the Salt River Valley became a major center of cotton production. The Elephant Butte Dam, on the Rio Grande River in New Mexico, had a similar impact in that state. However, the production of these two areas did not satisfy the growing needs of the automobile industry for cotton used in the manufacture of millions of tires, nor the wartime demands of the Allied powers for uniforms. As a result of this continuing economic demand, in central and western Texas cotton began to replace cattle as the primary economic base, and in Arizona and California farmers plowed up grazing land in order to increase their cotton acreage. These developments led to a critical need for farm workers, mostly in the irrigated areas of the borderlands, and to expanded recruitment of immigrants from the Mexican border region.

While increased agricultural production was creating a demand for more workers, completion of western railroad networks similarly put unskilled labor at a premium at a time when Oriental immigration rates dropped drastically. The Chinese had formed an important part of railroad construction gangs all over the West since their recruitment for the Central Pacific Railroad in the 1860s. When the severe depression of the mid-seventies hit the country, nativistic-oriented unions of the Pacific Coast became aroused at the competition of Chinese labor, because it brought lower wages and a lower standard of living. Pressured by unions and other exclusionist groups, the United States Congress passed a Chinese Exclusion Act in 1882. This act and the 1907 Gentleman's Agreement with Japan created a considerable vacuum in western labor by 1910. Into this labor vacuum quickly moved the dispossessed and displaced from Mexico.

As southwestern railroads continued to experience great need for workers, their agents successfully recruited workers both among the Mexican Americans along the border and among Mexicans in the adjoining northern states of Mexico. Beginning about 1900, the Southern Pacific and Santa Fe railroads seriously began soliciting Mexican workers at El Paso, Texas. By 1908 these two railroads averaged more than a thousand recruits per month among Mexicans on both sides of the border; this recruitment reached its peak in the years just prior to the outbreak of World War I.

When war erupted in Europe, American economic activity expanded rapidly in all sectors. The United States became chief supplier to the Allies, and the demand for industrial as well as agricultural workers soared. At the same time the European war drastically reduced trans-Atlantic immigration, and the American peacetime response of preparedness meant that many Americans were transferred from the labor market to the armed forces. To supply the thousands of new workers needed, additional Mexicans were recruited. These Mexican laborers worked not only in California's diversified agriculture, in Colorado beet fields, in Texas cotton fields, and in the copper mines of Arizona and New Mexico, but also in northeastern iron foundries and Appalachian coal mines.

Another aspect of this changing socioeconomic structure in the Southwest was the considerable modification of the traditional Mexican American life style. It centered on the relationships of Mexican Americans to the land. The new agriculture of the Southwest, based on a large-scale mechanized commercial operation, required considerable capital investment in machinery. Applying the technology of this new, highly competitive agriculture meant a greater per-acre investment in land preparation, such as land-leveling and extensive irrigation. These increased agricultural costs made it difficult for most Mexican Americans, who lacked capital, to remain competitive. Many were forced to sell their lands, or they eventually lost them through tax foreclosures, especially in New Mexico and Arizona. Others were displaced as irrigation dams continued to be constructed and their farmlands were flooded. Some discovered that the creation of national forests, with strict federal regulation of grazing, forced them to reduce their herds. As the result of the Forest Reserve Act of 1891 and presidential action setting aside thousands of acres for future national forests, some villages in New Mexico were eventually completely surrounded by federal lands. Traditional Mexican life patterns could not escape the impact of these changes; generally speaking, Mexican Americans had to reorganize their economic way of life. The more aggresive moved to the North and East to take advantage of new opportunities, but many merely became a part of the expanding migrant farm labor population of the Southwest.

The demand for migrants was particularly strong in the sugar-beet industry, and by the time the United States entered World War I, Colorado beet growers were already using large numbers of migrant workers, principally Mexican Americans from New Mexico and Texas. Within ten years Mexican Americans had become the mainstay of the industry and constituted more than half of the sugar-beet workers in Colorado.

In order to assure themselves of a regular and readily available labor supply, sugar-beet companies at this time began to develop local labor colonias, in which they encouraged migrants to settle rather than to return to New Mexico or Texas for the winter. Migratory workers, of their own volition, also began to winter in many of the larger cities within sugar-beet production areas, thus gradually eliminating the annual return southward. These settlements became the nuclei of today's large Chicano communities in many western cities. Denver, for example, quickly attracted a pool of Mexican American workers for the beet-growing area and soon developed into a major source of agricultural workers for the entire Rocky Mountain region.

Another socioeconomic change in the Southwest occurred when migrant Mexican American and Mexican labor began to replace southern tenant farmers and sharecroppers. This trend toward the greater use of migrant workers was accelerated by the large numbers of temporary workers who became available from 1910 to 1917. Following the pattern established in the sugar-beet industry, Arizona and New Mexico cotton growers by 1917 were recruiting thousands of harvest workers in northern Mexico. In California, the amazing development of more than 200 commercial crops in the first decades of this century was made possible largely by the recruitment of Mexican farm workers. In California, too, cotton was the catalyst. Although many California farmers preferred Chinese workers, whom they had traditionally used, growers in the Imperial Valley began recruiting Mexicans in Baja California and Sonora even before World War I. As wartime demands expanded cotton-growing into the southern San Joaquin Valley, the accompanying labor increase necessitated the recruitment of thousands of Mexicans. After the cotton harvest, many of these migrants wintered in the Los Angeles area, and as a result, large agricultural labor colonias developed there, as they had in the Rocky Mountain region. By 1916, this Mexican labor force had overflowed the traditional limits of Mexican settlement in Los Angeles, causing a movement from old Sonoratown eastward into the Belvedere section of the city.

Texas was also experiencing major socioeconomic changes

during this era, especially in agriculture. Farming development and expansion in the lower Rio Grande Valley in the early years of the twentieth century depended heavily on Mexican labor. Mexicans grubbed cactus and chaparral, cleared land, planted and harvested crops, and became indispensable to the Texas agricultural economy. Mexicans were especially important in the expanding cultivation of such crops as lettuce, spinach, carrots, and beans, all of which required many hours of hand labor. As the shift took place from tenancy and sharecropping to migratory labor, various techniques were developed to tie Mexican workers to local production areas. One device used by many farmers to retain a permanent work force was to provide migrant workers with a few acres for their individual use. Another widely employed device was de facto peonage, in which workers were kept from leaving their employers by salary advances, debts, and outright coercion. However, higher wage structures elsewhere in southwestern agriculture reduced the effectiveness of Texas growers in holding their labor force and resulted in extensive labor pirating. San Antonio and El Paso had become the earliest Mexican labor pools, and agricultural employers in these areas became particularly annoyed by persistent activities of railroad and sugar-beet labor recruiters.

Rapid changes in Mexican immigration patterns resulted from the United States entry into World War I. Passage of a general immigration act in 1917, which imposed an $8.00 head tax and literacy qualifications on all immigrants, temporarily checked the migrant tide from Mexico. Passage of the Selective Service Act also acted to deter immigration, since it applied to all those who declared their intention to become citizens. Soon railroads and large-scale agriculture, feeling the labor pinch more intensely because of wartime needs, started pressuring the United States government to permit recruitment of workers in Mexico. In response to these pressures, Congress in May 1917 waived immigration requirements for agricultural workers. A year later this waiver was extended to allow the importation of Mexicans to work on railroads, in coal mines, and on government construction work; and the 1885 prohibition against contract labor importation was ignored. These exemptions to the 1917 Immigration Act were extended until the end of June 1920. During this three-year period, approximately 50,000 Mexicans legally crossed the border into the United States on a temporary basis, and at least another 100,000 entered the country illegally. There existed no agreement between the United States and the Mexican government concerning these workers, and they had no guarantees of any sort concerning employment or living conditions. Low wages and poor housing prevailed, and often employment was of short duration, but many importers of labor refused to take any responsibility to repatriate unemployed Mexican nationals. One result of this appeared in the early 1920s in the form of widespread economic distress.

This heavy influx of Mexican workers into southwestern agriculture, mining, and railroading had a domino effect on Mexican American labor in the border areas. Pressured to move by increased low-wage competition from Mexican immigrants and attracted by wartime opportunities in industrial centers, Mexican Americans for the first time began to migrate to midwestern and northeastern cities. Many were able to take advantage of wartime opportunities and move into the industrial labor vacuum caused by World War I; others, not so fortunate, found menial jobs in agriculture and on railroads. Mexican Americans were able to move into industrial jobs far more readily than Mexican immigrants, because the former, having been exposed longer to Anglo society, were usually more acculturated than the immigrant. Most industrial work available to Mexicans and Mexican Americans was hazardous, dirty, unskilled, or arduous; nevertheless, it paid better than agricultural work, and thus it improved their economic position. Besides factory work, jobs on government construction projects, especially in the building of army camps, enabled many to move out of low-pay agricultural employment.

As a result of the wartime economy, Mexican Americans began to appear in such midwestern industrial cities as Saint Louis, Kansas City, Omaha, Chicago, Gary, and Detroit; small colonias began to develop in these and other cities as Mexican Americans obtained permanent employment and brought in their families. Later, coal mines, steel plants, packing houses, automobile plants, and other industries recruited Mexican Americans to work in Pennsylvania, Illinois, Ohio, Indiana, Missouri, and Michigan. By the end of World War I, Detroit had a Mexican American population of about 8,000, while the Chicago colonia had about half that number; another 55,000 were scattered elsewhere in the Midwest and Northeast. In contrast to the 70,000 living east of the Mississippi, there were approximately 700,000 living in the four states of Texas, New Mexico, California, and Arizona. World War I brought Mexican Americans widespread employment and relatively good wages; it also gave many of them valuable experience in the United States armed forces both at home and abroad.

The Selective Service Act of 1917 led to rumors in the Southwest which caused thousands of Mexicans to return to Mexico for fear they would be drafted into the United States Army. Legally, foreign residents who had declared their intent to become naturalized and all American-born children were subject to the draft; many of the latter group, however, spoke only Spanish and considered themselves Mexicans rather than Americans. It is only fair to point out that many Anglos also considered them as Mexicans. Despite urgings not to join the United States armed forces by some members of the community such as Ricardo Flores Magón, many thousands of Mexican Americans served valiantly in the Army and Navy, where their record for voluntary enlistment was proportionately greater than that of any other ethnic group.

Although Mexican Americans proved their loyalty by excellent armed services records and civilian support of the war effort, their patriotism was frequently questioned, and they continued to suffer discrimination. In southern Texas especially, Anglo-Americans often identified them with enemies of the United States.

One reason for this suspicion was the revelation in March 1917 of the German offer of an alliance with Mexico against the United States. The proposals of the famous Zimmermann note, intercepted by the Allies, promised Mexico that, in exchange for Mexican support of the Central Powers, lands lost to the United States by the Treaty of Guadalupe Hidalgo would be returned after the defeat of the United States.

Along with the implications of the Zimmermann note, other matters added to long-standing animosities between Americans and Mexicans along the border. Border banditry stemming from the Mexican revolution of 1910 and indiscriminate Texas Ranger retaliation, United States' seizure of Veracruz in 1914, and especially Pancho Villa's border raids in 1917 leading to General John J. Pershing's punitive expedition into northern Mexico—all contributed to exacerbating feelings between Anglo- and Mexican Americans. However, notwithstanding hostility, suspicion, discrimination, and prejudice encountered by Mexican Americans during this period, most remained extremely patrotic during the war.

Nevertheless, World War I left a considerable residue of alienation and mistrust of Anglo society and government by Mexican communities in the United States. Perhaps the most important development resulting from World War I for Mexican Americans was that for the first time thousands left their familiar Southwest environment. Furthermore, in the 1920s continuing waves of Mexican immigrants moving into the border Mexican American communities caused the already saturated local labor reservoirs to overflow, thus leading to depressed wages. Facing this stiffer job competition, additional thousands of Mexican Americans because of their greater familiarity with American society chose to leave their southwestern communities for opportunities elsewhere in the United States.

This important wartime and postwar experience broadened Mexican Americans' cultural horizons and raised their levels of expectations, thereby breaking traditional and long-standing patterns of isolation.

# eight

## Mande Vd., Señor

Deeply rooted in the Mexican past, Mexican immigration to the United States between 1890 and 1965 is one of the great population movements in the history of the Americas and is basic to an understanding of Mexican history. Over the years this migration has shown great variety: permanent immigrants, legal and illegal; temporary immigrants called braceros, on contract and on their own initiative; commuters, daily, regular, and seasonal; and businessmen, students, and tourists.

Anthropologists have pointed out that this migratory movement is deeply rooted in the Mexican past, and that in a sense it might be described as the return of the Indian Mexican to the area of his origins—Aztlán, the mythical homeland of the Aztecs. They also emphasize that for the most part, the move was not out of one culture into another, but within the same culture above and below the international border. The boundary established by the Treaty of Guadalupe Hidalgo in 1848 separated Mexico and the United States politically but not culturally. Crossings both ways continued without regard for the new border and in a highly informal manner. From Mexico, cowboys, sheepherders, miners, and farm hands crossed over to take advantage of higher wages in the Southwest, and political refugees from all economic levels fled to the safety of the United States. No one knows how many migrated or how many remained permanently in the Southwest, since little official concern about the movement evolved before 1900, and no records were kept. In relation to the sparse border population it probably was of fair size. More important, this regular and continuous flow of Mexicans established the conditions of twentieth-century migration patterns.

Three distinct waves dominate the history of Mexican migration to the United States since 1900. The first significant wave, made up mostly of Mexicans from central and eastern border states in Mexico, began at the turn of this century. The second and much larger wave came during the Mexican Revolution and continued through the 1920s. About half of this second wave came from the northeastern border states, and the remainder from west-central Mexico. Because of its volume, the second wave provided the matrix for most present-day Mexican American communities. These immigrants reinforced and underscored the existing Mexican American culture and gave it much of its specific shape and present-day content. The third wave was composed of braceros and mojados who came during and after World War II. This last wave came from no one specific geographic area, but from a distinct socioeconomic class—

the upwardly mobile part of the lower class. Braceros and mojados were attracted to the United States for economic reasons rather than sociopolitical conditions, which had been a characteristic of the two earlier waves of immigrants.

In the 1920s the second wave of migrants fanned out from its base in Mexico to the United States with its extremes extending to Pennsylvania in the East and California in the West. Proportionately more immigrants of this wave settled in California than had their predecessors, because of greater opportunity there for employment. As a result, during the twenties California had an annual increase in Mexican population of 20.4 percent; while Texas, favored earlier by Mexican immigrants, showed a yearly increase of only 7.6 percent. The attraction for this wave of migrants was primarily the demand for agricultural labor, but during the twenties important changes in immigration and settlement patterns began to emerge. In the later twenties immigrants began to settle outside of the traditional area of the Southwest; they, along with Mexican Americans, began moving into urban centers in larger numbers as job opportunities in industry increased.

As a result of these socioeconomic changes, shifting of the settlement pattern in the United States took place, as the accompanying table showing Mexican-descent population by states indicates.

| | 1900* | 1910 | 1920 | 1930 |
|---|---|---|---|---|
| Texas | 71,000 | 125,000 | 252,000 | 684,000 |
| California | 8,000 | 34,000 | 89,000 | 368,000 |
| Arizona | 14,000 | 30,000 | 62,000 | 114,000 |
| New Mexico | 7,000 | 12,000 | 20,000 | 59,000 |
| Colorado | 300 | 2,500 | 11,000 | 58,000 |

* These rounded figures for 1900, 1910, and 1920, taken from census reports, represent population of Mexican birth; figures for 1930 are for population of Mexican descent, i.e., both Mexican- and American-born.

The state with the most rapid rate of increase was California, in which the population of Mexican descent had grown to more than a third of a million by 1930. This sharp increase is undoubtedly explained by the greater economic opportunities stemming from California's booming agriculture, as compared with the slower rate of development in Texas.

The volume of the second wave of immigration (1910–1930) created great reservoirs of Mexican and Mexican American labor in many southwestern cities. By 1925, Los Angeles had a larger Mexican population than any other population center except Mexico City. Other important Mexican colonias had been established in California at Brawley, El Centro, Calipatria, and Calexico. With this rapid explosion of its Mexican-descent population southern California became an increasingly important source of migrant workers for west coast agriculture as far north as Washington. Unfortunately, little recognition was given to the importance of meeting the educational, residential, occupational, and social needs of this expanded Mexican American work force.

A similar expansion took place in Texas. By 1930 the Spanish-speaking population of that state had grown to more than two thirds of a million people, the majority located in the southern part. San Antonio, El Paso, and other cities became recruiting centers for the labor needs of the North, Northwest, and Northeast. These cities became temporary stopping-off places for Mexican immigrants, and from them migration routes developed, fanning out in all northern directions, forming an arc from California to New York. These routes northward usually followed railroad lines which often provided both transportation and jobs for the Mexican migrants.

Recruitment of Mexican workers became increasingly important after the 1921 and 1924 immigration acts which greatly reduced European immigration and thereby enlarged job opportunities in industry for non-European minorities. Western railroads were especially affected by this new legislation, and a new source of labor was necessary to replace Greeks, Poles, Italians, and other Europeans as they left menial work and moved up the economic ladder. In the early 1920s railroads such as the Southern Pacific employed increasingly large numbers of Mexicans and Mexican Americans as track maintenance workers. A study in 1929 showed that between 70 and 90 percent of track workers on southwestern railroads were Mexicans and that in Texas they were rapidly supplanting Negro railroad workers. The increased hiring of Mexicans by railroads led to the development of sizable colonias throughout the West. Often these colonias grew out of mobile boxcar work camps established along the various routes of western railroads.

Mexican railroad labor was recruited to work as far north as Detroit, Michigan, and as far east as Altoona, Pennsylvania. Although the Pennsylvania Railroad brought approximately 3,000 Mexican Americans northward to work on rail maintenance in the early 1920s, by the end of the decade only a few hundred of this group were still employed by that railroad. The Baltimore and Ohio Railroad had similar attrition rates with the Mexicans it brought to the North. Harsh climatic conditions in the North seem to have been an important factor in failing to attract and hold Mexican workers in this area. Within a few years most of the recruited Mexican Americans had either moved out of railroading into other industrial work in the North or returned to the Southwest.

Northern steel companies also recruited Mexican American workers. In 1923 Bethlehem Steel brought about 1,000 Mexicans from Texas to act as strikebreakers in its Bethlehem, Pennsylvania plant, and in the same year, National Tube Company, an affiliate of United States Steel, recruited about 1,500 Texan Mexican Americans for its Lorain, Ohio plant. The

Illinois Steel Mills, located in Chicago, also recruited Mexican Americans from the Southwest and in 1923 brought workers northward from the Fort Worth area.

Between 1920 and 1930 Chicago's Mexican American population expanded from 4,000 to nearly 20,000, making it the largest Spanish-speaking area in the United States outside the Southwest. Some of the Mexican Americans came to Chicago directly because of industrial recruitment, as in the steel industry; some came north in a series of short moves while working on railroads; and others were attracted to the city from Michigan's sugar-beet fields.

From their original occupations in steel and on railroads Mexican Americans in Chicago later took menial jobs in meat packing, utility companies, construction, trucking, dry cleaning, hotels, restaurants, and other service industries. These new jobs posed social and psychological problems for the Mexican Americans; many had difficulty in adjusting to the nature and tempo of industrial work. Adapting to a society different from that in the Southwest was a difficult aspect of this new experience. Forced to find housing in substandard overcrowded ghetto sections of Chicago, they were subjected to the prejudices of second-generation Poles, Italians, Slavs, and other European immigrant groups. Having become partially assimilated, these groups now identified themselves as 100 percent Americans and looked down on the newly arrived Mexicans in order to reinforce their own economic and social status. In this difficult situation, the Mexican community developed a number of organizations for mutual aid and security. In addition to various more or less ephemeral mutualist groups, they found succor in their church. In 1923 the Reverend William T. Kane, s.j., established the first Mexican Catholic parish among steel workers in South Chicago, Nuestra Señora de Guadalupe. It grew rapidly as the Chicago

Mexican population expanded, and by the end of the decade it had 8,000 parishoners. At the same time a 75-member Banda Mexicana de Chicago was formed, as well as a number of business and social clubs, all testifying to the growth and vitality of the Mexican American community.

While Mexicans were entering the lower ranks of industrial employment in the North, this movement was somewhat slower in California. Our knowledge of the economic role of Mexican Americans in the twenties is more detailed and complete for California as a result of government concern about the effects of heavy Mexican immigration into the state. In March 1928, Governor Clement C. Young created a Mexican Fact-Finding Committee, headed by the directors of the state departments of Agriculture, Industrial Relations, and Social Welfare, and instructed it to study the Mexican in California and the implication of continued immigration. The 1930 report of this committee indicated that about 28,000 Mexican Americans were employed in manufacturing (more than 50 percent of them in the Los Angeles area), another 21,000 in the construction and building industries, and about 3,000 in fruit and vegetable canning. Six of the larger railroads in the state employed some 11,000 Mexicans; however, the committee estimated that the total number of Mexican railroad workers was considerably larger. Most Mexicans working for the railroads (as well as other industries) were unskilled laborers; however, a few were employed as electricians, molders, machinists, woodfinishers, blacksmiths, upholsterers, painters, and pressmen.

The report further stated that by the 1920s Mexicans had become the main source of agricultural labor in California, replacing Chinese and Japanese workers who had supplied much of the needed farm labor since the turn of the century. Beginning at the time of World War I, an increasing number of California crops were being harvested by Mexican workers. The Fact-Finding Committee did not ascertain exactly how many Mexican farm workers were in the state, reporting only that they numbered in the tens of thousands. Like other casual labor, Mexican workers endured poor living conditions, low wages, and chronic unemployment; however, the committee seemed to be more concerned with the man-hour needs of the growers than with meeting the ordinary decent living conditions of the farm workers.

Elsewhere in the Southwest, economic conditions of Mexican Americans during the 1920s were less favorable than in California due to limited job opportunities. A sharp postwar business depression developed in the United States during 1920 and 1921, resulting in industrial layoffs and extensive business failures. This recession particularly affected the Mexican Americans because it had a severe and long-lasting impact on western agriculture. The recession also led a sizable number of Mexicans to be repatriated with financial assistance from the Mexican government. This repatriation weakened and severed the family and social ties that the returnees had developed during the time they spent in the United States.

The cotton industry was seriously affected by the recession; in 1920 the price of cotton plummeted from 38 to 18 cents a pound, and many growers went bankrupt. Thousands of Mexicans and other workers lost their jobs and were unable to collect their accumulated unpaid wages; many were obliged to accept charity. Angered by the growers' failure to pay the wages they had promised and by poor working conditions, 4,000 Mexican workers in the Salt River cotton area of Arizona went on strike in June 1920. The strike was unsuccessful, however, because the workers, who were not united, faced a solid front of growers and law enforcement agencies. Some growers used the strike as an excuse for defaulting on their commitment to provide return transportation to Mexico for their workers. Finally, arrests and deportations of the principal strike leaders brought the strike to an end. This method of strike-breaking established a pattern that was to be repeated time and again in the history of farm labor in the Southwest.

Along with a repatriation movement that developed because of the recession, an appreciable reduction of Mexican immigration to the United States took place as the wartime waiver of immigration restriction was now rescinded. With the recession acting as a motive force, illegal immigrants began to be deported on a larger scale than ever before. While mojados were forced to leave the United States, other Mexicans returned home voluntarily when economic opportunities in the United States declined. Some industries that had encouraged Mexican workers to come to the United States during World War I began to send them home in 1920. The Ford Motor Company alone repatriated 3,000 Mexicans at company expense during this period.

By 1923 the postwar recession and its effects were diminishing and the demand for workers increasing as patterns of agriculture in the Southwest underwent significant changes. A continuing decline in cotton prices caused Arizona Salt River Valley and California Imperial Valley growers to shift from cotton to lettuce production. Additional acreage was being added in the Imperial Valley through the extension of irrigation, and new citrus groves began to come into production in southern California. Agribusiness, therefore, began paying fees to labor contractors for the recruitment of farm workers. This practice led to a rapid development of the agricultural labor contractor, known in southwestern Mexican American communities and agribusinesses as the "contratista" or "enganchista."

Labor contractors served as brokers between Spanish-speaking Mexican laborers and agricultural employers. Typically they were Mexican Americans whose familiarity with the language and customs of la raza, as well as with the labor needs of the farmer, made it possible for them to secure Mexican workers for short-term jobs. Each contratista usually owned a number of trucks and would contract with farmers to provide a specified number of workers for a fixed fee per head. He played an important role for decades by recruiting, transporting, organizing, and supervising immigrant and Mexican American workers. Although both Anglo farmer-employers and Mexican workers needed the services of the contractor, he was usually disliked and despised, especially by Mexicans. He was often a shrewd businessman who exploited the workers he recruited by providing food, drink, and other necessities at outrageous prices. He was often accused—justifiably—of cheating on wages and contracts.

The enlarged demand for Mexican farm labor which produced the enganchista also led to a rapid rise in immigration, beginning in 1923. This resurgence in Mexican migration and reports of large numbers of mojados illegally entering the United States aroused concern at the national level, especially in Congress. Increasingly demands were made by nativistic and labor groups that the movement of Mexicans into the United States be restricted and controlled. The first evidence of these demands appeared in 1921, when an attempt was made in the United States Congress to include Mexico within the quota system in the Immigration Act of that year. When United States immigration policies were thoroughly revised in 1924, there was another attempt to place Mexican immigration under quota restrictions. Despite a growing exclusionist sentiment, the only restrictive clause pertaining to Mexicans in the 1924 Immigration Act was one that established a $10 visa fee. On the other hand, these two immigration acts were effective in reducing European labor sources at a time when the need for workers in the United States was increasing. This increased demand for workers was met by an expanded recruitment of Mexican workers, whose legal entry was officially encouraged, while illegal crossings were unofficially condoned.

Although efforts to restrict and reduce Mexican immigration continued throughout the rest of the twenties, western railroads and the southwestern farm bloc continued to lobby periodically in Congress to retain this source of cheap labor. Their lobbyists were successful in maintaining a steady flow of Mexican workers for their clients' benefit. However, the Justice Department, fulfilling its function of enforcing federal laws, in 1920 requested that Congress make unlawful entry a punishable offense in an attempt to reduce illegal Mexican immigration. Although this request was not acted upon until the end of the decade, in 1924 Congress did appropriate $1,000,000 to establish the Border Patrol. In July 1924, this agency began the almost impossible task of supervising and controlling the flow of migration with a staff of only 450 men.

A dramatic increase in the volume of emigration from Mexico in the mid-twenties led to a corresponding rise in nativism in the United States. A further attempt to include Mexico in the quota system took place in 1925, when William Harris and John Box introduced bills into Congress to restrict Mexican immigration. In 1926 the House Committee on Immigration and Naturalization began hearings on the Box bill, thereby initiating the first serious discussion of the widespread implications of heavy Mexican immigration to the United States. During these hearings testimony by representatives of the railroads, western farmers, sugar manufacturers, and cattlemen testified to their great need for Mexican labor. These groups maintained that a quota system or an end to Mexican immigration would be extremely detrimental to their businesses and drive them into bankruptcy. The State Department supported their position, arguing that the Box bill was inconsistent with traditional United States policies favoring Latin America. Because of this widespread and highly organized opposition, both the Harris and Box bills failed.

Nevertheless, similar bills were introduced in succeeding congresses, and two years later a Senate hearing was held on the issue of Mexican immigration. Numerous opponents of restricted Mexican immigration testified against the proposed legislation; only the California State Federation of Labor testified in favor of limitation. Restriction was also urged by the American Legion, public health agencies, teacher organizations, social service agencies, various nativistic organizations, and some racist groups. It is interesting to note that this coalition in support of restrictive immigration represented both extremes of the political spectrum. Similar coalitions against Mexican immigration have continued to the present.

Concern about Mexican immigration, both legal and illegal, continued into the late twenties, as record numbers entered the United States. A different approach to the problem of Mexican immigration was initiated at a meeting held in Mexico City in February 1929. American consuls in Mexico were instructed to reduce emigration to the United States by strict application of existing legislation, such as the Alien Contract Labor Law. Later that same year, the stock market crash and the great depression that ensued accomplished what restrictionists had been trying to achieve throughout the decade. Not only did the depression virtually halt Mexican immigration, but it also created a reverse migratory movement. During the thirties this southward migration included thousands of Mexicans who were forcibly repatriated as well as thousands who returned voluntarily. With this reverse movement, the second wave of Mexican immigration in the twentieth century came to an end.

This second wave of Mexican immigrants was especially

significant to Mexican Americans. Statistics on Mexican immigration are important, but they must be used with great caution, for they can only indicate general trends. There are large discrepancies between the Mexican immigration and repatriation statistics compiled by the United States and by Mexico. Until 1907, United States data on Mexican immigration referred only to seaport arrivals; since that time the United States has tabulated each individual legal entry, so that one person crossing the border into the United States five times appears in the statistical data as five immigrants. On the other hand, Mexican government figures on emigration have probably underestimated the numbers consistently. Furthermore, one must be aware of the distinction between gross and net immigration figures. The net figures represent the difference between the number of Mexicans entering and leaving the United States.

However, certain generalizations can be made from immigration and census statistics. In 1900, there were more than 100,000 Mexican-born Mexican Americans in the United States; an overwhelming majority of them—some 90 percent —were concentrated in Texas, California, New Mexico, and Arizona, with Texas having 70 percent of the total. Although immigration figures for the first decade of the century indicate that legal Mexican immigration did not exceed 40,000 net, the 1910 census listed 222,000 Mexican-born in the United States. The conclusion is obvious. In the decade 1900–1910 there must have been a net illegal immigration of approximately 80,000 Mexicans.

The same technique applied to the following census period indicates that illegal Mexican entrants for the decade of the twenties must have reached at least 112,000. However, the next decade was different. Between 1921 and 1930, gross legal immigration totaled 459,000; in addition there was considerable illegal immigration. However, the 1930 census showed an increase of only 155,000 Mexican-born in the United States. The explanation for this discrepancy between the 1920 and 1930 figures undoubtedly lies in the heavy rate of repatriation in the postwar recession of 1921–1922 and again in 1929 and 1930. While precise statistics on emigration are lacking, there is some evidence of the volume of this reverse migratory movement. In 1921–1922, the Mexican government spent $2,500,000 in aiding stranded persons returning to Mexico with food and transportation for the trip from the border back to their native towns and villages. This sum indicates a heavy movement of repatriation during this period as well as the Mexican government's concern for its nationals.

Before 1917 Mexico was not greatly concerned about the heavy emigration of its citizens, largely because of the chaos created by the 1910 revolution. However, in 1917, the Mexican government, in an attempt to implement Article 123 of its new constitution dealing with the rights of labor, requested that American employers give written job contracts to immigrants and that the United States government approve these contracts. At that time, the United States, which was involved in World War I, had neither the interest nor the motivation to assume this new responsibility. The Mexican government expressed disappointment with the American response, but it did little to discourage emigration other than to give notice of its disapproval. Because poor economic conditions in Mexico persisted into the 1920s and emigration acted as a safety valve, Mexico made no serious effort after the end of World War I to insure compliance with Article 123. Moreover, the dollar income that the emigrants were sending back to Mexico— between $5,000,000 and $10,000,000 per year—was a vitally needed addition to the Mexican economy.

Viewed from the perspective of the Mexican government,

this emigration also had some less positive aspects. The country lost a sizable part of its most able and enterprising population. In addition, other social problems resulted from the long absences of workers who were also heads of families. A less common but particularly serious problem was created by desertion of families resulting from these long absences.

One of the notable aspects of Mexican immigration to the United States in the twenties was the low level of naturalization. Of the 320,000 Mexican-born in the United States who were over 21 years of age in 1930, only 5.5 percent had become naturalized citizens, compared to 49.7 percent for the entire adult foreign-born population here. The most important reason for this low rate of naturalization was the recency of the heavy Mexican immigration; it usually took about 15 years for an immigrant to become a naturalized American citizen. Another reason was that many Mexican immigrants intended to return to their homeland. The fulfillment of this intent was far easier for the Mexican than the European, and this fact tended to deter him from seeking United States citizenship. Moreover, the ease with which a Mexican immigrant could retain his cultural identity tended to deter him further. Also, Anglo-American attitudes toward the Mexican which led to social isolation and discrimination had the effect of discouraging him. In addition, the fact of his illegal entry in many instances precluded the possibility of acquiring citizenship. Finally, from a pragmatic point of view, the Mexican stood to gain little from United States citizenship, for his basic needs were already being met in the barrio.

Between 1900 and 1930 more than half a million Mexican immigrants entered the United States legally. Of these, about one-half became permanent residents. Most of those who remained settled in the Southwest, usually after three or four trips back to Mexico. As a result of this migration, the Southwest, and especially Texas, became a great reservoir of cheap labor that could be exploited by both agriculture and industry.

The 1930 census indicated that there were about 180,000 Mexican Americans employed in agriculture and 150,000 in common labor. Of the latter group, approximately half worked in transportation, mostly in menial jobs on the railroads. The statistics also showed that some 16,000 were employed in mining, principally in the copper industry in the Southwest.

Despite the importance of their contributions, Mexican American workers continued to be socially and economically segregated. Since most agricultural work was seasonal, many Mexican families moved from area to area, thereby developing a migratory life style with little stability. Those employed on the railroads and in mining were often isolated physically and culturally from the mainstream of society because of the locations of their work. They received wages so low as to provide only a bare minimum subsistence; at the same time they met with a growing resentment on the part of organized labor, which refused to open up the doors of unionism to them. Although the economic importance of their labor was recognized, they were not rewarded adequately, and so their economic, social, and cultural isolation increased.

The expanding prosperity of the Southwest in the first thirty years of this century was in large measure based on Mexican American labor. This expansion could not have been achieved without the Mexican. One could even argue that much of this prosperity came out of the pockets of the Mexican in the form of low wages. Mexicans thus subsidized United States agriculture and continue to do so.

# nine

# Deporting Jesús

As the 1920s ended, the cold grip of the great depression began to be felt throughout the United States; between 1930 and 1933 the number of unemployed Americans rose from four million to more than thirteen million. In 1933, 25 percent of the labor force was unemployed and additional millions grossly underemployed. Hourly wages dropped from 35 cents to 14 or 15 cents, and job opportunities were greatly reduced.

The depression years brought economic misery and new problems to Mexican Americans in the Southwest as well as to the rest of the people in the United States. They found themselves competing for the fewer jobs available, often with unemployed Anglo workers. Especially affected by the depression were those Mexican Americans living in industrial areas, mostly in the Midwest, and the Hispano villages of the Rio Arriba region in New Mexico and southern Colorado.

As employment in meat-packing, automobile manufacturing, railroads, steel, and mining declined in the early thirties many Mexican Americans found themselves out of work or at best working only a few days a week. Despite pious assurances from the leaders of business and government that prosperity was just around the corner, employment conditions continued to deteriorate to the extent that work of any kind became difficult to find. Unable to continue in industrial work, many Mexican Americans, like other Americans, tried to return to their rural origins, hoping to resume their former ways of life. However, they found that the depression had seriously affected rural areas as well. Others became part of the estimated half-million or more Americans who, during the depression years, wandered back and forth across the land.

When large stock-raisers were forced to reduce the size of their herds of cattle and sheep as a result of the depression, many Mexican Americans in New Mexico were laid off. They failed to realize that the depression had drastically altered economic conditions throughout the nation, and so they continued to follow the traditional New Mexican pattern of economic life, leaving their villages to seek work elsewhere. Before the depression, thirteen thousand Hispanos from New Mexico had successfully obtained annual seasonal employment outside their villages.

Now this method of obtaining work failed to provide the needed jobs, as a study of eleven New Mexican villages published by the United States Department of Agriculture in the mid-1930s indicated. Before 1930, an average of 1,100 young men worked outside these villages each year in sugar beets, potatoes, mining, and on the railroads; however, in 1934 only 157 were able to obtain such work. Economic conditions for New Mexicans deteriorated further when, in April 1936, the governor of Colorado declared martial law in the state. Although previously Colorado agriculture had depended heavily on New Mexican workers, now there was a surplus of workers within the state and National Guard troops were ordered to patrol the border between Colorado and New Mexico to keep out job-seekers, who were mostly Mexican. This use of the National Guard was held to be unconstitutional, and fortunately the order was rescinded after several days. Nevertheless, the incident was yet another example of the manner in which Mexican Americans found themselves among the principal victims of the misuse of police power.

In addition to causing a lack of job opportunities, the depression also affected New Mexicans in many other ways. During the 1930s, about 8,000 New Mexicans, most of them Hispanos, lost their lands because they were unable to pay their taxes or the assessments of the Middle Rio Grande Conservancy District Project (MRGCDP). Ironically, this agency, established in 1927 to help New Mexicans by increasing the amount of land available for agriculture, was now having the opposite effect. Villagers had had no vote in establishing it, and now many had no way of paying the project assessments. However, some of the villages hardest hit by the MRGCDP assessments received aid from the federal government.

Nevertheless, this project was of dubious success, for at the same time that it increased total agricultural acreage, it made it impossible for many Mexicans who depended on land for survival to obtain good agricultural land. The result of this project, in which those who were supposed to gain actually lost, affords an example of governmental attempts to solve socioeconomic problems without sufficient consideration of the people involved.

As the depression continued, two distinct migratory patterns developed among Mexican Americans in the Southwest. One was a movement from urban barrios back to rural villages; the second was a movement from the villages to large urban centers of the Southwest. In the villages some of the poverty-stricken Hispanos learned the skills of eking out a living by combining subsistence farming and livestock-raising with welfare aid and occasional day labor. However, to survive, others moved to the city because they had lost their lands (and thereby their means of livelihood) through nonpayment of taxes or mortgage foreclosures. The majority left their villages principally to secure benefits of New Deal welfare programs they had heard about.

The depression caused urban as well as rural Mexican Americans to lose their means of livelihood. At the same time that villagers were moving to urban centers, many in the cities who lost their jobs were returning to their home villages, hoping to find greater economic security within the extended family and a familiar cultural milieu. Since they enlarged an already impoverished population, their return contributed to further deterioration of the already crippled village economies and a deepening of rural poverty. Their attempts to return to a subsistence way of life failed, and subsequently most went back to the urban centers from which they had come, thus becoming a part of the substantial migration to cities and towns of the Southwest during the depression years.

Thus there were "push-pull" factors which caused the numbers leaving villages for cities to exceed the numbers leaving the city for the village. The overall result of this two-way movement was a reduction of village populations by as much as one-third. From 1930 onward they became part of the expanding movement to the cities, so that by 1970 only 15 percent could be described as rural.

The majority of Mexican Americans moving to the city experienced only limited success in improving their economic condition. Although they did find some relief in the various welfare programs, jobs were extremely scarce and hard to find. Mexican Americans often lacked the training necessary for those jobs that were available; moreover, the depression increased job discrimination practices. Anti-Mexican feelings were widespread and overt throughout the Southwest in the 1930s. Signs reading, "Only White Labor Employed" and "No Niggers, Mexicans, or Dogs Allowed," were evidence of the feelings and attitudes of that time, which to a large degree continue till today, although in more subtle forms.

A California law passed in August 1931 prohibited the employment of aliens on all public works. Furthermore, this prohibition had the broader effect of discouraging contractors from hiring Mexicans even on jobs not specifically included in the law. Mexican immigrants found even pick-and-shovel work almost impossible to obtain, a difficulty shared by the American-born; for contractors, like earlier gold rush Anglos in the case of the foreign miners' tax law, failed to distinguish Mexican American citizens from Mexican nationals. As a result, many Mexican families were forced onto welfare rolls.

In the depths of the depression, Mexican Americans were denied even low-pay, back-breaking agricultural work as prices fell below costs of production. The total number of jobs in agriculture declined because of low prices and governmental crop-restriction programs, and there were then large number of Anglo-American competitors for the work available, as migrant Texas, Oklahoma, and other southern farm families began working in the West.

With dust-bowl conditions prevailing in Oklahoma and Arkansas in the mid-thirties, thousands of Oakies and Arkies, depicted so well by John Steinbeck's *The Grapes of Wrath,* abandoned their seared farms and headed west looking for work. Also migrating westward toward the fabled "Golden State" of California were tens of thousands of uprooted southern sharecroppers and tenant farmers who were likewise seeking new solutions to their depression-born economic problems.

No one knows how many took to the migrant circuit, but half a million is not an unrealistic estimate. Under the impact of this new addition to the southwestern labor pool, wages and working conditions fell to an even lower level than before. The results of these poor economic conditions and the added competition from the influx of Anglo migrants were especially devastating for Mexican Americans. Not only did Anglo migrants replace immigrant Mexicans, but in many cases they also replaced local Mexican American farm workers, just as Mexican nationals had earlier.

By 1937 more than one half the cotton workers in Arizona came from out of the state. This sort of competition made it increasingly difficult for local Mexican Americans to earn even a minimum living and forced many of them into the migrant-labor system. In Texas alone, the depression swelled this Mexican American migrant army to as many as 400,000. Perhaps more significant than has been heretofore recognized is that, as a result of economic competition between these two culturally different migrant groups, prejudices and social discrimination against the Mexican became more pronounced. Although both groups represented the same social class and worked equally hard, only the Anglos as a group achieved greater upward social mobility.

Because of the depression the Mexican Americans' progress toward a greater share in the American dream was slowed down and even reversed. For all Americans the thirties was a period of serious economic and social maladjustment, and the socioeconomic status of Mexican Americans reached an all-time low.

Franklin Delano Roosevelt's administration took the position that government was responsible for the economic and social welfare of its citizens. Efforts were made to alleviate the most serious problems of the 1930s under the three principal elements of the New Deal program—relief, recovery, and reform. Of these three components, the first, relief, was to have a most immediate and direct effect on Mexican Americans. In the Southwest, as in the rest of the United States, government agencies tried both to solve problems and to ease the difficulties that the depression brought, thereby providing Mexican Americans considerable assistance at a very trying time. In New Mexico the availability of range lands for subsistence use was expanded and an Interdepartmental Rio Grande Board was created, with the objective of giving first preference to subsistence farmers. Throughout the Southwest greatly expanded activities of federal agencies were factors in reducing ethnic conflict and improving the economic condition of Mexican Americans. For example, the Farm Security Administration established permanent migrant camps in a score of centers of large-scale agricultural employment such as the Salt River Valley, Coachella Valley, and the San Joaquin Valley and mobile camps elsewhere during peak employment periods. These camps were similar to Civilian Conservation Corps camps in construction and arrangement, and were superior to most grower camps of the period. Unfortunately, many frightened conservative farmers opposed these camps as hotbeds of radicalism whose spread they were determined to halt.

In towns and cities the Federal Emergency Relief Adminis-

tration of 1934 and 1935 also made an important contribution
to alleviating the socioeconomic distress of Mexican Americans
by providing critically needed employment during the winter
of 1934–1935. After 1935 the Works Progress Administration
(WPA) provided the bulk of jobs for the Mexican Americans
during the depression years and was both well-received and
useful. The WPA gave employment to carpenters, stone masons,
plasterers, and unskilled laborers in the construction of roads,
small bridges, libraries, city halls, and other municipal and
state buildings. An additional important aspect of the WPA
in the Southwest was that it not only provided employment
but also created a renewed interest in Mexican arts and crafts
of the area. This revival restored to Mexican Americans a
degree of self-confidence and cultural pride, for now the Anglo
government had recognized their skills and the value of their
art.

However, many Mexican Americans who needed help were
not able to obtain it because of legislative restrictions. The
WPA was allowed to employ only those referred from state
welfare departments, and in many states residence requirements for state aid were greatly increased by the legislatures
during the depression years in order to hold down relief costs.
This policy especially affected the Mexican American community. It meant that many migrant Mexican Americans could
not obtain state relief; nor could they be certified for possible
employment by WPA. Another program which provided some
help for Mexican Americans was the Civilian Conservation
Corps, but again employment in this agency was limited to
members of families qualifying for state relief, thereby ex-
cluding most migrant agricultural families.

Undoubtedly federal relief programs were generally less
helpful to Mexican Americans than to the rest of America's
poor. There were a variety of reasons for this. First, Mexican

American males were reluctant to seek public help because of pride and their attitudes of machismo. Coming from a folk culture, Mexican Americans were accustomed to solving their own problems without outside help. Many were denied benefits of various programs because they were aliens, while many more could not meet local residency requirements. Most Mexican Americans employed in agriculture were excluded from coverage by unemployment insurance, industrial accident insurance, and other social security benefits. In addition, even those Mexican Americans under social security programs often failed to benefit from them because of unfamiliarity with claim procedures. Thus, these benefits were less valuable to Mexican American society in general than to the population at large. Today agricultural employees, predominantly Mexican in the West, still lack basic social security coverage that other workers long ago achieved.

However, even with all these drawbacks, New Deal programs of the thirties greatly assisted the Mexican American minority. Without federal assistance in the thirties, many villages would have disappeared and the traditional New Mexican way of life have ended. That these things did not happen was largely the result of a number of federal programs. The implementation of these various programs provided some improvement in the immediate economic plight of Mexican Americans; however, overall the depression had a disastrous impact on their position in American society.

One of the dramatic occurrences of the 1930s was the repatriation of large numbers of non-naturalized Mexicans and American citizens of Mexican descent. In the preceding decade especially, Mexican immigrants had been made welcome in the United States, and hundreds of thousands had come to fill the expanding need for workers. All objections to heavy immigration in the twenties were minimized by agricultural employers, mining companies, railroads, and merchants of the Southwest. Both employers and merchants viewed suggestions of restriction on immigration as a labor union conspiracy. In 1928 and 1929 there was a decline in Mexican immigration from the earlier high levels, probably as a result of farm mechanization and the increasing difficulties of reduced agricultural prices at this time. Nevertheless, immigration for those two years still totaled nearly 100,000.

Then came the 1929 crash and accompanying depression. Suddenly the Mexican immigration question became academic, as a rapid and massive change in the direction of migration took place. From 1931 to 1940 inclusive, only about 20,000 Mexicans legally immigrated to the United States, and the border was strictly patrolled to discourage illegal entrants. As a percentage of all immigration to the United States, Mexican immigration dropped from 20 percent in 1927 to about 3 percent in the mid-thirties.

As a result of the depression, by early 1930 a change had begun to take place in the Anglo-American stereotype of Mexicans, at least in the Southwest. Added to the earlier picture of a docile agricultural worker was the widespread Anglo belief now that the majority of Mexicans had become public charges on the American taxpayer. Of course, because of chronic underemployment and low wages, Mexican Americans had not been able to accumulate savings; in the midst of the depression, some of them (together with many other poor) had become dependent on local and state relief.

During the depression years vast numbers of Americans received welfare payments at one time or another, and Mexican Americans were no exception. Among the major problems faced by many county officials was the matter of overburdened welfare rolls. Government officials, considering ways to reduce the numbers on welfare, reached the conclusion that repatriation of Mexicans was one of the most expedient solutions to their problem. Behind this thinking lay the rationale that Mexicans had always had a propensity to return to Mexico and that if their transportation costs could be paid by the government, many would be happy to realize this desire. This solution seemed simple because the transportation costs would be cheap and many Mexicans in the United States had a rather ambiguous status as citizens.

By 1930 local government faced the dual problem of low income from taxes and rapidly expanding relief costs; therefore, social agencies began to put pressure on Mexicans to return to their home country. Many Anglos in the Southwest considered Mexicans as foreign, short-term labor, who had no rights to welfare benefits. They thought the answer was ridiculously simple: send Mexicans back to Mexico. Even disregarding the ethical considerations of this pseudo-solution, the civil rights violations involved in repatriation programs were outrageous. Legally, the situation was extremely complex. Many repatriated Mexicans had been living in the United States for decades and had children who were United States citizens by birth, who therefore could not be legally deported. Even in the case of illegal entrants, the process for deportation required a public hearing and a formal order. The surprising aspect of repatriation is that very few Americans spoke out in defense of the constitutional rights of their fellow citizens, and a majority condoned these repatriation programs.

Although there are no adequate records to tell how many Mexicans and Mexican Americans were repatriated in the 1930s, census figures do indicate the gross trend. The 1940 census showed that there were 377,000 Mexican-born persons in the United States, while the previous census in 1930 had shown 639,000. The difference between the two census figures indicates the departure of slightly more than a quarter of a million Mexican Americans, but the actual number of repatriates was probably closer to half a million because of the large number of illegal Mexican immigrants living in the United States.

Basically there were three types of repatriates: those who were deported by immigration officials, those who returned voluntarily to their home villages in Mexico, and those who were threatened in various ways with deportation and left reluctantly. This last group, representing probably the majority of Mexican repatriates, was made up of those who were in the United States illegally and were forced by government agencies to repatriate. Methods used to persuade this group to return to Mexico ranged from inducement by official announcement of transportation aid to direct threats of termination of relief payments or physical removal.

In the columns of *American Mercury,* Carey McWilliams documented the story of this forced repatriation in the Los Angeles area during the early thirties. Here the process involved the Southern Pacific Railroad, which carried these repatriates to Mexico at low rates, approximately the cost of one week's relief payment. Because it was cheaper to repatriate Mexicans than to keep them on welfare, a trainload of repatriates per month was shipped to Mexico from Los Angeles from 1931 to 1933. The Los Angeles *Times* reported that more than 200,000 Mexicans were repatriated from the United States in 1932 alone. Of these, between 50,000 and 75,000 came from California, with about 35,000 from Los Angeles County. Los Angeles was only one of many centers for processing thousands of returnees to Mexico; Chicago, Detroit, Denver, and other cities served in this capacity as well. Other thousands of men, women, and children arrived by the truckload at border towns all along the frontier from Tijuana to Brownsville.

As indicated earlier, statistics on repatriation may be misleading. In general, Mexican statistics concerning repatriates are probably closer to reality, since American figures reflect only those repatriates who were aided in their return to Mexico by various government agencies. For example, in the three years 1930 to 1932, United States immigration statistics indicate that 68,000 Mexicans were repatriated, while Mexican government statistics show four times that many for this same period. However, emigration statistics may tend to distort and overemphasize this displacement of Mexicans in the thirties. For example, Mexican statistics on repatriates for a comparable three-year nondepression period, 1924 to 1926, are 251,000, or nearly as many as the 275,000 for the 1930–1932 period. In other words, there had always been a heavy movement in *both* directions across the border. The chief difference between the two three-year periods was that the earlier group was not as gravely affected socially and economically as were the repatriates of the thirties.

During the 1930s the largest number of repatriates, about 132,000, came from Texas, which had the largest Mexican community in the United States at that time; California was second, and the Indiana-Illinois area third in number of repatriates. It is interesting to note that one-half of the Mexican-descent population of Indiana, Illinois, and Michigan were repatriated during this period. In comparison, only one-tenth of New Mexico's Spanish-speaking population was repatriated. The explanation of this disparity in repatriation percentages lies in the fact that the three midwestern states were more industrialized and therefore harder hit by the depression than were the southwestern states. Moreover, the Mexican American population of Indiana, Illinois, and Michigan had immigrated more recently and thus were more likely to consider returning to Mexico than those in the Southwest. Having been forced to leave the United States, many of the repatriated were re-recruited by the southwestern growers, and some were undoubtedly re-repatriated.

In the mid-thirties, much legislation was introduced in Congress to restrict Mexican immigration. Southwestern ranchers and growers again successfully opposed restrictive legislation, but not for humanitarian reasons. Many greedy growers ignored the obvious injustice of inviting Mexicans to come into the country as cheap labor and then sending them back during the depression. Another injustice of the repatriation was that it included many United States–born children, whose civil rights were clearly violated. Recent research indicates that approximately half of the returnees in the thirties were American-born. When these children later wished to come back to the United States in the belief that they were citizens, many found that they had unwittingly lost their citizenship by serving in the Mexican army or by voting in a Mexican election. Most responsible for these injustices was the failure on the part of government officials to inform these American citizens of their rights.

Most repatriates received little help in making the transition to their new life in Mexico. However, some efforts were made, such as those of Dr. C. N. Thomas, who helped sixty Santa Monica (California) Mexican families establish themselves at Valle de las Palmas in Baja California.

The Mexican government established a program for resettling the repatriates in special colonies. Four centers were established—one each in the states of Guerrero, Michoacán, Oaxaca, and Chiapas; these centers, however, had limited success in relocating the returnees, since only 5 percent were settled in this fashion. At the very end of the 1930s, President

Lázaro Cárdenas established a small colony near Matamoros in the state of Tamaulipas and proposed expanding the program for the resettlement of repatriates. However, Mexico had always been a poor nation and was also a victim of the depression; as a result of her economic conditions she was unable to develop an effective and viable repatriation program. Moreover, the political priorities of the Cárdenas administration emphasized continuing efforts to implement the objectives of the 1910 revolutionary reforms for all Mexicans; few resources could be diverted to meet the unexpected problems of repatriates. Only a very small portion of the repatriates were accommodated, and Mexico's total efforts were only slightly successful. Even these were terminated by the beginning of World War II, which reversed the migrant flow.

The experience of Mexican Americans during the 1930s confirmed their earlier mistrust of Anglo society, and strengthened the conviction of many that the United States government was something to fear and avoid. One result of forced repatriation in the thirties was the further disillusionment of Mexican Americans, who were already alienated from the mainstream of American life. They became more acutely aware of their role as pawns on the chessboard of the American agricultural economy. Before the thirties, they had suspected and distrusted employers, labor contractors, merchants, landlords, school officials, and Anglos in general. Now their suspicions and distrust were confirmed by government actions which obviously operated against their welfare. Politically ambitious Mexican American leaders were pushed one step closer to making effective demands for equality as American citizens—but only one step.

In general, the attitude of American government and society in welcoming the Mexican with open arms when his labor was wanted, in paying him a bare subsistence wage at most, and in then unceremoniously sending him destitute back to Mexico when times were bad did nothing to enhance trust in the United States government or to improve relations with Mexico.

However, there was a positive aspect to the Mexican experience in the thirties. The depression, in addition to creating problems for all United States citizens, also led to increased interest in their problems, with special attention given to those of Mexican Americans. Illustrative of this concern were California Governor Clement C. Young's Mexican Fact-Finding Committee, President Herbert Hoover's Committee on Social Trends, and the Texas State Educational Survey. The reports of these committees brought to light the growing problems of Mexican Americans; but only a small number of persons, mostly social workers and academics, became informed about the conditions of Mexican Americans as a result of this research. In the early thirties New Deal reform programs stimulated greater interest in seeking the causes of socioeconomic problems and especially of those related to underprivileged groups, particularly cultural and racial minorities. This rising tide of social concern manifested itself during the late twenties and early thirties in the publication of a wide variety of scholarly studies about the problems of Mexican Americans.

A leading contributor to these studies was Paul Taylor, an economist at the University of California in Berkeley, whose series of detailed studies of agricultural workers aroused greater interest in Mexican Americans. Taylor's work called attention especially to the problems of migrant Mexicans and Mexican Americans in California and Texas. Emory Bogardus, a prominent sociologist at the University of Southern California, focused his attention on race relations, emphasizing the role of leadership among Mexican Americans. At the University of Texas Herschel Manuel, the educational psychologist, began studying the obstacles encountered by Spanish-speaking children in an English-speaking environment. In New Mexico, Lloyd Tireman initiated studies of the unique educational problems of teaching Mexican American children with their dual cultural background. Also in New Mexico, Professor George I. Sánchez was beginning a lifetime of study devoted principally to Mexican Americans and their education. The conclusions and recommendations of these scholars were in vain. Published in scholarly journals and other publications of limited circulation, they failed to reach the attention or to stir the moral conscience of America; and they failed to move those with political power to take remedial action.

It is tragic, not only for Mexican Americans but also for society at large that these recommendations were never effectively implemented. The few attempts that were made were mainly only token in nature. In the 1930s New Mexico initiated a few reforms aimed at accelerating the rate of acculturation of Mexican Americans. Broad changes were made in the sources and distribution of school funds in order to bring this about. Improved public health services were made more widely available to all segments of society. Furthermore, Mexican Americans did begin to take an increased and more effective role in politics, but not enough to reduce their political isolation.

Similar slight improvements occurred in California, Arizona, and Colorado. However, Texas, historically notorious for its anti-Mexican attitudes, lagged far behind in every respect. Mexican Americans of Texas suffered under discriminatory law enforcement agencies (such as the Texas Rangers), had the least responsive political leadership in all southwestern states, and had the lowest levels of health, education, employment, and living conditions. Fortunately, the demands of World War II in industry and agriculture were to bring some improvement for Mexican Americans in the Southwest, even for those who lived in Texas.

# ten

## ¡Basta Ya!

At the beginning of the twentieth century the emergence of large-scale commercial farming linked to a mass market became one of the characteristics of agriculture in the Southwest. This trend was especially notable in California, where, just before the turn of the century, the organization of large companies like the Kern County Land Company, the Newhall-Saugus Land Company, and the Di Giorgio Fruit Corporation gave impetus to this movement. Commercial farming conducted by these organizations, referred to collectively as agribusiness, was characterized by employment of a seasonal labor force which tripled or quadrupled at the peak of the harvest season by adding temporary (usually migrant) labor from Mexico and southwestern Mexican American labor pools.

Because most of the crops were extremely perishable, southwestern agriculture was highly vulnerable to labor shortages and union pressures. Farmers, therefore, preferred an abundant supply of highly mobile and unorganized farm workers. This attitude explains why agribusiness supported the unlimited admission of Mexican nationals so strongly during the 1920s and even during the depression. Their inability to speak English, their ignorance of personal rights under American law, and their recent experience as virtual serfs under the exploitative dictatorship of Porfirio Díaz made them ideal workers from the growers' viewpoint. Nevertheless, Mexican and Mexican American workers of the Southwest did unite in protest on occasion against poor working conditions, thus invalidating stereotypes of Mexican passivity or apathy.

The rise of large commercial farm operation in the Southwest was accompanied by the beginning of labor organization there. Since Mexican Americans and Mexicans formed a large part of the southwestern work force, they also understandably played important roles as leaders and activists in the development of labor unionism in the area. An early indication of this activity was seen in 1883, when several hundred cowboys in the Texas panhandle went on strike against a number of large cattle companies and won their demands for better pay. Among the leaders of this strike were a handful of Mexican vaqueros.

Also in the 1880s an organization called the Caballeros de Labor, patterned after the Knights of Labor, was begun in the Southwest. Recognizing that ownership of land was a more important issue in the Southwest than wages and hours of labor, it concentrated its efforts in fighting Anglo land-grabbing schemes, however, with only moderate success. Since its objectives were largely political rather than those of a regular trade union, it had little influence among the masses of Mexican American workers.

In the mid-1890s the Western Federation of Miners began organizing in the West with greater impact than the Caballeros de Labor. The success of this organization stemmed in part from its ability to develop union leadership among the Mexicans who made up an important segment of the mining population in the Southwest during this period.

Greater union activity among Mexican Americans began to appear in the first decade of the twentieth century. In the southeast Arizona copper mining region of Clifton-Morenci, a walkout developed in June 1903 from a conflict over an hourly pay reduction. Initiated by Mexican miners, the strike failed to attract the support of Anglo workers. It was finally ended by the unusual combination of a disastrous flash flood (in which more than fifty persons lost their lives, causing some Mexican miners to have second thoughts about the strike) and the concurrent suppression of the strike by the arrest, trial, and conviction of its leaders. Another example of the difficulties experienced by mine workers in unionizing was the quashing of a strike by the Western Federation of Miners in the Colorado coal fields. By refusing to negotiate and importing Mexican strikebreakers—a common and long-continuing practice of mine owners—the strike was ended in 1904.

Unlike Texas, New Mexico, and Arizona, California did not have a nineteenth-century history of Mexican American involvement in union organization. From the beginning of the American period, labor needs in California had been met by the use of Oriental workers, and not until the turn of the century did Mexicans become an important part of the state's labor force.

In 1903, a strike of sugar-beet workers near Ventura, California, took more than a thousand Mexican and Japanese workers out of the fields. After two months of strife and some violence on both sides, workers won the right to negotiate directly with the grower rather than with the Western Agricultural Contracting Company, a labor contractor. This strike gave further rebuttal to the idea that Mexicans were completely docile workers. Additional evidence of early involvement of Mexicans in labor disputes can be seen in the Los Angeles street railway workers' strike in 1910. Early in the year, Mexican workers walked off the job, demanding higher wages, and soon the strike spread to the metal trades, leather, and brewing industries. Support for this strike rapidly subsided when the strongly anti-union Los Angeles *Times* building was dynamited in September, resulting in the deaths of twenty-one *Times* employees. This occurrence became an important factor in crippling the strike and led to its eventual failure.

In the history of American labor unionization, migrant farm workers have been the most difficult of all workers to organize. The difficulty of agricultural union organization stemmed principally from the instability of a labor force made up largely of minorities, the existence of large labor pools, a limited and seasonal need for workers, and a distinct life style based on day-to-day struggle for survival. In the final analysis, however, the chief obstacle to unionization of farm labor has been the strong opposition of farmers and farm organizations, because they had become accustomed to keeping production costs down by using cheap labor. This economic attitude and a lack of social and economic concern for their workers has characterized many grower groups, just as it has other businesses.

An excellent example of this attitude and a major milestone in the history of migrant labor conflict was the Durst Ranch affair of August 1913. Durst was no more inhumane than other agricultural employers, but he was not greatly concerned with the conditions of filth and poverty under which his migrant employees worked and lived. Housing on the ranch was virtually nonexistent and the nearly three thousand workers were provided with only eight toilets. In addition, the combination of daytime temperatures in excess of 100 degrees with a lack of garbage disposal, of organization for sanitation, and of drinking water in the fields created animallike conditions of existence.

Workers, led by Industrial Workers of the World organizers Herman Suhr and Blackie Ford, rose up in protest against these subhuman conditions on the Durst hop ranch near Wheatland, California. In the emotionally charged atmosphere, a deputy sheriff, by firing a warning shot in the air, touched off a riot which left four dead. On the following day four companies of National Guard troops were brought in, and about 100 migrant workers were arrested. As a result, the strike was broken. Eight months later Ford and Suhr were tried and sentenced to life imprisonment for their roles in the riot, while other leaders received long prison terms.

The widespread publicity received by this strike led to creation of the California Commission on Immigration and Housing. The report of this commission substantiated and articulated the plight of migratory workers, thereby arousing awareness of their problems. Its recommendations led to state regulation of California's farm labor camps, but there were only negligible improvements in working and housing conditions.

In September 1915, Mexican copper-mine workers in the non-union towns of Morenci and Clifton, Arizona, became incensed at the traditional pay differential between Mexican and Anglo workers. About 500 Mexican workers belonging to three unions affiliated with the Western Federation of Miners went on strike over this and other grievances. In this instance Mexican miners were joined by many Anglo workers. The National Guard was called in, but negotiations went on, and after five months the strikers obtained an agreement that guaranteed equal rates for Anglos and Mexicans, banned the Western Federation of Miners, and set up committees and procedures for dealing with grievances. Labor unrest erupted again in the Clifton-Morenci area during 1917 and 1918, when both Mexican and Anglo copper miners staged walkouts. These strikes were broken by vigilante action encouraged by the mine owners and by wholesale deportations of hundreds of Mexicans.

During the 1920s, labor unrest among Mexican Americans spread from mining to agriculture. A decline in agricultural prices and wages caused considerable dissatisfaction and unrest among Colorado beet workers, and some unions began to organize under the leadership of the IWW and AFL. In 1928, C. N. Idar of the American Federation of Labor directed the organization of Mexican Americans in Colorado, Wyoming, and Nebraska, and was successful in forming a Beet Workers Association of about 10,000 members. However, it never became affiliated with the AFL. Furthermore, the depression at the end of the decade and competition with non-union dustbowl migrants brought about its decline.

In California, the history of labor organization among Mexican Americans in the 1920s was more encouraging than in other areas of the Southwest. At the 1927 convention of the AFL held in Los Angeles, the delegates discussed the negative effects of Mexican immigration on American labor and supported a restrictive immigration policy. Although the AFL conference did not result in any organizational efforts among Mexican Americans, in November of the same year a committee representing the Federation of Mexican Societies in Los Angeles took a first step in this direction. It passed a resolution calling on its affiliates to lend moral and financial support in a drive to organize Mexican American workers of the area. As a result of this effort, a number of local unions were organized, and these then formed the Confederación de Uniones Obreras Mexicanas (cuom), modeled after the chief Mexican labor union, the Confederación Regional Obrera Mexicana (crom). In March 1928, this new labor organization (the cuom) drew up a constitution which declared that its purpose was to organize all Mexican workers in the United States, to achieve wage parity with Anglo workers, and to end discrimination against Mexicans. Another objective of the organization was to persuade the Mexican government to restrict the flow of Mexican immigrant labor to the United States and to assume a more positive role in meeting the economic needs of repatriates by establishing agricultural colonies in Mexico.

A month later, a general cuom convention was held in Los Angeles at which twenty-two unions were represented. The crom in Mexico demonstrated its support by sending Emilio Mújica as its representative. He served as an adviser and even remained a month longer to help unionize Mexican American and Mexican workers in southern California. The initial enthusiasm of this organizing effort was considerable, and by 1928 the cuom claimed to represent twenty locals, with about 3,000 workers. However, a year later there were only ten locals with about 200 members still functioning.

Despite its decline, the cuom was important in the history of labor because of its goal of organizing Mexican American workers in order to improve their economic welfare. Its constitution clearly expressed Mexican American views on many issues of prime importance to la raza; and the union provided leadership training for organizers who later helped to establish more successful labor organizations.

A labor dispute in the Imperial Valley illustrates the difficulties Mexican Americans faced in dealing with problems of a large labor pool and a limited and seasonal need for workers. In April 1928, melon pickers, with the help of the Mexican consul at Calexico, established the Mexican Mutual Aid Society of Imperial Valley (MMAS). Early in May this organization delivered to the growers an ultimatum on conditions for harvesting the melon crop, including acceptance of the union as the workers' spokesman with the growers and the elimination of the labor broker—the contratista. The latter demand was a long-standing goal of farm laborers, since the contratista represented the most exploitative aspect of the worker's life. The workers also demanded a raise of 1½ cents to 15 cents per crate, with a minimum hourly wage of 75 cents, and that the grower provide picking sacks and crates, better housing, and ice for drinking water. The growers accepted some of these conditions but not all. As a result, cantaloupe pickers, unwilling to accept the growers' compromise, refused to harvest the crop.

However, because of threats and coercion the workers eventually were forced to accept the growers' terms. A combination of large-scale arrests by the local sheriff, Charles Gilbert, threats of deportation to Mexico, accusations of Communism, and use of anonymous circulars threatening to bring in workers from Texas—all worked together to break the strike. Although the strike was broken, it helped to increase unionization efforts in the area.

One unforeseen result of the Imperial Valley melon strike was that the district attorney urged revision of the standard harvesting contract widely used by growers. The California Department of Industrial Relations called a meeting of growers at El Centro in December, and a revised harvesting agreement was written. This contract, drawn up after much negotiation and discussion, made growers rather than contractors responsible for wages, and it eliminated the much disliked, common practice of withholding 25 percent of the workers' wages until the end of the season. In place of this withholding practice, the agreement added a bonus to achieve the desired effect of keeping workers until completion of the harvest. Although the use of this harvest contract form was not mandatory, its formulation was a significant victory for the MMAS, since it was developed by a state agency and it recommended the abolition of deeply entrenched abusive practices on the part of the growers. Nevertheless, early in the 1930 harvest season, Mexican American workers once again went on strike in the Imperial Valley for improved working conditions and the restoration of a wage cut. Although the growers made some concessions to the workers, they also continued their bitter attack on the MMAS, successfully using the usual strikebreaking techniques.

Agriculture was hit especially hard during the depression. There was an unusually large number of strikes between 1930 and 1935, due especially to the fact that agricultural wages had fallen from their already depressed levels of the twenties to all-time lows. Other grievances included widespread use of contratistas, default on wage payments to agricultural workers, deterioration of housing conditions, and poor sanitation facilities. Radical labor groups, capitalizing on the rising discontent, began to win new adherents. The Communist-affiliated Cannery and Agricultural Workers Industrial Union (CAWIU) and the Trade Union Unity League (TUUL) succeeded in recruiting Mexican American workers.

Much of the agricultural unrest of the 1930s in the Southwest stemmed from two sources—Mexican American workers and the TUUL, one of the most active radical labor groups in the West. The basic tactic of the TUUL was to move into an incipient strike situation, providing leadership and counsel for the workers at a time of confusion and uncertainty. Because the TUUL was widely involved in agricultural labor disputes throughout the West during this period, the growers often equated labor organizing with Communism.

The TUUL was actively interested in Mexican American migrant workers from the beginning of the depression. For example, the League held a conference in 1929 at which the problems of Mexican workers were discussed. The TUUL organized several hunger marches; a notable one, which took place in December 1931, included many Mexican Americans from Los Angeles.

Throughout the Southwest at this time Mexican Americans were active in organizing labor and in leading strikes. Their training in radical unions and the regimentation experienced by la raza in various government relief programs facilitated these activities. By mid-1934 in California Mexican American workers had effectively organized some forty agricultural unions, but most of these were short-lived. The most successful was the Confederación de Uniones de Campesinos y Obreros Mexicanos (CUCOM), which developed out of the El Monte berry strike in Los Tngeles County.

Dissatisfied with wages that had dropped to as little as 9 cents an hour, several thousand Mexican American pickers walked out of the strawberry fields at El Monte in May 1933. The strike was characterized by a power struggle for control of the workers between local Mexican American leaders and outside representatives of the radical CAWIU, who attempted to dominate the movement. With the help of the Mexican consulate in Los Angeles, Mexican American leadership was successful in forming a new organization around some of the former CUOM leaders. As the strike continued, other locals were organized among strawberry workers throughout Los Angeles County and beyond; finally an agreement was signed on July 6, 1933, establishing a wage of 20 cents an hour. However, by that time the berry season was over, and so the workers received no benefits from the settlement. Nevertheless, ten days after the strike was settled, a permanent organization, the Confederación de Uniones de Campesinos y Obreros Mexicanos was established; it became the most active agricultural workers' organization in California, with 50 locals and more than 5,000 members by the end of 1933.

Many other strikes took place among migratory agricultural workers in California during 1933, and Mexican Americans were active in all of them. There were strikes by pea-pickers in Hayward; cherry-pickers in the Mountain View–Sunnyvale area; peach-pickers at Merced, Sacramento, and Gridley; pear-pickers in the Santa Clara Valley; Filipino and Mexican American lettuce-workers in Salinas; fruit-pickers at the Tagus ranch, south of Fresno; and grape-pickers in the Fresno-Lodi area, with 6,000 workers participating.

The most significant strike was called by the San Joaquin Valley cotton-pickers of the CAWIU in October 1933. The strike began at Corcoran with 5,000 workers, and soon encompassed the entire southern part of the valley. Eventually 18,000 workers walked out, principally over demands that the rate per hundredweight be increased from 60 cents to a dollar. Evicted from the growers' camps, cotton-pickers set up a "strike city" headquarters at the outskirts of Corcoran on a rented farm. The workers had the Herculean task of picketing along a hundred-mile front, and in addition they faced hostile vigilante action. Intense feelings were generated among the strikers on October 12, 1933, when the union hall at Pixley was riddled by rifle fire, killing two strikers and wounding several others. Labor tension increased when a striker was shot to death on the same day farther south in the valley at Arvin, another center of strike activity.

This tense and inflamed situation forced Governor James Rolf to mobilize the National Guard. To further calm down the strikers, Enrique Bravo, a Mexican consul, was brought in to address the workers and try to persuade them to end the strike. Meanwhile, the governor appointed a fact-finding commission which recommended setting up a state mediation board; this board, headed by Archbishop Edward J. Hannah, worked out a compromise which gave the strikers a 25-percent wage increase. By the end of October most of the strikers had returned to work at a wage of 75 cents per 100 pounds of cotton.

To thwart the legitimate desires of agricultural workers to organize, the Agricultural Labor Subcommittee of the California Chamber of Commerce held a meeting in Los Angeles in November 1933. At this meeting a resolution was passed calling for use of the state's criminal syndicalism laws in labor disputes and for passage of legislation to outlaw picketing. This resolution was intended to suppress agricultural union agitation. The delegates then formed the Associated Farmers of California, an organization opposed to unions in general as "red" movements and devoted to combatting unionism by education, persuasion, and a permanent lobby at Sacramento. Well-financed and supported by law enforcement agencies, in 1934 this group turned to more overt means of suppressing labor union activity. Clearly, the Associated Farmers contributed substantially to the demoralization and decline of Mexican American labor in the 1930s; it was also responsible for much of the labor violence which occurred during the period.

In a 1934 strike at Brentwood, California, deputies and vigilantes penned up 200 Mexican strikers and later shipped them out of the county. Eight strike leaders of the Cannery and Agricultural Workers Industrial Union were tried and convicted under California's criminal syndicalism laws. Three years later all eight convictions were reversed by the appellate court. The CAWIU participated in the famous San Francisco general strike of 1934 initiated by the International Longshoremen's Union. In July, the police raided the Sacramento headquarters of the CAWIU and arrested its leaders. Eighteen were subsequently tried under the criminal syndicalism laws, and eight were eventually convicted and sentenced to jail terms. Despite appeals, these convictions were upheld. The CAWIU's parent organization, the Trade Union Unity League, was dissolved by the Communist Party in 1935, and its own organizers were harassed by mounting police suppression, and so, in time, the CAWIU became crippled and went into decline.

As the influence of the CAWIU decreased, the Confederación de Uniones de Campesinos y Obreros Mexicanos became more active in farm labor disputes. In 1935 one-third of eighteen important farm worker strikes were led by the CUCOM; in a number of instances, it was able to achieve its objectives without striking. During this period there was a move to affiliate agricultural unions with the AFL, but Mexican unions, including the CUCOM, felt that their members could not afford the high AFL initiation fees.

However, the Mexican American unions were aware of the benefits to be derived from the federating of small unions, as is indicated by the establishment of the short-lived Federation of Agricultural Workers Unions of America, founded in Los Angeles in January 1936. The key to this new federation was the CUCOM, which furnished the leadership necessary to bring together many independent Los Angeles County Spanish-speaking unions. In April this new federation called a strike of workers in the Los Angeles celery fields. Led by a dynamic labor leader, Guillermo Velarde of the CUCOM, 2,600 strikers walked out of the fields. The growers, mostly Japanese, resorted to traditional strikebreaking techniques: police, guards, tear gas, harassment, and violence. Finally in August the strike was settled. The workers achieved a number of gains, including an improved wage scale. In June, while the celery strike was still on, the CUCOM called a strike in the Orange County citrus groves. Velarde again led the CUCOM in demanding that the California Fruit Growers' Exchange (Sunkist) recognize the union and improve working conditions. The usual methods of repression were again used by the growers: evictions, tear gas, night-riding vigilantes, and accusations of Communism. One hundred and fifteen Mexican American strikers were arrested for trespassing on a public highway. The jailed strikers were illegally detained for fifteen days, which helped to demoralize the workers; by the end of July the strike had lost its appeal for most of them, and they returned to the groves with only a slight wage increase.

Mexican farm labor continued to be interested in a large and more effective agricultural organization. The CUCOM and other California farm labor groups held several conferences in 1935 and 1936 to form a statewide organization, but they had little success. Nevertheless, the first national convention of agricultural workers, held at Denver, Colorado, in 1937, attracted delegates from most of the California Spanish-speaking unions. Many of them joined the United Cannery, Agriculture, Packing, and Allied Workers of America, an affiliate of the Congress of Industrial Organizations (CIO). However, most Mexican unions eventually affiliated with the AFL, and some remained independent.

There were few strikes among field workers in 1936 and 1937 and only two important labor disputes in California agriculture during this period; both concerned packing and cannery workers. In September 1936, the Vegetable Packers Association, an AFL affiliate, went on strike in the Salinas lettuce fields. In response, the Associated Farmers raised a strikebreaking fund of $225,000 and, announcing that it was "against the unionization of farm labor on any basis," eventually crushed the strike. The following April, cannery workers struck in Stockton. Again, the Associated Farmers moved quickly to suppress the strike.

In this instance the strikers were compelled to return to work by the deputizing of over 1,200 farmers.

In December 1937, the Associated Farmers met at San José and organized the broader-based United Farmers of the Pacific Coast. This organization continued to repress labor activity in California agriculture to the end of the decade.

The last important prewar California farm workers strike was in Ventura County in January 1941. Here 1,500 lemon-pickers, mostly Mexican Americans, organized the Agricultural and Citrus Workers Union, which became affiliated with the AFL. Rejecting union demands and refusing to negotiate with union representatives, the growers brought in strikebreakers. When the United States Department of Labor proposed arbitration of the issues, the growers rejected its mediation. After four months the strike collapsed, and the workers gave up in defeat; they lost not only the strike but also their jobs, which were taken mostly by dust-bowl refugees.

While Mexican American labor leaders in California were primarily involved in organizing farm workers, union activity elsewhere in the Southwest occurred largely among non-agricultural workers. Unionism played a less important role in New Mexico, Arizona, and Texas; and its activities, usually led by Anglos, were often directed against Mexicans as a source of cheap, strikebreaking labor. At the beginning of the 1930s the only Mexican American union of any real importance outside California was the Sheepshearers Union of North America, an AFL affiliate. It differed from most of the California Mexican unions in that it was a strongly cohesive and relatively well-financed organization; in the early thirties it launched an aggressive unionization drive in Arizona and Texas. With 750 members in the San Angelo, Texas area by 1934, the union felt strong enough to launch a strike there for higher wages. This strike was defeated by the use of threats, strikebreakers, arrests, and vigilante activity, setting a pattern of defeat for similar strike efforts later on.

At this time there were also a number of strikes near San Antonio, where the pecan industry employed thousands of Mexican and Mexican American workers. In the mid-thirties the pecan-shellers' piece-rate earnings dropped to 4 cents an hour, and in 1938 this starvation rate caused pecan workers to strike against the Southern Pecan-Shelling Company, which dominated the industry. While the strike was somewhat successful in raising wages, resort to the National Labor Relations Board proved more productive. Wages in the pecan industry were increased to 25 cents per hour. The higher wages, however, led the industry to mechanize its operations, thus depriving most of the workers of their jobs. By 1941 the Southern Pecan-Shelling Company had reduced its labor force from more than 10,000 to 600 workers.

In New Mexico, the organization of Mexican labor received an impetus in 1934 when Jesús Pallares founded La Liga Obrera de Habla Español (The Spanish-Speaking Labor League). Active primarily among the coal- and copper-miners in the area around Gallup, it soon claimed a membership of 8,000 in northern New Mexico and southern Colorado. In 1935 it achieved some success in striking for better working conditions in the mines of the Gallup-American Company; however, because of these strikes, some workers were arrested and deported, including Pallares. Thereafter, the Liga lost its influence and rapidly declined.

A significant problem of Mexican American industrial workers throughout the Southwest was the general practice of paying Anglo and Mexican American workers different wages for the same work. This form of discrimination was energetically fought by the Union of Mine, Mill, and Smelter Workers, which had some Mexican American leaders. This union achieved redress of differential wages and other grievances after 1937 through the intervention of the National Labor Relations Board. However, differential wages continued to be a major problem as mining expanded during World War II. Finally the issue was brought before the National War Labor Board, which in 1944 ordered copper-mining companies to cease this discriminatory practice. This practice was so entrenched that two years later, in March 1946, the Mine, Mill, and Smelter Workers union had to resort to a strike to hasten compliance with the 1944 order.

Unionization among Mexicans and Mexican Americans in the 1920s and 1930s took place predominantly in agriculture, where most of them were employed. During this period, radical and Communist leadership was extremely aggressive and exploited labor discontent, not only in the Southwest among Mexican Americans but throughout the rest of the country as well. At this time (and even today) the government has used Mexican consuls to stifle Mexican American organizational efforts. During the twenties and thirties the Southwest had small Mexican unions, whose energies and weak finances were quickly sapped by the oppressive tactics of growers, such as indiscriminate arrests, deportation, excessive bail, expensive litigation, vicious vigilante assaults, and other forms of intimidation. Although Mexican Americans gained much labor union experience from 1900 to 1940, their organizations achieved only limited success. Some gains were made in wages and working conditions; however, the hopes and aspirations of Mexican American workers continued to be frustrated by repression and discrimination.

# eleven

## Heroes, Second Class

World War II provided Mexican Americans with new opportunities for improving their economic and social conditions. Within both the armed forces and industry they discovered immediate and potential avenues for achieving a higher standard of living. This is not to say that they all profited from the improved conditions brought by the war, however. Traditionally isolated from the mainstream of American life by their distinct barrio and village culture, Mexican Americans were now abruptly uprooted and obliged to become part of the labor force of a massive war machine.

Wartime manpower requirements not only forced industry

to open new doors for the Mexican American; they also led to unprecedented numbers of Mexican Americans entering the United States armed forces by enlistment and by induction. For example, New Mexico, the state with the highest percentage of Mexican Americans in its total population, also had the largest number of volunteers per capita of any state. Wartime legislation also facilitated the enlistment of Mexican nationals in the United States armed services. Urged by President Manuel Avila Camacho to forget their lingering animosities, considerable numbers of Mexican nationals living in the United States also enlisted for war duty.

Mexican Americans tended to be overrepresented in the armed services for a number of historical reasons. One of these was that service in the armed forces afforded an easy means of naturalization for a large number of immigrants who had not yet become citizens. Also, Mexican American communities had a high percentage of draft-age youths, but relatively few who qualified for job deferments. Finally, because Mexican Americans generally had fewer opportunities for economic security in civilian life than Anglos, many viewed military service as a possible route to security, recognition, adventure, and equality in treatment. However, this view proved to be illusory, for the military only reflected civilian society.

More than one-third of a million Mexican Americans served in all branches of the armed forces during World War II. However, most of them enlisted in the army, and it is notable that more Mexican Americans served in combat divisions according to their percentage of the total population than any other ethnic group in the United States. Possibly because of such factors as patriotism and machismo, a high percentage of Mexican Americans volunteered for the more hazardous branches, such as the paratroops and marines.

By the end of World War II, seventeen Mexican Americans

had earned the Congressional Medal of Honor for their valor above and beyond the call of duty. Of fourteen Texans winning the Congressional Medal of Honor, five were Mexican Americans. Others were awarded the Silver Star, the Bronze Star, the Distinguished Service Cross, and other medals. Thus, by serving so well in the armed forces, they proved their loyalty and dedication to the United States.

Mexican American soldiers were among the first to face the enemy in the Philippines. A few months before Pearl Harbor the 200th and the 515th Coast Artillery arrived at Clark Field near Manila. These two outfits were part of the New Mexico National Guard, which was made up mostly of Mexican Americans. After the attack on Pearl Harbor (December 7, 1941) came the attack on and invasion of the Philippines. On Bataan, Mexican Americans made up one-fourth of combat troops defending the area.

After the surrender of Corregidor to the Japanese early in 1942, there was the infamous Bataan Death March, in which many of the marchers were of Mexican descent; large numbers died as a result of severe hardships on the forced march, and those who survived suffered long and wretched imprisonment. Few history books have mentioned the participation of Mexican Americans in these early stages of World War II.

Mexican Americans participated in most campaigns of World War II. When the North African offensive began in November, 1942, Mexican American soldiers were in the front lines, battling Nazi Panzer units of General Erwin Rommel, the famous "Desert Fox." When Rommel's forces were defeated, the major thrust of the war shifted to the invasion of Sicily and Italy. In the Italian-Sicilian campaign Mexican Americans played important roles in two infantry units, the 88th Division and Company E, 141st Regiment of the 36th Division.

The 88th Division, an elite group of combat troops, was made up principally of officers and men from la raza. Initially there was some concern among the general officers about the division's fighting abilities because of its draftee composition— probably because of the predominance of Mexican Americans. However, in battle the men of the 88th Division quickly dispelled all doubts about their combat effectiveness, and became widely known as the "Blue Devils."

Company E of the 141st Regiment, a Texas National Guard unit, most of whose men were Mexican Americans from the El Paso area, achieved an equally outstanding record. Company E was initiated into combat during the bloody invasion at Salerno in September 1943. The following January, Company E took another murderous pummeling farther north, when it crossed the Rapido River. After having fought the entire length of the Italian peninsula, Company E participated in the August 1944 invasion of southern France. Company E's battle-hardened veterans later fought their way the entire distance from southern France to the heart of Germany.

By early 1944, the Allies had won air supremacy over Europe, making it possible to launch a direct attack on Hitler's Fortress Europa. The costly and crucial invasion of Normandy began on D-day (June 6, 1944). The following day, the 2nd (Indian Head) Division, which included many Mexican Americans from southern Texas, landed and began to push across northern France into Germany. In December, German forces launched a counterattack against the center of the Allied lines at Ardennes. For his great valor in holding back this German counterattack almost singlehandedly, José López of Brownsville, Texas, won the Congressional Medal of Honor. After the war he had the unusual distinction of also being awarded the highest Mexican military honor, the Aztec Eagle, by President Miguel Alemán.

Mexican Americans also fought in the China-Burma-India

theaters and in the Pacific. During the Battle for Saipan, Guy Gabaldón performed one of the most amazing feats of the war, which earned him the Silver Star. Gabaldón, a Mexican American who had been raised by a Japanese American family in East Los Angeles, spoke Japanese fluently. On Saipan he used his proficiency in Japanese to persuade more than a thousand Japanese soldiers to surrender, a deed without parallel in World War II.

In May 1943, on the Aleutian Islands, José Martínez of Ault, Colorado, became the first draftee to earn a recommendation for the Congressional Medal of Honor. The award was made posthumously for extraordinary bravery and valor in the invasion of Attu. Today he is memorialized by creation of the José Martínez American Legion Post #623 in Los Angeles and the José Martínez Disabled American Veterans chapter in Colorado.

World War II experiences were extremely valuable for many Mexican Americans. For the first time Anglo-Americans in large numbers worked together with Mexican Americans for mutual objectives of security and survival. The latter found little discrimination in actual combat, although it persisted in other areas. Because the army has a promotional system based on individual merit, many Mexican Americans obtained the recognition and promotions that would have been impossible in civilian life. Few, however, became officers because of their relatively low educational levels. Because Mexican Americans as a group were aware of their excellent military record, they achieved a new sense of confidence and worth.

After the war Mexican Americans returned home with new aspirations and ambitions. The G.I. Bill provided la raza veterans with opportunities for job training, education, and home loans which had not been available before. Some took advantage of the educational opportunities of the G.I. Bill, while others used the bill to go into business for themselves. Many returning veterans had acquired strong new feelings of self-awareness and self-esteem in the armed services, ending their traditional provinciality and making them aware of new possibilities for improving their social status.

This new self-confidence led Mexican Americans to establish a number of important social, political, and service organizations: the Mexican American Political Association, American G.I. Forum, Community Service Organization, and Political Association of Spanish-Speaking Organizations. The returning Mexican American veterans took the lead in new attempts to achieve civil rights, thereby replacing traditional attitudes with a new spirit of hope and activism.

Most Mexican American veterans, however, even the heroes, failed to find appreciation on the part of the larger society for their contributions and talents. Instead, many found, to their dismay, that little had changed in the way the majority society viewed them. Even in death they found that they were not accepted by Anglo society.

In 1948, the remains of Félix Longoria, who had been killed in the battle for the Philippines, were returned to the United States for burial. There was a bitter dispute in his home town over his burial. The only mortician in Three Rivers, Texas, refused to hold services in his chapel for Longoria, and the story quickly made newspaper headlines. Most Texans opposed the mortician's refusal, and the Texas Good Neighbor Commission, which was appealed to in the case, declared that the funeral director's refusal was discriminatory. Intervening in the case, Lyndon B. Johnson, then senator from Texas, succeeded in obtaining burial for Longoria in Arlington National Cemetery. This was one of many unfortunate racist incidents which increased the awareness and aggressiveness of the Mexican

American community and provided its leadership with ammunition in the battle for civil rights.

Earlier incidents of discrimination against civilian Mexican Americans also contributed to their growing assertiveness. In the early 1940s recruitment by wartime employers brought Mexican Americans to the attention of many urban Californians for the first time. Economic competition for semi-skilled industrial jobs soon brought to the surface latent racial tensions between Mexican Americans and Anglos in the Los Angeles area. These tensions produced racial conflicts, thus belying the great freedoms for which the war was being fought.

One major conflict was called the "Sleepy Lagoon case" by the Los Angeles press. On August 2, 1942, young José Díaz was found unconscious on a rural road near Los Angeles, apparently the victim of a severe beating. He died without regaining consciousness; the autopsy showed that death had resulted from a fracture at the base of the skull. No weapon was found nor proof of murder established, but Díaz had participated in a gang clash the preceding evening at a nearby swimming hole. As a result twenty-three Mexican youths and one Anglo who had participated in the fighting were charged with murder.

Two of the indicted youths asked for separate trials and were subsequently released. The other twenty-two were tried together on sixty-six charges. The judge in the case, Charles W. Fricke, made no secret of his bias against Mexicans, and the prosecution repeatedly called attention to racial aspects of the trial. Throughout the court proceedings the defendants were denied haircuts and a change of clothing, and soon they began to resemble the prosecution's stereotype of the unkempt Mexican.

In January 1943, the jury found three of the youths guilty of first-degree murder, nine guilty of second-degree murder, and five guilty of assault. The other five were found not guilty. This verdict led to the creation of the Sleepy Lagoon Defense Committee, headed by Carey McWilliams, and which was organized to appeal the convictions. In October 1944, the California District Court of Appeals unanimously reversed the lower court's verdict, dismissing the charges for lack of evidence.

Although all charges were dropped, the Sleepy Lagoon case had widespread negative repercussions. It became a focal point for extensive anti-Mexican feelings, and the Los Angeles press exploited the situation by using sensational journalism to emphasize Mexican American crime. This "crime wave" campaign in the newspapers in turn put public pressure on the police department, which reacted with systematic roundups of Mexican American teenagers and with other suppressive measures in the Los Angeles area. These included police harassment of Mexican American youth clubs, extensive arrests based on race and mere suspicion, and general overpolicing of Mexican American areas. Because of the adverse effects of this police repression on wartime hemisphere relations, Washington put pressure on the newspapers to stop using the label "Mexican" in crime stories. It was replaced with the nonspecific but recognizable negative racial epithets of "Pachuco" and "zoot-suit."

At the time of World War II, Los Angeles had a large second-generation Mexican American teenage population, children of the immigrant wave of the 1920s. Some belonged to gangs whose members affected a distinctive dress style known as the zoot-suit, consisting of a broad-rimmed, flat hat; a long draped coat; and high-waisted, baggy-legged trousers with tight-fitting pegged cuffs. A long duck-tailed, squared-off hair style and a lengthy, elaborate key chain usually completed the outfit. This dress style was not originated by Mexican American youths, but had been adopted from a widespread style which became associated with the jitterbug dance craze originating in the East.

In April and May 1943, a few months after the convictions in the sensational Sleepy Lagoon case, there were some minor clashes between zoot-suiters and military personnel in Los Angeles. Rapidly mounting tensions soon led to serious rioting in the first days of June 1943, when clashes broke out between zoot-suiters, including Mexican American youths, and groups of disgruntled sailors and soldiers stationed in the area. Military personnel roamed the streets of Los Angeles seeking out and attacking those whom they thought were zoot-suiters. Streetcars and buses were stopped, and zoot-suiters were pulled off; theaters were entered and zoot-suiters were dragged out. Many were assaulted and had their clothes ripped off, their lank hair cut. These vicious attacks quickly extended to everyone who seemed to look like a Mexican. For all intents and purposes, there was an undeclared war on Mexican Americans by roving packs of undisciplined servicemen. This war reached a peak on June 7, when fleets of taxis filled with sailors cruised the streets of Los Angeles seeking victims. To make matters worse, the shore patrol, city police, and county sheriff's officials responded to this action by following the cabs at a distance, and then arresting the victims of the attacks rather than the attackers.

In this emotion-laden situation, the conservative Spanish newspaper, *La Opinión,* called for a cooling off and asked Mexican American youths to give up their rights of self-defense in the face of these unjustified criminal attacks. Retaliation by gangs of adolescent Mexican Americans was inevitable, however, and occurred wherever concentrations of la raza existed. Meanwhile, the Los Angeles English-language press caused further agitation with sensational headlines, inflammatory stories, and editorials against—of all people—the victims of these servicemen's attacks!

What had begun as a series of street brawls turned into a full-fledged race riot inflamed by the press and condoned or ignored by the major law agencies. Outbreaks similar to the Los Angeles rioting occurred in Pasadena, Long Beach, and San Diego. This violence in southern California triggered similar race riots against Mexican Americans in midwestern and eastern cities such as Chicago, Detroit, and Philadelphia during the summer of 1943. All over the country there was reaction to these occurrences, and *Time* magazine later called the riots in Los Angeles "the ugliest brand of mob action since the coolie race riots of the 1870s."

Finally, the Mexican ambassador in Washington, Francisco Nájera, requested the State Department to look into the Los Angeles situation. This pressure, along with reports that the riots were being used in Axis propaganda, caused the State Department to insist that military police take steps to bring rioting servicemen under control; consequently overnight passes and leaves were canceled and strict controls instituted. As a result of these measures the rioting tapered off by mid-June, and order was restored.

The final version of the Los Angeles rioting by city and county officials was that soldiers and sailors had acted in self-defense and that no element of race prejudice was involved. However, a citizens' committee appointed by Governor Earl Warren and headed by Bishop Joseph McGucken of Los Angeles found that these riots were caused principally by racial prejudice which was stimulated by police practices and by inflammatory newspaper reporting. In the Mexican American community the reaction to the servicemen's attacks stemmed in part from such long-standing conditions as poor housing, overcrowding, and lack of recreational facilities.

In reality Mexican American young people in the Los Angeles area had a good record as law-abiding citizens. In his study of the riots, sociologist Emory Bogardus estimated that only 3 percent of Mexican American youths participated in zoot-suit gangs and that only a slightly higher percentage even wore such outfits. Nevertheless, because the press overused the term "zoot-suit," guilt was often determined by length of hair and cut of trousers rather than by any evidence of wrongdoing. The matter reached such ridiculous proportions that on June 10 the Los Angeles City Council seriously debated a proposed ordinance that would have made it a punishable offense to wear a zoot-suit.

In the long run, the Sleepy Lagoon affair and the zoot-suit riots had a few positive results. The former led to open grand jury hearings on the problems of Mexican Americans, and the latter produced—at least temporarily—some Anglo concern about Mexican Americans. For example, in 1944, a Los Angeles Commission on Human Rights was set up, and for the next two or three years considerable interest was shown in the "race question." A large number of conferences, institutes, and meetings on the problems of la raza were held and still continue. Another byproduct was the creation of the Civic Unity Council which came out of the zoot-suit emergency committee headed by Carey McWilliams as a result of liberal demands for an agency which would give ethnic minorities greater representation in civic matters. Unfortunately, after a few years the Civic Unity Council became increasingly conservative in its makeup and ineffective in its operation, and it finally disappeared in 1948. However, politicians continued to pay lip service, at least, to the idea of fair treatment and political representation for Mexican Americans.

Another aspect of the Mexican American experience during World War II in the Southwest was the rise of sinarquismo.

Sinarquismo, an extreme right-wing political philosophy with Spanish and German fascist connections, developed in Mexico in the 1930s under Salvador Abascal, Manuel Zeremo, and Oskar Schreiter in precisely those areas from which most immigrants to the United States had come. This philosophy strongly emphasized Mexican nationalism and opposed both United States and Mexican involvement in the war against the Axis powers. Concurrently with the outbreak of World War II, an attempt was made to spread the doctrine of sinarquismo to Mexican barrios in the United States, especially in centers of heavy Mexican population such as Los Angeles.

Two local leaders, Pedro Villaseñor and Martín Cabrera, had direct links with sinarquistas in Mexico, and provided leadership for southern California by publishing *El Sinarquista* in Los Angeles. This newspaper served as a vehicle for spreading sinarquismo, and its pages carried various rumors intended to discourage Mexican Americans from actively supporting the war effort. Sinarquistas advocated the return of the Southwest to Mexico, an attitude known as irredentism, which was appropriate to the way some Mexicans and Mexican Americans viewed the Southwest. This movement was taken seriously enough by both the United States and Mexican governments, and the former made efforts to counter its propaganda by sending a special agent to the Southwest to inform Mexican Americans of its threat and the latter infiltrated secret agents within its ranks. At its peak sinarquismo made wild claims of large membership, but the evidence indicates that Mexican Americans overwhelmingly rejected its divisive appeal. In all the Southwest the organization probably never attracted more than two or three thousand members—a testimonial to the loyalty of Mexican Americans to the United States.

The appeal of sinarquismo to Mexican Americans was further diminished by improved economic opportunities created by the industrial war effort, whose manpower needs increased rapidly as the war progressed. Because of wartime employment opportunities in the burgeoning industrial centers of the Midwest and the West Coast, many Mexican Americans obtained jobs and acquired union membership on a much wider scale. Mexican American family incomes rose substantially because of higher wages and several family members were able to get jobs. Mexican American women in large numbers were able to break away from their traditional roles and obtain employment outside the home. A new socioeconomic pattern was thus introduced to underscore even further the change for Mexican Americans from a rural, agricultural life style to an urban, industrial one at the same time that World War II was expanding the urban American population.

In New Mexico the war years saw considerable development of federal defense agencies. Projects at Los Alamos, Alamogordo, and White Sands provided many Mexican Americans with high-paying industrial jobs. Between 1939 and 1942, about one-half of all men and working-age boys left the rural villages of New Mexico. Some of these went into agriculture and herding; however, many were able to go into defense plants and other war industries as the result of skills acquired by participation in the various federal programs of the depression years.

During World War II, the New Mexico Department of Vocational Education greatly expanded the training program that it had started among the Hispanos in the thirties. Also, by September 1942, federally sponsored programs had trained some 3,500 Mexican Americans in such critically needed wartime skills as welding and mechanics. These trainees were able to obtain jobs in new industrial centers throughout the Southwest, especially in California, where shipyards and other war industries had created great demands for skilled and semi-skilled workers.

Although many employers were still reluctant to hire Mexican Americans, the federal Fair Employment Practices Commission enabled many of them to secure jobs commensurate with their training. Most Mexican Americans performed well on the job, thereby opening the door wider to others who followed, but at the war's end many found themselves the first to be laid off.

Although Texas had less wartime industrial development than other parts of the Southwest, the oil business expanded greatly between 1940 and 1946, and as a result, Mexican Americans were able to establish a foothold as petroleum workers. They often found discrimination, however. To try to cope with this age-old problem from another perspective, President Franklin D. Roosevelt appointed the well-known historian, Professor Carlos E. Castañeda of the University of Texas, as his special assistant on Latin American problems. In his role as assistant to the chairman of the Presidential Committee on Fair Employment Practices, Dr. Castañeda helped to improve opportunities and working conditions for Mexican Americans in Texas. Early in 1945, the FEPC ordered the Shell Oil Company to revise its work contracts in compliance with the Fair Employment Practices Act and to give promotions to three Mexican Americans it had failed to promote. Meat packing in Texas also opened its doors to Mexican Americans during the war. Although unionized plants practiced relatively little discrimination, non-unionized plants discriminated in both wage differentials and job opportunities.

During the war, attempts were made to end discrimination in public schools—by curtailing the segregation of Mexican American children and by fostering appreciation of Mexican and Latin American history and culture. In January 1944, the Texas Supervisory Committee on Inter-American Education recommended setting up teacher-training institutes to implement these objectives; therefore, summer workshops were established for public school teachers.

These workshops encouraged the teachers to develop more open attitudes toward Mexican American students and to appreciate their civil rights. Curriculum materials and teaching units were prepared. One session chaired by Dr. George Sánchez concluded that most Spanish-speaking children were in need of curriculum enrichment to compensate for environmental, social, and economic deficiencies, but no action was ever taken on these conclusions. Although these initial efforts toward helping the Mexican American child were weak and hesitant, they were at least the first step—a recognition that problems existed. Much time has elapsed since these recommendations were made, and we are still diagnosing and defining problems that have already been articulated, but little effective remedial action has been taken.

One interesting effort to improve relations between Anglos and Mexican Americans during World War II was the creation of the Spanish-Speaking Peoples' Division in the Office of Inter-American Affairs. Although the Office of Inter-American Affairs was not created to deal specifically with the problems of Mexican Americans, its coördinator, Nelson Rockefeller, was inundated with suggestions that it focus its primary attention on the Spanish-speaking. Thus, the Spanish-Speaking People's Division was set up in April 1942, with Carey McWilliams as operational officer.

This division wanted to eliminate discrimination against Mexican Americans and to develop programs that would enable them to participate more fully in American society. Although the plan was never fully implemented, a series of important conferences on the problems of Mexican Americans was held in the Southwest during 1942 and 1943. The division organized a number of teachers' workshops, and provided a few fellowships for Spanish-speaking students.

By the end of World War II the economic status of Mexican Americans had improved slightly. There was less discrimination, greater access to union representation, opportunities in the semi-skilled and skilled trades, and increased small-business ownership.

Socially, more Mexican American children were obtaining better educations than ever before. More were completing elementary school, and many were entering high school. However, they were handicapped by inferior education and unequal educational opportunities.

This hindrance to Mexican American social progress arose in part from continuing deep prejudices about the racial and cultural background of the group. These prejudices and misconceptions about the Mexican American's intellectual and technical abilities continue to prevail as the result of widespread acceptance of I.Q. tests based on middle class Anglo-Saxon cultural values and therefore biased against minority groups like the Mexican Americans.

World War II had a wide variety of impacts on Mexican Americans in the Southwest. The war provided new and enlightening experiences, technical training, expanded job opportunities, and new goals for Mexican Americans. The war also provided new sources of income. Armed services allotments considerably reduced the desperate poverty and hopelessness of the 1930s. In addition, money sent home by soldiers had a dramatic effect on the economic welfare and stability of their home communities.

Education, acculturation, and wartime experiences modified the attitudes of younger Mexican Americans but had less effect on the older generation. Spanish-language newspapers, magazines, and radio stations, as well as greater possibilities for traveling to Mexico, all helped to preserve the Mexican life style. Because World War II provided Mexican Americans with new views, needs, and desires, they became increasingly motivated to attain higher economic and social levels; toward this end they began to form their own organizations and to seek ways of developing ethnic political power.

# twelve

## Braceros

The Mexican term "bracero" comes from the Spanish word *brazo* (arm) and has several meanings. In its widest sense it has the same general meaning as the English "hired hand." In the following chapters it is used to refer to Mexican nationals recruited under various Mexican-United States arrangements. Brought into the United States under programs organized by the two governments for seasonal employment, they normally returned to Mexico at the end of their contracts; however, some stayed over to the following year, while others, having returned to Mexico, came back in succeeding years—often to the same area and employer.

Basically the bracero program in the United States covers two periods. The first period began in August 1942 and ended in December 1947; the second ran from February 1948 to December 1964. While the first period was very important for the United States war effort, it was relatively small in scale and did not exceed 250,000 braceros in the five years of its existence. In this first phase, Mexican workers were recruited under executive agreement as well as Public Law 45, passed by Congress in 1942.

The second, postwar period of the program was far more important both to Mexico and the United States since it lasted seventeen years, during which some 4,500,000 Mexican nationals were brought temporarily to the United States. This second period can be divided into two subperiods. The first of these extended from 1948 to 1951, during which the importation of workers was on a semi-individual basis under several executive agreements. The second subperiod began largely as a result of the Korean War and led to the passage of Public Law 78, under which large numbers of braceros were brought annually into the United States until 1965, when the bracero program officially terminated.

Of course, this large scale program did not spring fullblown into existence at the beginning of World War II. Its faint beginnings go back to World War I, when in 1917 the Mexican government requested the United States to guarantee contracts of immigrant workers, a proposal which the American government rejected. A second stage of the bracero program beginnings took place during the heavy immigration wave of the mid-twenties, when the Mexican consul general at San Antonio, Enrique Santibáñez, suggested in 1926 an organized program of seasonal migration, to be supervised by the two governments. This suggestion went unheeded by the American government. Subsequently, however, the Mexican Congress passed labor legislation in 1931 designed to regulate migration for employment. It required that all contracts provide certain basic needs, such as free housing, free medical service, and half-pay during illness, and that all contracts for temporary agricultural employment of sixty days or more be in writing. These regulations proved ineffectual, since they could be implemented only with United States coöperation, which was not forthcoming.

In the 1930s dust-bowl migrants contributed significantly to the makeup of America's farm labor force. By the latter part of the thirties they formed about 50 percent of all migratory workers in western agriculture. When World War II broke out in Europe in 1939, domestic labor continued for a while to meet most United States needs for agricultural workers. However, American agricultural workers were increasingly attracted to expanding defense industries, especially in West Coast cities like San Pedro, San Diego, Los Angeles, Richmond, Seattle, and others. As a result of this farm labor drain, by 1941 the United States was making its first informal inquiries to Mexican government agencies about the possibilities of recruiting agricultural workers in Mexico. The Mexican government responded that such recruitment was possible only if conditions of work were guaranteed and immigration supervised by the American government.

This reply and the entrance of the United States into the war after Pearl Harbor marked the beginning of a large-scale, organized bracero program. Early in 1942, California sugar-beet growers asked the United States Employment Service (USES) for permission to bring in Mexican workers. Immediately thereafter, the citrus industry and the railroads added their voices to this request. However, the USES first undertook recruitment of domestic labor, and not until the middle of May 1942 did it certify the probable need for 3,000 Mexican workers. Growers wanted an open-border policy such as had existed in World War I, and California growers especially kept pressuring the United States government for Mexican workers under some such broad arrangement. Mexico, plagued by memories of the recent repatriation, was not enthusiastic about supplying workers on any basis. However, at the end of May, Mexico declared war on the Axis powers and as an ally indicated its willingness to supply workers to the United States as a part of its contribution to the war effort.

A mixed United States–Mexican committee began working out details of a bracero program, incorporating some of the ideas of the noted Mexican anthropologist Manuel Gamio. In the 1920s he had carried on extensive research on Mexican immigration, supported by the Social Science Research Council. His general findings were published by the University of Chicago Press under the title, *Mexican Immigration to the United States: A Study of Human Migration and Adjustment.* In this work, Gamio proposed a regulated migration, which he hoped would improve both Mexican income and agricultural practices.

In July 1942, an executive agreement was signed by the two governments, and the accord was ratified at Mexico City two weeks later. It included the following provisions: workers not to be used to displace American workers or to lower wage rates, minimum guarantees governing wages and working conditions, pay at the prevailing rate for at least 75 percent of the contract period, the right of workers to request termination of contract at any time, free transportation of workers to and from their homes, and subsistence to be provided en route. This agreement emphasized the temporary nature of the arrangements, but it did not set any specific time limit to them. Either government could terminate the pact on ninety days' notice. To a considerable degree the United States was assenting to the 1917 position of the Mexican government, which at that time asked for guaranteed labor contracts to insure the well-being of migrants and legal recourse in case of noncompliance. These arrangements to protect workers' rights were considered by grower groups to be excessively protective of Mexican nationals but were accepted reluctantly because of the dire need for labor.

In April 1943, this basic agreement was modified in view of the first year's operational experience, and subsequent minor changes were made at the request of Mexico. The United States Congress, under heavy pressure from agribusiness lobbyists, made some assertion of growers' viewpoints in the details of actual operation of the accord. Thus, general policies of the bracero program were determined, often through pursestring control, by a congress which was very sensitive to the desires of agricultural interests. An example of this influence was Public Law 45 of April 29, 1943, which, among other things, authorized spending public funds to implement the agreement with Mexico. Under its provisions, the United States Department of Agriculture had responsibility for recruiting, contracting, and transporting braceros. In addition, its agents determined prevailing wage rates and interpreted details of policy virtually without restriction.

At the Mexican government's request, the Farm Security Administration of the Department of Agriculture was at first placed in charge of the program. However, it was considered too idealistic and reformist by growers and their congressmen, and they worked to remove the program from control of the FSA. By the end of June 1943, direction of the bracero program was turned over to another Agriculture Department agency, the War Foods Administration. There, farmer and grower groups dominated the program, and some reversion to the earlier patterns of foreign worker treatment occurred. The bracero program did not eliminate exploitation; it merely set limits on it.

The total cost to the federal government of the World War II bracero program amounted to more than $450 per bracero, or more than $113 million. This partial payment of labor costs by the United States government was in effect a subsidy to large-scale agricultural enterprises and railroad companies. Although the Mexican government did the recruiting, the United States financed a large part of the recruiting costs. In addition, the United States government paid medical costs of eighteen to twenty dollars per bracero annually, plus minimal educational costs; it also operated reception centers, paid part of transportation costs, and provided subsistence during transportation.

During the five-year period from 1942 to 1947, a total of more than 200,000 braceros were employed in twenty-one of the United States. Beginning in 1942 with 4,000 men, the number quickly rose to 52,000 the following year, reached its peak in 1944 with about 62,000 workers, and then tapered off rapidly to about 30,000 in 1947. More than half the braceros were employed in California agriculture, while the remainder were used principally elsewhere in the Southwest. At the peak of the 1944 harvest season, braceros made up 9 percent of all agricultural workers in the Pacific states, and in that same year they supplied the United States with 10,000,000 man-days of farm labor, harvesting crops estimated at $432-million in value.

Growers appreciated bracero workers, both because they were an able and dependable labor force and because they enjoyed a draft-free status. Generally, the bracero program in agriculture proved very successful; bracero labor made it possible to raise and harvest the crops required by expanded wartime demands. Unquestionably, there would have been greater food shortages during the war years had it not been for the bracero program.

However, not all World War II braceros worked in agriculture. Many thousands worked at transporting harvested crops and other needed goods and supplies to the civilian population and the armed forces. Late in 1941, the Southern Pacific Railroad requested that the Immigration and Naturalization Service grant permission to bring in Mexican nationals for track-maintenance work. However, organized labor emphatically opposed the use of bracero labor on railroads, and the Southern Pacific withdrew its application. But the need for laborers continued, and early in 1942 railroads were running advertisements in metropolitan newspapers asking for weekend recruits to work on track maintenance. In May, the Southern Pacific again filed application to recruit Mexican workers, arguing that it found itself unable to fill nearly a thousand jobs from the domestic labor supply. No action was taken on this request, and through the Railroad Retirement Board a large number of retired workers were recruited for the jobs. In October 1942, Joseph Eastman, the director of the Office of Defense Transportation, successfully petitioned the War Manpower Commission to take steps to obtain Mexican track workers for western railroads.

As a result, recruitment of railroad workers began in Mexico the following May. During the war years, thirty-two railroads requested and secured Mexican workers under an agreement which included a minimum wage (45 cents per hour at first; later 57 cents) and a guarantee of 90 percent employment during the normal six-month contract period, at the end of which they usually returned to Mexico. Later this arrangement was modified to allow Mexican nationals to be transferred from track work to various semi-skilled job categories in railroad work. Eventually, more than 80,000 Mexican braceros were recruited for the railroads, over half of them working for the Southern Pacific and Santa Fe lines.

With the end of World War II in mid-1945 recruitment of railroad workers in Mexico came to an end. The railroads requested extension and renewal of the bracero program, but their requests were denied. Railroads reacted to this refusal by delaying repatriation of nationals for several months. Both the Mexican Ministry of Labor and the American Federation of Labor lodged complaints at this footdragging, and finally, in April 1946, the last of the Mexican railroad workers were sent back to Mexico.

Texas did not participate in the bracero program. Texas growers and ranchers favored the "open-border" policy, which had functioned profitably for Texas during World War I. This open-border policy was, of course, directly contrary to Mexican–United States agreements of 1942 and early 1943.

Nevertheless, Mexican migrants were recruited outside these agreements by private labor contractors for work in Texas, and the Immigration Department, on May 11, 1943, authorized issuance of one-year work permit cards, which in effect provided Texas with a legally sanctioned open-border policy. Some 2,000 Mexican workers quickly crossed over into Texas before the border was again closed, an action prompted by protests from the Mexican government. This flouting of Mexican national feelings was only one part of the Mexican complaint against Texas. In June 1943, the Mexican Secretary of Foreign Affairs, Ezequiel Padilla, announced that no braceros would be authorized for work in Texas because his office had received an excessive number of complaints from Mexican consuls about discrimination against Mexicans in the state. While discrimination against Mexican workers was common in all states, the Texas attitude was so intolerable that the Mexican Labor Minister, Roberto Medellín, made a similar policy statement in support of Padilla's position.

Responding to Mexico's refusal of workers, Texans reassessed the implications and consequences of prevalent racial attitudes and practices in their state. As a result, on May 6, 1944, more out of necessity than altruism, the Texas legislature passed the Caucasian Race Resolution, which endorsed the idea of equal rights in public places of business and amusement for all Caucasians. In mid-June, Texas governor Coke Stevenson informed Secretary Padilla that measures were being taken to reduce discrimination, and he promised enforcement of the recently passed resolution. Governor Stevenson also informed Padilla that he intended to create an executive anti-discrimination commission; however, Stevenson did not actually appoint this commission until September. Replying to Stevenson's promises of reform, Padilla simply said that the solutions promised were unequal to the magnitude of the problem. Texas obtained no braceros during 1943.

In 1944 and 1945 Mexico reconsidered its firm position regarding braceros and Texas discrimination. During this time, both Padilla and President Manuel Avila Camacho considered sending braceros to Texas; however, they feared that once Texas received approval for braceros, enforcement of anti-discrimination legislation would cease. Many Mexican officials shared this fear, which was substantiated and reinforced by the failure of the Texas legislature to pass a bill proposed in 1945 to end discrimination in restaurants. Meanwhile, lacking braceros, Texas filled her labor needs during World War II by recruiting local Mexican Americans, school children, college students, and even prisoners of war. Also a noticeable increase in the number of illegal immigrants took place; these illegal entrants were commonly referred to as "wetbacks" or mojados, because they presumably swam the Rio Grande to enter the United States.

Lack of braceros in Texas during the war years benefitted American workers in the state. In order to attract more do-mestic workers into farm labor, a program was initiated in January 1945 to improve housing, education, and working con-ditions. As one aspect of this program, some Texas farm com-munities even provided reception centers for migrant workers in the spring of 1945. As a result of these measures, some Texas migrants found living conditions improved, but the effort proved inadequate.

Governor Stevenson created the Texas Good Neighbor Com-mission in 1943, feeling that an official organization was neces-sary to attack effectively the problems of discrimination. In its early years, the commission emphasized educating people about the evils of discrimination rather than by proposing anti-discrimination legislation. Between 1943 and 1947, the com-mission could claim that it had brought about better Anglo un-derstanding of Mexicans and Mexican Americans than had existed before. In 1947 it was made a permanent state agency.

Unfortunately, Governor Beauford H. Jester, who succeeded Stevenson, had a different view of the commission's function, and it became largely ceremonial. In April 1947, Pauline Kibbe, executive secretary of the commission, strongly criticized the 25-cent hourly wage authorized in the lower Rio Grande Val-ley of Texas. This position brought her into direct conflict with powerful interests and resulted in Miss Kibbe's resignation in September of that year. Within two years the agency had com-pletely redirected its focus, and its activities became largely focused on visiting Mexican dignitaries. After oilman Neville Penrose was named chairman in 1950, the commission con-cerned itself more with being a good-will diplomatic agency than with championing farm labor rights. Thus the commission's original objectives of improving Mexican American relations in Texas were completely lost. A continuing basic weakness of the commission was that it seldom included more than a few Mexican Americans and sometimes none at all.

While the bracero program had differing impacts north and south of the Rio Grande, it was favorably received on both sides of the border. Whatever the reservations of Mexican government officials, the average Mexican had only the greatest expectations about working in the United States, and economically he usually fared better there than in Mexico. This led to the problem of there being many more people trying to get into the program than could be accepted. Fearing the population movement and pressures this eagerness might generate, the Mexican government preferred to recruit in the interior rather than at the border, and as a result, most wartime braceros were recruited from around Mexico City. When the news of the program broke, so many thousands of Mexicans jammed the Mexico City recruitment center that on the first day, twenty died from the crush and suffocation.

Although most braceros were recruited in central Mexico, they came from a wide range of economic backgrounds, and only about 20 percent came directly from rural farm backgrounds. There was wide variation within bracero ranks, but the typical bracero grew up in a small, isolated village, and had moved from his village to a Mexican urban center; he was in his mid-thirties, male, married (although he usually had left his family at home), barely literate in Spanish, and unable to speak English. He became a bracero because of defects in the economy of Mexico, where unemployment and underemployment have always been high, especially in the rural parts.

Bracero experiences in the United States were often unpleasant; however, since jobs in Mexico were scarce and pay below subsistence levels, the workers usually wanted to return. About 70 percent of the annual quota of braceros was composed of returnees from earlier years. Encouraged by growers, who naturally preferred experienced help, many veteran braceros returned year after year with the hope of working for the same companies or growers. This attitude reflected to a degree the patrón-peón relationship of an earlier period in Mexico and the Southwest. The most important factor in the willingness of the bracero to endure hardship and separation from family was financial; the average bracero annually was able to send home a sum sufficient to maintain his family and himself in Mexico until the next recruitment cycle.

Criticism concerning the bracero program came from both the United States and Mexico; however, it was never taken seriously enough for either side to request termination of the program. Although a majority of growers preferred bracero workers, many of them resented guarantees stipulated in the program, especially those concerning minimum wage requirements suggested by the Mexican government. On the other hand, United States labor complained that growers used braceros to hold down agricultural wages. It may be pointed out that cotton wages in Texas, which obtained no braceros, rose 236 percent during the war years, while in California, which used more than half the bracero quota, cotton wages increased only 136 percent. In addition wages were held down in other ways as well. In 1943, at the growers' request, the War Food Administration set wage ceilings on asparagus, tomatoes, grapes, and cotton—all crops heavily using bracero labor.

Braceros had their own lists of complaints, many reflecting their exaggerated hopes and expectations. These included poor food, excessive charges for board, substandard housing, prejudice and discrimination, physical mistreatment and exposure to pesticides, excessive deductions from wages, and unsatisfactory earnings. Extravagant claims regarding wages and the quality of life in the United States had been made and were readily accepted by naïve and credulous Mexicans. Tales of daily wages of $25 to $35 deceived some; many more were misled by honest statements of probable earnings. It was difficult for them to realize that the cost of living in the United States was so much higher than in Mexico and that it would so greatly diminish their real wages.

In addition, there was widespread unhappiness at the failure of farmers and farmers' associations to provide continuous employment. Often braceros were idle through no fault of their own, either because of inclement weather or insufficient work. Weekly earning at times were below the cost of room and board, which averaged about $12 a week. The average earnings of wartime braceros did not exceed $500 per year.

Perhaps the most frequent complaints, although not the most serious, concerned the food provided in the farm labor camps. Braceros had little choice about housing and eating accommodations, and charges for room and board were deducted from their pay. They complained that food prepared for them was often of inferior quality, uninspired in preparation, and foreign to Mexican tastes.

Often the meals in the bracero camps, prepared by concessionaires, were unfit for human consumption, and cases of food poisoning, though fairly common, often went unreported. The menu was frequently arranged around such things as chitterlings, beef hearts, tripe, oxtails, pig feet, chicken necks, and sheep heads. Noon lunches in the field were usually made up of leftovers from earlier meals. Furthermore, most braceros felt that food costs were inflated and that, in fact, their menus were planned solely on the basis of providing food at minimal cost—a feeling often corroborated by Mexican consuls to whom complaints were made.

More serious were the complaints voiced by braceros about housing, which generally was substandard, often pest-ridden, and bare to the point of providing only minimal shelter. Braceros were often housed at first in converted chicken coops, railroad cars, and dilapidated farm structures. However, the construction of ninety-five farm labor camps by the end of 1943 somewhat alleviated this situation. In addition to complaints about the poor quality of housing, there existed much unhappiness that labor camps were usually located far from population centers, making it difficult for braceros to make use of business and social services. This isolation added to their natural feelings of homesickness and nostalgia. They especially felt the need for someone they could trust and to whom they could take their problems. There were, of course, Mexican consuls; but they were relatively few and often little concerned with the problems of braceros, since their offices primarily dealt with trade and tourism. While braceros themselves did not stress discrimination, perhaps for fear of being returned to Mexico, the Mexican press carried considerable criticism of discrimination as well as poor working conditions and the manpower loss to Mexico. This discrimination and the poor working conditions have been verified and documented by many investigators such as Dr. Ernesto Galarza and Carey McWilliams.

The victory over Japan early in September 1945 brought World War II to an end. A year later, on November 15, 1946, the United States Department of State notified the Mexican government of its wish to terminate the bracero agreement. Employers, however, continued to plead a need for braceros, arguing that the demand for agricultural workers was still acute and that they needed time to adjust to their former sources of labor. In an effort to secure continuation of the wartime supply of Mexican workers, a bill was introduced in the House of Representatives in January 1947 to extend the bracero program to June 30, 1948. This bill was modified in Congress and passed in June 1947 as Public Law 40, which provided for the program's termination and repatriation of all braceros by December 31. Officially the program came to an end at that time.

However, only the special legislation implementing the program was abrogated; the habit and rationale of bracero labor still remained an important factor in American agriculture, and its use was to expand in the 1950s and 1960s. Braceros continued to be brought across the border as agribusiness returned to the familiar patterns of the prewar years, the contracting for labor being carried out directly between braceros and farmers or farm organizations without any specific arrangements between the two national governments and with supervision only by the Mexican government. The fifties and sixties, with their high levels of illegal immigration, also proved that Mexican workers could not be prevented from crossing the border so long as the attraction of high wages and expectations of a better way of life persisted.

# thirteen
## Mojado, Bracero, and Mexican American

Of all the workers in the Southwest during the years following World War II, mojados unquestionably became the most outrageously exploited. Not only did they receive the lowest wages, endure the worst working conditions, and live in the poorest housing, often without sanitary facilities, but they also suffered from discrimination, chiseling, and racketeering by Mexicans, Mexican Americans, and Anglos. In spite of all this, mojados had considerable impact on the socioeconomic development of the Southwest. Their contribution of labor to southwestern agriculture made expansion of intensive-cultivation crops possible. At the same time, mojados, forced, because of their illegal status, to accept virtually any wage offered them, depressed wages and living standards of local workers, predominantly Mexican Americans. Therefore, the general reaction to mojados on the part of Mexican Americans was at best ambivalent, and it often involved suspicion and distrust. Mexican Americans recognized mojados as members of la raza, but they also saw the illegal immigrants as a direct threat to them and their family's economic welfare.

In order better to understand the Mexican migratory patterns of the postwar years, it is important to trace the historical pattern of this phenomenon. Movement of Mexicans north and south of the political border between the United States and Mexico has a very long history. In the nineteenth century the unimpeded flow of migrants both ways across the border aroused little interest in either country. The passage in 1882 of the first restrictive immigration legislation—against the Chinese—only increased the demand for labor in the Southwest, thereby enlarging the movement of people north from Mexico. As time went on, other factors also encouraged the expanded use of Mexican labor. These were: the absence of legal penalties; agribusiness employment of contratistas; the difficulty of distinguishing the immigrants from Mexican American workers; the exploitative motives of agribusiness; cultural protection and security provided by Mexican American communities in the Southwest; and widespread public indifference.

World War II enabled many Mexican Americans to move out of central and southern Texas into urban centers of Texas and elsewhere in the country. Many Mexican Americans also moved into geographical areas where their presence had previously been minimal. For example, in Arkansas by 1948 about 13,000 Mexican Americans and Mexican nationals had replaced Negroes in the cotton harvest. This internal migration after

World War II was of major significance to present-day settlement patterns of Mexican Americans, equal in importance to the waves of migration which resulted from the 1910 Revolution.

In the postwar years, mojados replaced those Mexican Americans who had migrated from the lower Rio Grande Valley, and from 1946 to 1954, they supplied the main source of cheap labor for agribusiness throughout the Southwest. A congressional committee was appointed in 1948 to investigate the flow of illegal traffic across the border. However, no action was taken and nothing changed until 1954, when the Immigration Bureau organized a massive drive known as "Operation Wetback," designed to curb the illegal flow of workers from Mexico. This roundup, like other efforts, did not stop the flood of mojados into the United States; in fact, the termination of the bracero program in 1964 further increased illegal crossings, which continue to the present time.

At the end of World War II two new factors worked together to increase greatly the number of migrants moving illegally from Mexico into the Southwest. In the decade between 1940 and 1950, widespread expansion of irrigated cultivation in northern Mexico brought large numbers of Mexican workers to the border cities. Many of these, attracted by higher American wages, crossed over into the United States. Recognizing that the attraction of higher wages in the United States would continue to deplete their labor supply, Mexican employers recruited many more workers than they needed. As a result of this overrecruitment, the population of most Mexican border towns more than doubled between 1940 and 1950. At the same time that this excess number of Mexican laborers was being drawn to the Mexican border regions, irrigated agriculture was being expanded in the southwestern United States.

The addition of 7,500,000 acres to the agricultural lands of the seventeen western states between 1945 and 1955 rapidly increased the need for stoop labor.

There is also considerable evidence that the introduction of braceros under a formal program in 1942 and their continued use in the 1950s tended further to stimulate illegal crossings. Many returning braceros enthusiastically described the opportunities and comparatively high wages available in the United States to other Mexicans. Bureaucratic red tape and expense inherent in the bracero program, however, forced anxious Mexican workers to choose the easy and expeditious alternative of crossing the border illegally. However, widespread availability of legal braceros during the war years (except in Texas) held the mojado flow in check to some degree at first. Up to the end of World War II, the number of illegal entrants was relatively small, and they usually worked in areas close to the border.

With the termination of the wartime bracero program in December 1947, mojado smuggling, which previously had been important only in Texas, now became a thriving and lucrative business along the entire southwestern border. No one knows exactly how many entered the United States, but in the nine-year period from 1947 to 1955, more than 4,300,000 illegal immigrants were apprehended and returned to Mexico. How many avoided apprehension is not known, but estimates run into the millions.

The floodtide began in 1949, when an estimated half-million Mexicans illegally crossed the border. This very rapid expansion was the product especially of two factors; first, Mexican workers, by crossing over as mojados, could save money, waiting time, and travel expense; second, American growers by hiring mojados, could save money by evading minimum wage and employment standards, bonding and contracting fees, and the restrictions of the bracero program. Extremely important in this illegal labor development was the Spanish-speaking Mexican American labor contractor, the contratista or enganchista. He often headed a highly organized system which included fleets of trucks and buses, secret hideout-camps, and counterfeit documents.

As a result of this increased mojado influx, the lower Rio Grande Valley became a great labor reservoir into which legal and illegal immigrants moved because of easy accessibility and cultural affinity. As illegal immigrants moved in, local Mexican American labor, unable or unwilling to compete for low-paying jobs, sought better opportunities through seasonal migration to the North and Northwest, thereby swelling the annual migrant stream from Texas. In some areas as many as half the local workers moved out when mojados entered in large numbers. During the postwar years Texas paradoxically became both the largest importer and exporter of migrant labor.

Like braceros, mojado ranks included workers with a wide variety of skills, and many used agricultural work as an intermediate position before taking industrial jobs in the United States. They moved into construction work, service industries, hotel employment, and other low-status jobs, where they became increasingly a matter of concern to American unions because of their depressant effect on wage levels.

During World War II, little effort was made by the Immigration Service to keep illegal Mexican immigrants out of the United States, especially in Texas, where the majority of them crossed and settled. As the mojado movement increased toward the end of the war, the United States and Mexico reached an understanding in an attempt to reduce illegal entry. However, political and community pressures often hampered work of the Immigration Service and the Border Patrol. Both agencies were to a degree subservient to southwestern farm interests, and as a result of pressures brought by these interests, enforcement of immigration laws was often lax. On occasions the Immigration Service made arrangements with state employment agencies not to enforce immigration laws strictly until after harvest. The only enforcement improvement in the postwar years was a sharp rise in the number of deportations.

Immediately after the war, the Immigration Service introduced a new method of dealing with illegal Mexican entrants by converting their status into that of legal braceros through a process known as the "drying-out" technique. This technique involved giving mojados employed by American farmers identification slips, sending them back across the border and then allowing them to reënter the United States legally. Thus farmers benefitted by having experienced workers, and the former illegal entrants were given legal status, providing them some minimal guarantees as legal foreign agricultural workers. Had the drying-out process been successful in checking the mojado flow, it might have aided Mexican-American efforts for better socioeconomic conditions; however, it did not.

Concerned about the treatment of mojados, the United States and Mexico early in 1947 held a series of meetings to discuss possible solutions to the problem. On January 31, the two governments agreed that the estimated 120,000 illegal entrants living in the border region would be legalized at the border and given contracts that would provide some guarantees, especially that of a minimum wage. Texas growers responded to this agreement by certifying a wage of 25 cents an hour, despite higher prevailing wages in most of the Southwest. Reacting to this "magnanimous" wage offer, Pauline Kibbe, executive secretary of the Texas Good Neighbor Commission, publicly criticized the low rate certified. Dissatisfied with the unjust position on wages taken by Texas growers and also their failure to live up to other agreements, Mexico again put Texas on the blacklist and ended the legalizing of mojados in September 1947, after about 55,000 had been "dried out."

Termination of the wartime bracero program had not ended legal importation of Mexican workers into the United States; it merely ended the large-scale, two-government cooperative arrangements. In January 1948, control of importing alien workers was transferred from the Department of Agriculture to the Department of Labor. Importation continued on a semi-individual basis under a series of executive agreements with farmers' associations that often undertook responsibility for making the necessary arrangements with American and Mexican officials.

In February 1948, the United States and Mexico reached an agreement on the importation of agricultural workers which retained few wartime bracero guarantees. The United States Employment Service then established 40 cents an hour as the prevailing wage in the Rio Grande Valley, despite the complaints of Texas growers that they would be bankrupted. Using the wage scale of 40 cents an hour as a yardstick, agribusiness interests extended this wage to include not only imported Mexican labor but also Mexican American labor. The attitude expressed here might be interpreted as "A Mexican is a Mexican is a Mexican."

A similar wage situation developed in the fall of 1948 as the cotton harvest approached; growers established a rate of $2.50 per hundred pounds, although the going rate for that amount was $3.00. Responding to this arbitrary wage-setting by the growers, the Mexican government insisted that the workers be paid at the $3.00-rate or the use of Mexican workers would not be approved. Early in October, the Immigration Service was told that the cotton crop would rot in the fields without Mexican nationals to pick it, and as a result the Texas border at El Paso was opened to Mexican nationals from October 13 to 18.

Despite efforts of the Mexican government to stop Mexicans from crossing into Texas, including the use of army troops, nearly seven thousand, lured by job opportunities even at low wages, streamed across the border. As they crossed, they were placed under technical arrest by Immigration Service representatives and "paroled" to local United States Employment Service centers. Loaded into trucks of various growers' agents with the approval of the Employment Service, they were taken to labor camps.

Strong protests against this unethical but legal maneuver were made by the Mexican government, various labor organizations, and many Mexican American groups. A few days later, the Mexican Secretary of Foreign Relations, Jaime Torres Bodet, abrogated the February bracero agreement. Subsequently, the United States expressed regret for this unfortunate El Paso incident, but only after the cotton crop was saved!

For the next nine months no United States–Mexican agreement existed on braceros; during this time the number of mojados—especially in Texas and California—increased appreciably. Both governments, concerned about this rapid increase, pushed for further discussions, which finally led to a new agreement on braceros in August 1949. This accord put stress on suppression of the number of mojados and included a denial of braceros to growers using illegal workers. It also provided for the legalizing of mojados already in the United States.

As a result of this new agreement, 87,000 illegal immigrants were "dried out" in 1949, while at the same time almost 280,000 were apprehended and deported. In the following year, 96,000 more mojados were legalized and 459,000 deported, as illegal entrants continued to pour into the Southwest. In 1951, the Presidential Commission on Migratory Labor substantiated this trend by reporting that the legalization of workers already in the country illegally had made up the bulk of United States contracting activities since 1947. At the beginning of this legalization effort, officials hoped that extensive legalization would reduce mojado crossings. However, these expectations were not realized, because the possibility of eventually being given legal status encouraged many Mexicans to cross the border illegally. As the program continued Mexico became increasingly unhappy with this "drying-out" arrangement as well as with the ill-treatment of her nationals and violations of contracts by growers, especially in Texas and Arkansas.

The Korean War, which broke out in 1950, became the occasion for returning to stricter controls on the importation of Mexican labor. The Mexican government informed the United States that if it wanted large numbers of workers, it would be necessary to reëstablish guarantees agreed upon during World War II. Because of this strong stand by Mexico, President Harry Truman appointed a commission, which included Archbishop Lucey of San Antonio, to study the problems of migrant labor. As a result of the commission's work and the demands of the Mexican government, on July 12, 1951, a Migratory Labor Agreement, more commonly known as Public Law 78, was passed by Congress as a temporary two-year Korean War measure.

Public Law 78 basically outlined a new bracero program, detailing the provisions for improved administrative control of migration and, in effect, making the Department of Labor the labor contractor. Under this new arrangement, the Secretary of Labor certified the need for braceros, authorized their recruitment in Mexico, transported them from recruiting centers to labor camps, and guaranteed that all contractual terms would be met. Public Law 78 specified that braceros were to be contracted for periods of from six weeks to six months, during which they were guaranteed work for 75 percent of the time, and were to be paid the prevailing wages established by the Secretary of Labor.

In August 1951, Mexico and the United States signed a treaty formalizing the details of Public Law 78. This treaty led to a sharp rise in the use of braceros; their numbers rose from 67,000 in 1950, before Public Law 78 and the treaty, to 192,000 annually in 1951 and 197,000 annually in 1952. The popularity of this program among growers caused negotiations to be undertaken in 1953 to renew the provisions of Public Law 78 for two more years. While debate on the measure mounted, Mexican government officials now threatened termination of this labor supply unless an improvement was made in the bracero wage structure. The United States, in a coercive effort, then announced, in January 1954, a temporary policy of recruiting at the border outside the bracero agreement. This move paralleled an earlier attempt by the Associated Farmers of California to recruit South Korean workers, when it seemed that Mexico might refuse to extend the treaty agreement. This new border-recruitment policy led to a second incident similar to the one which took place at El Paso in 1948. Despite Mexican government efforts to restrain her nationals from crossing the border at Calexico, about 3,500 of them crossed, were certified, and assigned to growers in complete defiance of Mexico's protests. This border recruitment ended early in February; however, at the same time, many illegal immigrants were "dried out" through the technicality of temporary recrossing.

Meanwhile, the new bracero program did not have the effect of reducing the mojado flow; in fact, the number increased. In 1951 and 1952 more than 500,000 were apprehended and returned to Mexico, and the following year their numbers reached approximately 875,000. Not all deportees had been employed in agriculture, as indicated by Immigration Department statistics. By 1953, immigration authorities were picking up 2,000 mojados per month from within industrial occupational ranks, and by mid-1954 this figure increased to 3,500 per month. As more illegal entrants moved into industrial work, opposition from organized labor increased. In December 1953, the AFL and CIO joined Mexican labor groups at a Mexico City meeting in protesting illegal traffic as deleterious to both United States and Mexican labor union welfare.

The increasing use of illegal rather than contract Mexican labor was abruptly reversed by sudden, strict enforcement of immigration laws, which came about when the United States Attorney General, Herbert Brownell, Jr., ordered a massive deportation drive in June 1954. Brownell cited the possible illegal entrance of political subversives as the chief reason for his action. "Operation Wetback," as this drive became known, was widely publicized beforehand in order to discourage employers from hiring mojados and also to encourage the illegal immigrants to leave the United States voluntarily.

Operation Wetback affected many segments of the agricultural and, to a lesser extent, the industrial economy. A specific impact of Operation Wetback can be seen in its effect on cotton wages in the Lower Rio Grande Valley of Texas. Before Operation Wetback, Texas cotton growers were paying as little as $1.50 per hundred pounds of picked cotton. After Operation Wetback, the corresponding wage rose to $2.05—a 36 percent wage increase almost overnight! Similar changes in wage structures took place in other commercial farm crops and truck gardening; generally speaking, these changes also resulted in improved working conditions and housing.

Operation Wetback came as a mixed blessing, however; although it served to improve the lot of Mexican Americans economically, its results in social terms were ambiguous. A total of 1,075,000 illegal entrants were rounded up by a special mobile force and deported to Mexico in 1954. Many deportees had been living in the United States for long periods —some for ten years or more. In meeting the goals of Operation Wetback, some of the basic civil liberties and human rights of deportees and their families were often brutally ignored, and physical treatment of deportees was marked by disrespect, rudeness, and intimidation. From 1950 to 1955, approximately 3,700,000 mojados were deported; of this number only 63,500 were expelled through formal deportation proceedings. Others left the country "voluntarily."

A further negative aspect of the 1954 operation was the manner in which it affected family units. Disruption of families occurred when heads of households were deported, leaving their wives and children to fend for themselves and often to become burdens on society. Although some of these wives and most of the children were United States citizens, the over-whelming majority chose to leave the country in order to remain with husbands and fathers in Mexico rather than jeopardize family unity. Many Mexican American communities still feel the effects of the legal but inhumane treatment inflicted by Operation Wetback in negative attitudes toward government agencies and programs and in the sociological results of families being left without fathers. Nevertheless, Operation Wetback had some beneficial results, especially for Mexican Americans in southwestern agriculture. Included among these benefits were expanded job opportunities and some improvement in wages, working conditions and housing.

Traditionally, Mexican Americans had held ambivalent feelings about mojados and their effect on the community. Everyone recognized that they constituted a force which tended to hold down wage scales and to retard Anglo acceptance of Mexican Americans. Yet they were members of la raza. Mexican Americans and Mexican nationals felt that no moral or social stigma attached to mojado status, and many illegal immigrants became well integrated into the community life of the Southwest. Their massive deportation in the early 1950s affected the stability of the Mexican American communities of which they had long been a part. Their expulsion reinforced traditional mistrust of the United States government among Mexican Americans and further increased feelings of alienation from Anglo society.

Extended for two-year periods in 1954, 1956 and 1958, Public Law 78 was kept alive by a coalition of conservative Republicans and southern Democrats largely from the farm states. The postwar bracero movement reached its peak in 1956, when approximately 445,000 Mexicans were processed under Public Law 78 and were approved to work in the United States. The approximate breakdown by state was: 193,000 in Texas; 151,000 in California; 30,000 in Arkansas; 22,000 in Arizona; 20,000 in New Mexico; 7,000 each in Colorado and Michigan; and 15,000 in other states. Between 1955 and 1959, the average number of braceros entering the United States per year approached 430,-000. They constituted roughly 25 percent of all farm workers hired during this period in the four southwestern states of Texas, California, Arizona, and New Mexico, thus underscoring their significance to the farm economy.

Prompted by criticisms of inhumane treatment of braceros from various socially conscious groups such as the National Catholic Welfare Council, the Labor Department in 1958 initiated a two-year study of the implementation of Public Law 78. Results of the investigation substantiated most of the charges made by critics of the program and led to minor improvements in working and housing conditions for some braceros. Criticisms and controversy surrounding the bracero program led to introduction of a bill in the House of Representatives by which Congressman (later Senator) George McGovern proposed to phase out the bracero program; however, his efforts were unsuccessful. When Public Law 78 came up for renewal in 1960, a seven-month debate ensued, finally ending in a compromise six-month extension. This long debate on continuing Public Law 78 greatly aroused public opinion regarding the use of Mexican labor. The National Catholic Welfare Council, the National Council of Churches of Christ in America, the National Consumers League, Americans for Democratic Action, the National Farmers Union, the Agricultural Workers Organizing Committee of the AFL-CIO, and other organizations demanded that the bracero program be terminated. The establishment of a $1.00-per-hour minimum wage for braceros in 1962 by Secretary of Labor Arthur Goldberg, although fought bitterly by growers, further discouraged use of braceros. Increased mechanization, especially in the growing of cotton and tomatoes, and a union prohibition against using bracero labor on power machinery were other factors contributing to the decline in bracero use. In May 1963, Congress defeated a bill to extend Public Law 78 for a period of two years; however, in December it voted to extend the program for one more year. This latter bill obtained sufficient votes for passage only because it included an amendment specifically stipulating that this was the final extension of Public Law 78. This congressional prohibition forced growers to seek other sources of farm labor, one important source being "greencarders," permanently admitted legal immigrants from Mexico authorized under the McCarran-Walter Immigration Act of 1952. In December 1964, Public Law 78 finally expired amid predictions that its end would mean a billion-dollar crop loss per year and a great decline in southwestern agriculture. Just days before its expiration, the Labor Department issued "eleventh-hour" admissions standards for future Mexican workers. Discussions were then held between United States and Mexican authorities about the future use of Mexican labor in the United States.

While this discussion concerning Mexican workers was taking place, a new general immigration act was passed in 1965, with implementation to begin June 30, 1968. This new immigration legislation set an annual limit of 120,000 immigrants to come from all western-hemisphere countries and a 20,000 maximum from any one country. The long-term impact of this law on Mexican immigration remains to be seen, but in the short time that the law has been in effect, Mexico continues to be a main source of immigrants from the western hemisphere. Mexico complains that the 20,000 maximum from any one country is an unrealistic quota for her because of socioeconomic and geographical relationships to the United States.

In addition to illegal immigrants and braceros under various programs, immigration under permanent-visa status has contributed to the growth of Mexican American communities in the United States in recent decades. Immigrants entering on this status between 1941 and 1950 numbered 61,000; from 1951 to 1960 the total rose to 300,000; and from 1961 to 1965, the number reached approximately 220,000. The volume of this immigration, primarily from lower socioeconomic classes in Mexico, has swelled and somewhat unbalanced the existing social and economic bases of the Mexican American population. One major significance of these Mexican migration patterns and trends is that, unlike members of other ethnic groups, Mexican Americans have had constant reinforcement from their mother culture and therefore greater retention of traditional cultural patterns and a resultant disparity of acculturation levels.

Since the termination of Public Law 78, various attempts have been made to revive the bracero program, but in recent years these efforts have had little effect. A major effort was initiated in May 1964, when the National Council of Agricultural Employers was organized to undertake the task of lobbying and propagandizing for braceros. Early in 1965, growers demanded the privilege of employing braceros, arguing that not enough domestic workers were available for their needs. Although Secretary of Labor Willard Wirtz did not accept this argument, he approved the use of the McCarran-Walter Act to bring in about 20,000 temporary Mexican workers in 1965. Pressure from agribusiness interests in the same year caused Governor Ronald Reagan of California to allow the use of prison labor in agriculture. Since then, however, shortages in farm labor have declined, as growers have worked more successfully to develop domestic sources of labor.

Historically, another source of Mexican labor in the United States has been the commuter, especially in the border regions. With the elimination of the bracero program in December 1964, a noticeable increase in the use of commuter labor took place. Commuters may be divided into "greencarders" and "bluecarders." Those classified as greencarders are legal permanent immigrants entitled to residence in the United States; the bluecarder is also an immigrant permitted to enter the United States legally, but with his residency limited to not more than seventy-two hours at one time. Since the end of Public Law 78 commuters have taken over much of the work braceros performed earlier. In 1970, there were an estimated 100,000 to 150,000 greencarders and bluecarders working in the United States.

Only 40 percent of the commuters work in agriculture, the rest being employed largely in cheap-labor industries located in the larger cities on the American side of the border. The ready accessibility of low-cost labor from Mexico has attracted many garment factories and other cheap-labor industries to border towns such as El Paso and Brownsville. American labor unions have consistently fought against this exploitation of foreign workers whose employment tends to hold down wages and reduce employment of union members. In 1965, commuters formed 23 percent of the work force in Brownsville, Texas; 17 percent in El Paso; and 5 percent in San Diego, California. As was true of braceros and mojados, competition from commuter labor results in low wages, an exodus of local workers, mostly Mexican Americans, and unemployment. For example, the unemployment rate in California's Imperial Valley, where in 1969 commuters formed about 85 percent of the farm work force, was twice as high as the state average.

Commuters have been a matter of concern not only to American labor and government but also to Mexico. The Mexican government initially responded to the commuter problem by promoting on their side of the border in-bond-industries heavily dependent on unskilled and semi-skilled workers. The economic rationale behind this response of the Mexican government was that goods would move back and forth across the border instead of workers. This innovative approach to a long-standing problem has had considerable economic success but has met with criticism in both the United States and Mexico. American labor was and is strongly opposed to this policy, because it is unable to compete with lower foreign labor costs. The Mexican industrial sector also did not completely approve of this policy because of the fragmented, isolated location of these factories, compared to the established Mexican industrial complex, and their orientation toward the United States. As a result of this criticism, in 1961 Mexico moved toward a gradual "Mexicanization" of border industries in an attempt to tie them more closely to the general Mexican economy.

The use of Mexican labor has always had a strong influence on the socioeconomic development of the Southwest. There has been a close relationship between Mexican immigrants, regardless of their status, and the Mexican American communities of the Southwest. These communities have acted as a buffer between the immigrants (braceros, mojados, and commuters) and Anglo society. In turn, immigrants have produced a continuing infusion and reinforcement of Mexican culture and cultural values. They have also helped to perpetuate ethnic characteristics that make Mexican Americans highly visible as a minority. As a result, many Mexican Americans have felt socially, as well as economically, threatened by this influx of their Mexican brethren.

Encouragement of Mexican immigration has created a labor surplus in the Southwest, especially in low-skill jobs, in which Mexican Americans have been concentrated and in which unemployment has been heaviest since World War II. In the past few years there have been indications that the use of mojados as laborers is sharply on the increase. Smugglers continue to do a thriving business in illegally importing laborers into the United States at $150 to $200 per person. Although they use highly sophisticated and organized techniques, the inhumane treatment and casualty rates of this trafficking are reminiscent of the African slave trade. Various devices and methods have been developed in attempts to outwit border authorities. Tied to the undercarriage of vehicles, hidden in false compartments, stuffed into trunks of automobiles, illegal immigrants have suffered not only gross indignities but also severe physical pain. There have been numerous instances in which they have been transported worse than animals, being locked for long periods of time in closed vans or auto trunks, sometimes causing illness and death from dehydration and carbon monoxide poisoning. Despite all this, there are between a half-million and a million illegal immigrants from Mexico in the United States, according to authoritative estimates.

Unquestionably, extensive use of immigrant labor has a depressing effect on wage structures in industries in which it is employed. Immigrant wages tend to become the norm, and in turn low-wage competition drives domestic labor out of the kinds of work in which Mexican nationals are used. In many cases employers have deliberately discouraged local workers so that they could use braceros, a practice resulting in greater unemployment of domestic workers, many of whom were Mexican Americans. For example, in 1960, the San Joaquin Valley tomato harvest employed 8,530 braceros but only 860 domestic workers.

Employment of Mexican nationals has depressed and discouraged local workers and has forced them to migrate from the Southwest to other areas. Widespread employment of Mexican nationals has therefore resulted in unemployment and underemployment of domestic workers, with a concomitant rise in welfare costs. Also, the heavy influx of Mexican nationals has placed a serious burden on the resources and leadership of Mexican American organizations in the United States.

# fourteen

## Chicano Voices

The development of Mexican American organizations is not something new, for it dates back to the last century as indicated in earlier chapters. However, extensive development of leadership and organization in the areas of labor, politics, and civil rights have occurred during this century, closely paralleling (but remaining independent of) the black civil-rights movement. Largely a byproduct of the two world wars, today a wide variety of organizations speak for the various geographic, economic, and social sectors of the Spanish-speaking Southwest. There is notably no single organization with the scope of such groups as the NAACP or the Urban League, such as exist within the black community.

However, a number of factors have contributed to the potential development of a viable, representative national Mexican American organization. Some of these are: an increased awareness and expanded horizons of many Mexican American veterans of World War II and the Korean conflict; influence of returning veterans in Mexican American organizations such as the G.I. Forum, the Community Service Organization, and the Mexican American Political Association; rising educational levels among Mexican Americans (especially after World War II); increased national awareness of the civil-rights movement during the late sixties; emergence of nationally significant Chicano leaders in community organizations and governmental positions; and introduction of multi-ethnic curricula at various levels of education (especially development of Chicano studies departments and programs in many colleges and universities).

Of the wide variety of Mexican American organizations, most have been and continue to be local and regional. Their goals and philosophies are very diverse. At one end of the organizational spectrum are most of the older groups, which advocate total assimilation or integration into American society; at the opposite end are recently founded organizations, which advocate a nationalistic militant philosophy and the retention of Mexican values and life style. Many organizations mix these goals in varying proportions, with the result that gross contradictions and inconsistencies sometimes exist between philosophies and practices. Most organizations seem to occupy a central position between the two opposite ends of this continuum. These centrists advocate variations of a culturally pluralistic society in which the best of each culture would be retained. Moderate in approach, their organizations usually prefer to improve socioeconomic conditions for la raza within the structure of existing institutions.

Mexican Americans have always recognized the many problems confronting them in American society and their need to organize to solve them, but not until after World War II did they gain intraethnic support for their organizational goals. Many social scientists have argued that their lack of unity and success in achieving socioeconomic and political rights has been due to a cultural emphasis on individual rather than group action. However, history shows that, in the struggle by Mexican Americans to obtain civil rights, both individual and group efforts have been represented. Mexican American efforts to achieve their rights have been unsuccessful, not so much because of cultural factors but rather because of overwhelming political, social, and economic forces controlled by the dominant society. Nevertheless, unlike other immigrant groups in the United States, until recently there has been minimal effort in Mexican American communities to educate recent arrivals from Mexico concerning their rights and responsibilities as members of American society.

The economic and social needs of Mexican American communities in the United States led to the development of organizations originally formed to furnish some small measure of mutual aid and security in an often hostile environment. These mutualist groups provided the foundations for labor and civil-rights organizations which were to follow in later years.

One of the oldest of these societies, the Alianza Hispano-Americana, was founded in Arizona in 1894. Initially mutualist in nature, the Alianza is organized into regional lodges or chapters, somewhat paralleling the organization of the Masonic order, each with a considerable degree of local autonomy. Members of the Alianza are provided with sickness and death benefits. These organizational benefits attracted membership at a time when social security was not available. In response to new needs, the Alianza organized a civil-liberties department in 1954 and today is still active, with over 260 lodges in the Southwest. Some other early organizations of a similar nature and with parallel objectives were the Sociedad Mutua Hijos de Hidalgo, Sociedad Benito Juárez, and the Sociedad Española de Beneficencia Mutua.

During World War I, a large influx of Mexican immigrants to the United States and their orientation toward Mexican consulates contributed to a sense of common heritage, destiny, and need to organize. As a result of this need, new organizations developed, basically alike in their stress on social and mutualistic aims and emphasizing Mexican nationalism; among these were La Sociedad Ignacio Zaragoza, La Cámara de Comercio Mexicana, La Sociedad Cervantes, and La Sociedad Mutualista Mexicana. These societies served as meeting places where members could voice their feelings and attitudes about their problems, mutually support each other, and find some help in coping with the American way of life.

In 1921, an important organization known as the Comisión Honorífica Mexicana was founded in Los Angeles by the Mexican consul, Eduardo Ruiz. At about the same time a Comisión was also established in Dallas, and subsequently hundreds of similar chapters developed. Although its original purpose was to assist Mexican nationals until consular aid could be obtained, the Comisión later developed much broader goals, and it often became accepted as ombudsman and community spokesman, especially in cities and towns with a large recent middle-class Mexican immigration. Since World War II, local Comisión organizations have centered their concern on providing scholarships for Mexican American youths, and in recent years they have tended to act as a counterforce against more militant Chicano activist leadership.

Military service during World War I had a valuable educational impact on Mexican Americans and produced the most important early organization, the Order of the Sons of America, founded in 1921 in San Antonio. Many returning veterans, imbued with ideas of educating their fellow Mexican Americans about their political rights, became active in developing organizations for this purpose. The basic objectives of this organization were to enable Mexican Americans to achieve acculturation and integration, principally through political action. Ultimately, the order sought to end prejudice against Mexican Americans, to achieve equality before the law, to acquire political representation at all levels, and to obtain greater educational opportunities. Restricting membership to United States citizens of Mexican or Hispanic background, it strongly emphasized that its members learn English and work toward gaining citizenship.

From its original chapter in San Antonio the organization expanded to seven councils throughout Texas, with the San Antonio and Corpus Christi councils becoming more active than the others. However, soon thereafter, there developed within the organization a conflict which resulted in the San Antonio council's reorganizing as the independent Knights of America. This split prompted Benjamin Garza, a leading figure in the Corpus Christi council, to call a meeting of Mexican American community leaders. As a result, in August 1927, a meeting was held at Harlingen, Texas, to discuss Mexican American problems—especially the lack of unity. At this meeting, a decision to reorganize was reached; however, when the Order of the Sons of America was invited to be part of this reorganization, its leadership refused to coöperate. Finally, after considerable discussion, debate, and further conferences, the League of Latin American Citizens was organized with objectives similar to those of the Sons of America.

In February 1929, the Corpus Christi council of the Sons of America, under Garza's leadership, voted to withdraw from the order and also to call a convention to unite all Mexican American organizations. Ten days later, representatives of the League of Latin American Citizens, the Knights of America, and the Order of the Sons of America met in Corpus Christi where they formed the League of United Latin American Citizens (LULAC).

At a meeting held in May of the same year, this new organization adopted a constitution, which stressed as its major goal the achievement of economic, social, and political rights for all Mexican Americans. In its objectives LULAC sought to end discrimination and mistreatment of Mexican Americans; to achieve equality in government, law, business, and education; to promote education in order to produce more doctors, lawyers, engineers, and other professional people of Mexican descent; to develop pride in Mexican ancestry; to promote the learning of English by Mexicans as a means of achieving a greater degree of equality; and to encourage the effective exercise of United States citizenship by active participation in politics.

With its direction firmly established, LULAC spread rapidly, and by 1930 it was beginning to exert considerable influence through eighteen councils. From Texas it soon extended its membership into Arizona, New Mexico, California, Colorado, and urban centers elsewhere in the country having Mexican American communities. In the late thirties a junior LULAC developed, and a women's auxiliary was authorized. World War II had a very negative effect on the junior movement, but indirectly it encouraged expansion of the parent organization. After the war, LULAC grew to two hundred councils, extending from California to the District of Columbia and having a membership of approximately 15,000.

Somewhat modifying its initial, broad-ranging goals, LULAC, its membership drawn principally from the middle and upper economic classes, has not had a primary interest in direct political action. From its inception, the organization concerned itself with problems related to education—particularly segregation in public schools. Through its national education committee, organized in 1931, LULAC pressured the Texas State Education Department to end discrimination in Texas schools. In addition, it directed its efforts to such issues as the exclusion of Mexican Americans from jury service, the exploitation of migrant labor, and the demoralizing economic effects of both bracero and illegal labor. *LULAC News*, the official newspaper of the organization, was used to promote a LULAC viewpoint, often publishing articles on these and other matters of concern to its membership.

After World War II, LULAC, increasing its struggle for equality of educational opportunity, achieved two notable successes. In 1945, it initiated legal action against four Orange County (California) school districts, alleging de facto segregation of Mexican American students. This case, Méndez *v.* Westminster School District, was decided in favor of the complainants by a federal court which enjoined the school districts from continued segregation. Upon appeal to the circuit court, this decision of the lower court was upheld in 1947. In Texas also LULAC successfully fought against intentional segregation.

In the Delgado case, the state courts held in June 1948 that segregation of Mexican American children in schools was unconstitutional. In the aftermath of the case, there was a policy statement by the Texas Board of Education instructing local districts to eliminate any segregation of Mexican Americans (although this did not apply to Negroes). These two court decisions, based on constitutional guarantees, and others in the succeeding decade clearly established the illegality of deliberate segregation of Mexican American school children, but they by no means ended it. In New Mexico, LULAC had a third success. There it led a movement against job discrimination and was influential in persuading the New Mexico legislature to pass a fair employment practices law in 1949.

In 1938, nearly a decade after the founding of LULAC, another, less permanent organization developed, called the Mexican Congress. Labor-oriented, this federation of Mexican American groups worked for a better general understanding between Mexican and Anglo-Americans in order to achieve social and economic improvement of la raza, but it especially devoted its attention to trade unionism. At its peak, it had about 6,000 members; however, its decline during World War II eventually led to its dissolution.

In January 1945, the Catholic bishops of Los Angeles, Santa Fe, Denver, and San Antonio called a meeting in Oklahoma City to discuss social problems confronting the Spanish-speaking. At the meeting these Catholic prelates organized the Bishops Committee for the Spanish-Speaking and set as its goal the betterment of Mexican Americans in the areas of religion, health, and social aid. Since its inception this organization has promoted a variety of programs to assist in alleviating the socially critical conditions in Mexican American communities of the Southwest by developing credit unions and coöperatives, by organizing citizenship classes, various special institutes, recreational projects, and health programs. It has also established medical clinics, health centers, and settlement houses. Personally concerned about the condition of Mexican Americans, Archbishop Robert Lucey of San Antonio quickly became the moving force behind the Bishops Committee. Although it has been an important agency in helping the Mexican American to help himself, in recent years it has come under critical attack from various Chicano community organizations for its limited approach.

Generally speaking, Mexican American organizations declined during World War II, but the war's end brought renewed and expanded organizational activity. A powerful force awakening Mexican Americans to their rightful place in American society, the war brought significant changes in the direction and goals of postwar Mexican American organizations. A strong emphasis on direct action—especially on active participation in politics—characterized organizational activities in the late forties and early fifties. Expanded opportunities in the military had enabled Mexican Americans to acquire leadership experience, with the result that, while in the armed forces and as veterans, they were unwilling to accept discriminatory practices aimed at themselves and their community. These attitudes, coupled with a determination to better their position in American society, became the driving force behind the resurgence of organizational activity.

An early expression of this new mood came with the development of the Community Service Organization. In 1946, Edward R. Roybal, a Mexican American from East Los Angeles, ran for the city council and lost. Born in Albuquerque during World War I, Roybal had come to maturity in the depression years and served in the Civilian Conservation Corps during the mid-1930s. He subsequently moved to California, becoming active in public health education. During World War II he served in the Army for two years and then returned to Los Angeles, where he quickly became involved in city politics. His defeat in the city council contest led to his realization that to win, development of a community political organization was imperative. Therefore, in preparation for the 1948 elections, his campaign committee formed the Community Service

Organization. Based on Saul Alinsky's community organizational theories, the cso deëmphasized an ethnic Mexican image and emphasized mass political involvement. In 1948 cso precinct workers pounded pavements and registered 15,000 new Mexican American voters in Los Angeles. This cso effort resulted in victory; Roybal won by 20,000 to 12,000.

With Roybal elected, the cso became involved in nonpartisan civic action. In its constitution, drawn up after the elections, the organization declared its objectives to be an awareness and discharge of citizen responsibilities, the protection and furtherance of democratic rights, and the coördination of efforts for community good. Without qualifying restrictions on membership, the cso today numbers more than 50,000, and its ranks include people from varied economic and social backgrounds.

Having twin goals of social and political integration, the cso has organized mass registration drives and emphasized naturalization and assimilation of Mexicans. In 1952, with the passage of the McCarran-Walter Act, which allowed immigrants over 50 years of age to qualify for citizenship in their native language, it conducted a very successful citizenship drive among older Mexicans. It continues to emphasize these traditional objectives, and in recent years it has been active in breaking down barriers of discrimination, especially in housing.

A second Mexican American organization coming out of World War II was the American G.I. Forum. Its development was directly associated with the previously mentioned Felix Longoria case in Three Rivers, Texas, in 1947, which aroused many Mexican American veterans and caused strong protests. During the following year, a group of these aroused citizens met in Corpus Christi to discuss what might be done to protest the poor service and discrimination that Mexican Americans encountered in veterans' hospitals. Dr. Hector García, a World

War II combat surgeon with a distinguished record, led in organizing the G.I. Forum, which spread rapidly throughout Texas and beyond.

Dr. García subsequently went on to a second career as a civic leader and diplomat. During the Johnson administration, he was appointed to a number of diplomatic posts, including that of alternate delegate to the United Nations. He was also a member of the United States National Commission for UNESCO in 1968 and was sworn in as a member of the United States Commission on Civil Rights in the same year. He has been the recipient of numerous other honors and awards.

Although the Forum developed in response to immediate and concrete problems of hostility and discrimination, its organization has expanded beyond any narrow confines. With broad and balanced goals, it aims to aid needy and disabled veterans, to advance the principles of democracy, to promote mutual understanding among ethnic and religious groups, and to develop leadership among Mexican Americans by encouraging them to participate widely in community, civic, and political spheres of action. It is composed largely of middle-class Mexican Americans and has had its viewpoint respectfully heard by such influential officials as mayors, state officials, and even governors.

Like the cso, the G.I. Forum heavily accents political action. Nominally nonpartisan but predominantly Democratic in its sympathies, it is active at all levels of the American political system. It employs a full-time lobbyist in Washington. During the 1950s, through registration drives and other political activities, the Forum successfully increased Democratic strength in the Southwest; later its leaders were prominent in organizing Viva Kennedy clubs in the 1960 presidential election. Today it is one of the most important and widespread Mexican American organizations, with chapters not only in all the Southwest but also throughout the rest of the United States.

A third organization developing out of World War II, the Mexican American Political Association, arose out of the dissatisfaction of Mexican Americans with their lack of representation in the Democratic Party. Although a majority of Mexican Americans voted with the Democrats, the party, even after the war, showed little interest in integrating them into its structure. In addition, activist Mexican American politicians found their efforts to become part of the party hierarchy rebuffed. Many became convinced that Democratic leaders took them for granted. These feelings and attitudes finally led a number of political activists, including Bert Corona and Edward Quevedo, to call a meeting at Fresno, California, in 1959 to consider what might be done to promote Mexican American political interests. As a result of this conference, they decided to form a separate political organization known as the Mexican American Political Association (MAPA).

As originally formed, MAPA owed much of its form and content to Corona and Quevedo. The former, a clever and astute student of politics, has had a long history of leadership in Mexican American organizations, having helped establish a youth conference in the mid-thirties. A pioneer in working for social reform and greater educational opportunity for the Chicano, he also was active in the establishment of the CSO during Roybal's campaign. Edward Quevedo was likewise dedicated to the political improvement of the Mexican American, having expended both his physical energy and his savings over the years in pursuit of his goal of creating a Chicano political force.

The overwhelming concern of MAPA has been and continues to be the combination of political and ethnic interests. Drawing its membership almost exclusively from the Mexican American community, in 1968 it claimed over sixty chapters, involved in a wide spectrum of political activity. It takes public positions on issues affecting Mexican Americans and also urges elected and appointed officials to consider matters of concern to Mexican Americans. During election years, it seeks out Mexican American candidates for various state and local political office; it endorses and supports them financially as well as morally. It has also conducted successful voter-registration drives and get-out-the-vote campaigns. Traditionally, it has taken only limited action in seeking to better social and economic conditions for Mexican Americans; however, recently a considerable change in the philosophy of the organization has led to greater involvement in issues of discrimination and civil rights.

Initially generating widespread interest and support in the Southwest, MAPA quickly extended its influence and was instrumental in the development of similar groups. A similar organization (with an identical acronym), Mexican Americans for Political Action, was formed in Texas early in 1960, but it was soon overshadowed by the more charismatically appealing Viva Kennedy clubs of the 1960 presidential campaign. These clubs captured Mexican American imagination and support throughout the Southwest; their popularity soon caused the Texas MAPA to wither on the vine.

After John Fitzgerald Kennedy's election to the presidency in 1960, a group of Mexican American leaders met at Phoenix to discuss possibilities of political unity. At this meeting of representatives from California MAPA, CSO, LULAC, Viva Kennedy, and other politically oriented groups, California mapistas urged the creation of a national Mexican American political organization along MAPA lines through a coalition. However, a majority of delegates favored a broader structure, which would include Cuban, Puerto Rican, and other Spanish-speaking Americans. Out of these discussions emerged the Political

Association of Spanish-Speaking Organizations (PASO or PASSO; both usages are accepted), although MAPA and CSO refused to take part. Albert Peña, a commissioner of Bexar County and organizer of the Viva Kennedy clubs, played an important role in fashioning PASO. As a result, PASO became an organization largely made up of Texas Viva Kennedy clubs. Almost completely Mexican American in makeup, PASO has concentrated its efforts in Texas and chiefly concerns itself with political action and civic education rather than assimilation. Its most notable success took place in Crystal City, Texas, where in 1963, it led a number of groups in a successful campaign to elect an all-Mexican American city council and mayor, defeating the Anglo machine which had previously dominated the overwhelmingly Chicano city. Election success was quickly followed by a pattern of harassment of Mexican Americans by the sheriff and other Anglo officials. This strong reaction to the victory may be explained by the fact that Chicanos at the time were a majority lacking any real political representation in twenty-six Texas counties, and it was feared that their success in one place would bring on a domino effect.

Stunned by success at Crystal City and lacking both organizational support and an articulated program, Chicanos soon abandoned their candidates, and in the 1965 elections Anglos and "vendidos" (Mexican American term for "sell-outs") returned to power. Although this battle was temporarily lost, from it Chicanos recognized the need to develop continuing programs with both immediate and long-range goals and to provide sustained support for them.

As Mexican Americans moved into cities in great numbers during the postwar years, and as more moved into middle-class positions, they became increasingly dissatisfied with the limited and inferior roles assigned to them in American society by the Anglo majority. Courage to express their dissatisfaction with discrimination, prejudice, lack of status, and inequality of opportunities in education, housing, and employment came from developments in the civil-rights movement during the late fifties and early sixties.

In the second half of the 1960s new goals and organizational techniques of Chicano leaders resulted in an intensified campaign to demand a rightful place in society. These new directions encouraged many young Chicanos to become involved for the first time in an aggressive social movement whose prime objective was to force society to recognize members of la raza as fellow human beings. As a result of this intensification during the latter sixties changes began to be seen in the areas of civil rights, union organization, education, politics, and economic status.

Chicano youths made an important contribution to this new development by their commitment to and involvement in all phases of the movement. Ignoring the passive role prescribed by their elders and unwilling to accept the limitations of previous organizations, these youths for the first time provided leadership as well as support in every part of the struggle for Mexican American rights. In this effort many organizations, groups, and individuals have played and continue to play important roles; despite varying philosophies underlying these new organizations, a crystallization of structures and leadership has taken place, and a unity of effort is evident.

Beginning about 1966, a new sense of ethnic worth manifested itself among Chicano youths, giving them the impetus to demand recognition from the middle-class educational system. Critical of its predecessors, the young leadership of this movement turned to direct action and militant confrontation in order to achieve its goals. This dynamic new force soon attracted thousands of followers, appealing overwhelmingly to young people, although Chicanos of all ages became involved.

From the ranks of this youth-oriented movement an energetic, politically minded, and revolutionary leadership began to grow. Motivated by a new ideology, Chicanismo, and inspired by Cuban and Mexican revolutionaries such as Ernesto "Che" Guevara and Emiliano Zapata, this new leadership quickly developed student organizations throughout the Southwest. Permeated with a cultural consciousness, emphasizing their language, heritage, and ethnic contributions, the new militant organizations appeal to nationalism and urge Chicanos to unity and action at all levels. These student groups have been forming not only in universities and colleges but also in junior and senior high schools.

Student organizations are most strongly developed in California, which has taken an outstanding leadership role in the Chicano movement. In the Los Angeles region in 1968 college students formed an organization called United Mexican American Students (UMAS), with representatives from various local Mexican American Student Association (MASA) chapters. In the San Francisco Bay area, a similar regional organization known as the Mexican American Student Confederation (MASC) developed during this same period. Recently a new organization has emerged, Movimiento Estudiantil Chicano de Aztlán (MECHA), which has quickly become the important umbrella organization for most Chicano college and university groups. At the high school level, there are a number of student clubs; Mexican American Youth Organization (MAYO) is one of the most active throughout the Southwest, especially in California and Texas.

While the college organizations have a wide range of objectives, high school groups usually stress the goal of getting more Mexican American youths to attend and complete college. In California, demands of these groups for larger enrollments at state colleges and universities and for departments of ethnic studies at these institutions have generally received sympathetic interest. However, in most cases educational institutions have taken action only after considerable student pressure on the administration.

Calling for reform of poor school conditions, demanding the firing of prejudiced teachers and administrators, insisting that school curricula be revised to acknowledge Chicano contributions to American society, Chicano students staged walkouts in the latter sixties in California, Texas, Colorado, New Mexico and other areas. Student walkouts became the focal point around which Chicano communities rallied forces and commenced their struggles for self-identity. Student walkouts were followed by increased police harassment, felt not only by students but by the entire Chicano community. Chicano student leaders in Los Angeles, Denver, San Antonio, San Jose, and El Paso were accused of conspiring to disturb the educational processes and were jailed. Those charged with leading the walkouts were tried and, in many cases, convicted, sent to prison, fined, or placed on probation. The end result? Many organizations, left without effective leadership and with their memberships demoralized by continual harassment, were forced to reëvaluate their structures and to plan new tactics and strategies. Student walkouts clearly indicate the nature of today's Chicano youth. Through their protests and walkouts students have had a measure of success in changing their own educational environment. Today, they have become a dynamic and powerful force throughout the Southwest, not only in education but also in politics. Many have developed well-articulated programs, while others are still groping in search of direction.

In addition to campus groups, Chicano students have also been active in developing organizations with objectives beyond education. Perhaps the best known of these is the Brown

Berets, made up essentially of students organized throughout the Southwest, and active especially in California and Texas. Founded in Los Angeles by David Sánchez, the Berets have approximately thirty chapters throughout the Southwest and in large Chicano communities elsewhere. Committed by their bylaws to keep informed of political and social issues affecting Chicanos, Brown Berets are usually present at meetings or events which concern the Chicano community. They hope to unite the community and ensure that Chicanos are treated justly by giving the example of a disciplined and dedicated life based on principles of brotherhood.

Patterned along similar lines, with goals of justice and dignity for Chicanos, the Black Berets was founded in Mountain View, California, in the latter sixties. Not a student organization, it is a brotherhood of Chicanos, with a regional structure composed of chapters. It is militant but allegedly nonviolent. In recent years, both the Brown and Black Berets have been deeply involved in action-oriented activities in Chicano communities throughout the Southwest.

Although Chicano students have made education the focal point of their activities, their influence and involvement go far beyond the field of education. With students in the vanguard, the Chicano movement has led to an increased interest in Mexican cultural life. A resurgence of ethnic awareness has taken place and has provided inspiration for numerous Chicano writers, playwrights, journalists, poets, novelists, and artists.

Prominent among these writers are the novelists Raymond Barrio (*Plum Plum Pickers*), Richard Vásquez (*Chicano*), José Antonio Villarreal (*Pocho*); short-story writers Tomás Rivera, winner of the Quinto Sol Publications' award for the best literary work written by a Chicano in 1970, Daniel Garza, Enrique ("Hank") López, Nick Vaca, and others; and poets Alurista, Miguel Ponce, Tomás Rivera, Roberto Vargas, José

Montoya. Chicano playwrights include Luis Valdez, whose Teatro Campesino has achieved a national reputation and has also served as a model for other teatro groups. Among leading Chicano artists are Malaquías Montoya, Harry S. Israel, Ricardo Cuadra, Ebel Villagómez, Esteban Villa, Manuel Hernández Trujillo, René Yáñez, José Ernesto Montoya, Raul Espinoza, "El Queso" (Roberto S. Torres). The literary and artistic output of these new artists and writers have appeared for the most part in periodicals which were nonexistent as recently as 1966.

These militant-activist publications, born in the past few years, have definitely contributed to a rising sense of unity among Chicanos. Attacking and criticizing police, growers, government agencies, the educational system, politicians, and the *tio tacos* of the community, most articles in these periodicals are subjective and heatedly polemical in tone. The best-known publication of this genre is undoubtedly *El Grito,* edited by Octavio Romano; it deserves much credit for introducing Chicano writers and a Chicano perspective to Anglo society. Also included in this group are *Bronze, El Machete, La Raza, Con Safos, El Pocho Che, Regeneración, El Malcriado, La Voz Mexicana, El Gallo, La Verdad, El Tecolote, El Grito del Norte, Carta Editorial, El Papel, Basta Ya, Inside Eastside, Adelante, Inferno, Trucha, Qué Tal,* and others. Chicano prison inmates (pintos) have also begun to publish their own newspapers; *El Chino, La Voz del Chicano,* and *Aztlán.* Most of these newspapers are members of The Chicano Press Association, a confederation of community newspapers dedicated to promoting unity among Chicanos and the movement for greater self-determination of la raza.

One type of Chicano publication that has yet to be developed fully is that of professional journals. At present there are two, in an embryonic stage: *Aztlán: Chicano Journal of the*

*Social Sciences and the Arts,* published at UCLA since mid-1969, and *The Journal of Mexican American History,* published at Santa Barbara since the fall of 1970.

Underdevelopment in professional journals is symptomatic of a shortage of Chicanos in all the professions and results from a shortcoming in American institutions of higher learning. Indeed, a crying need of the Chicano community has always been and continues to be the creation of a stronger and more committed corps of trained and experienced professionals and leaders. As yet, no institution has assumed the responsibility of initiating a center for the development of Chicano leaders.

As a result of activist student pressures, Chicano study programs and departments have been organized in a number of colleges throughout the Southwest and in other areas having high concentrations of Mexican Americans. Unique in this development is the fact that most of these programs have been articulated and staffed by young Chicano professionals with support from the community and a handful of older leaders. In addition to undergraduate programs, there is one Chicano center concentrating on work at the graduate level, the Mexican American Graduate Studies Department organized at California's San José State College in 1969. Another undertaking holding out high expectations was the inception in the fall of 1970 of a new Chicano-Indian university—D.Q.U. (Deganiwidah-Quetzalcoatl University) near Davis, California, which began its first year of instruction in a program concentrating heavily on Indian and Chicano cultures.

Some gains have been made by many other forces at work within la raza. Hundreds of regional and local groups, although differing widely in their objectives and constituencies, all complement each other and form an integral part of the

Chicano movement. For example, in Colorado, there are the Colorado Federation of Latin American Groups, the Spanish American Citizens Association, the Latin American Council, the Latin American Educational Foundation, the Latin American Service Clubs, and other groups. In Arizona, one of the more important local organizations developed out of an attempt to establish a PASO chapter; instead, the American Coordinating Council of Political Education (ACCPE) was formed. It spread quickly in Arizona and within two years boasted a membership of over 2,500.

Southern California organizations include Unity Leagues, the Alliance of Layman Mexican Americans (ALMA), Congress of Mexican American Unity, Chicano Legal Defense Fund, and many other groups; while in the northern part of the state, there are, among others, the Mexican American Legal Defense and Educational Fund, La Confederación de la Raza Unida, Operation Ser (a national organization), the Mexican American Community Organization, the Spanish-Speaking Citizens Foundation in San Francisco, the Spanish-Speaking Unity Council in Oakland representing eighteen groups, the Community Alert Patrol and Mexican American Community Service Agency in San Jose, the Concilio in Sacramento and the Mexican American Citizens League of Santa Clara County. In addition, there are many more Mexican American societies in the states of the Southwest and beyond: The Southwest Conference of La Raza, Latinos Unidos por la Justicia, Mexican Civic Committee, Mexican American Registration League, IMAGE, Mexican American Council on Higher Education, Association of Mexican American Education, the National Education Task Force of La Raza, Spanish American Alliance, Spanish Surnamed Political Association, and others. Much work remains to be done!

# fifteen

# The Four Horsemen

During the 1960s, large numbers of Mexican Americans, for the first time encompassing all social and economic sectors of the community, developed programs and organizations known collectively as the Chicano movement. World War II had made them aware of their political and economic rights as American citizens and conscious of widespread denial of those rights. Returning to their communities, they found themselves still limited to the poorest-paying jobs and to the most dilapidated housing and with only limited access to education and other public services.

Up to the early 1960s, organizational development in the

Mexican American community was overwhelmingly local in activity and membership. Little had been done to form national organizations, and few leaders with national exposure had appeared; in recent years, however, activist spokesmen of prominence have arisen. These new leaders range from fiery militants to moderate advocates of nonviolence. Four of these young leaders have had considerable impact, especially since 1965: César Chávez of California, 44 years old in 1972; Rodolfo ("Corky") Gonzales of Colorado, 43 years old in 1972; José Angel Gutiérrez of Texas, 27 years old in 1972; and Reies López Tijerina of New Mexico, 45 years old in 1972. Through their actions these Chicanos have received national attention from the news media and have built up reputations and followings in the Chicano community with varying degrees of success. The first of these four to attract national attention was César Chávez.

Whatever else may happen to César Chávez in the future, and whatever criticism may be leveled at his activities, he must be given credit for bringing the benefits of union organization to the last large segment of unorganized American labor. Viewed as a Chicano, Chávez is symbolic of the long struggle la raza has had to wage, with all its obstacles, tribulations, and reverses. He was the first Chicano to achieve national recognition through his farm worker organizational activities and has become a national unifying force for Chicanos from quite diverse social and economic levels.

In the early spring of 1962, a quiet young Mexican American moved to Delano with his family; since then neither Delano nor California agriculture has been the same. César Chávez, a gentle apostle of a nonviolent approach to reform, quickly became recognized as a spiritual leader of Chicanos. Through his efforts to improve the conditions of agricultural workers, the attention of the entire country has been turned to César Chávez and one of the last strongholds of cheap labor in the United States—agriculture.

But the story does not begin with the Delano grape strike in 1965, nor with César Chávez' arrival three years earlier. It has its roots in California's agricultural history. Indians formed California's first source of cheap labor, and when they declined in numbers as California agriculture expanded, they were replaced by the Chinese. In 1882, the Chinese Exclusion Act, passed by the United States Congress, began to cut off that source of labor, and farmers turned to Japanese workers until they, too, were eliminated as a cheap labor supply by the Gentlemen's Agreement of 1907–1908.

The resultant scarcity of cheap labor forced American farmers to look elsewhere for a source of workers. Beginning about 1910, growers found an answer to their labor problem in the multitudes of destitute refugees forced to flee Mexico because of the revolution in that country. Mexican immigrants quickly became the backbone of California's farm-labor supply and held this position until the influx of the dust-bowl migrants of the 1930s. Following publication of John Steinbeck's novel on migrant life, *The Grapes of Wrath,* the La Follette Committee of the United States Congress held hearings on migrant workers in 1939 and 1940 and in its report made the following recommendations: passage of an agricultural employment stabilization law, with provisions for unemployment insurance and social security; creation of an Agricultural Wage Board to determine fair wages; an Agricultural Fair Labor Standards Act to extend the Fair Labor Standards Act's benefits to agricultural workers; an Agricultural Labor Recruitment Act to regulate the hiring of farm workers; and an Agricultural Labor Relations Act to give farm workers the right to organize and bargain collectively. None of these recommendations was implemented.

After World War II, Fred Ross of Saul Alinsky's Industrial Areas Foundation began community organizational work among Mexican Americans in California. Ross and others traveled over the state in the late 1940s organizing Community Service Organizations among working-class Mexican Americans. At the same time, workers on the large DiGiorgio Fruit Corporation farm near Arvin formed the National Farm Workers' Union, and in October 1947, more than a thousand of them went on strike. These strikers held out for over a year, but they were unable to obtain redress of their grievances in the face of violence, smear tactics, and imported Mexican strikebreakers.

Continuing this organizational effort, the United Packinghouse Workers of America began to organize field workers in the mid-fifties, and between 1954 and 1959, these workers went on strike several times. Each time the strike was broken by the use of scabs, mostly Mexican nationals. Further organizing efforts by the AFL-CIO in 1959 established the Agricultural Workers Organizing Committee (AWOC), which concentrated on recruiting members among workers in the Imperial Valley. Two years later AWOC successfully organized lettuce workers there, but a subsequent labor dispute failed when 7,000 braceros were used as strikebreakers, despite the Mexican government's request for their removal.

In May 1965, AWOC struck the Coachella Valley vineyards for union recognition and the same rate of pay ($1.40 per hour) that braceros were receiving. Although growers refused to grant union recognition, they later met with union leaders and agreed to pay $1.40. As the grape harvest moved northward through the San Joaquin Valley to Delano, members of AWOC found prevailing wages at $1.20 per hour. This wage differential quickly led to another labor dispute.

Led by Larry Itliong, 1,300 Filipinos of AWOC walked out of the vineyards on September 8, demanding union recognition and $1.40 an hour. The hiring of local Mexican Americans as strikebreakers caused Itliong to go to César Chávez and ask him to persuade the members of the National Farm Workers' Association to join the walkout. Although Chávez' union was not prepared for a strike, on September 16, Mexican Independence Day, he called for a strike vote, and it was unanimously approved. The famous Delano grape strike had begun; it was to become a long, drawn-out affair dominated by one man, César Chávez.

Chávez came out of the largely inarticulate subculture of the migrant farm worker, characterized by extreme poverty, lack of organization, and paucity of leadership. César Estrada Chávez was born into a family of five children on a farm near Yuma, Arizona, in 1927. Eleven years later, during the depression, the family was forced into the migrant stream when their farm was sold for taxes. Chávez grew up as a typical Mexican American migrant. Following the crops, he attended about thirty different schools and eventually reached the seventh grade. After serving in the Navy for two years, in 1946, he returned to migrant life. Two years later he married Helen Fabela of Delano. In 1950, Chávez settled in San Jose, California, and there met Fred Ross of cso, in which he became active; subsequently he rose to the position of cso director for California and Arizona. Chávez' political and economic ideas matured, and he soon began to advocate a program of organizing farm workers. When his proposals for an organizational campaign were voted down at a Calexico meeting of the cso in 1962, he resigned as director.

Turning down several job offers, Chávez soon moved to Delano, went to work in the vineyards, and dedicated himself to creating a farm labor group, the National Farm Workers' Association. This organization, today known as the United Farm Workers' Organizing Committee (ufwoc), is more nearly a coöperative than a union and incorporates earlier ideas of nineteenth-century Mexican mutualist organizations. Within its structure, it has developed for its members a death benefit plan; a coöperative grocery, drug store, and gas station; a credit union; a medical clinic; a social protest theatre group, the Teatro Campesino; and a newspaper, *El Malcriado*. Furthermore, the UFWOC has extended its efforts beyond helping farm laborers and concerns itself with problems affecting the broader Chicano community, providing a unifying force in the struggle for Chicano civil rights.

Chávez patiently established locals in the southern San Joaquin Valley, and in two years NFWA had 1,000 members. By the time of the Delano strike in 1965, NFWA membership had risen to about 1700. César Chávez and the NFWA completely molded and dominated the Delano grape strike. Chávez felt that the strike had possibilities of sucess because of the termination of Public Law 78 and the bracero program in 1964, plus the relatively large core of active union members living in the Delano area. He viewed wages and collective bargaining as only part of the strike's objective, which, in a broad fashion, was intended to restore human dignity to farm workers. Skillfully using America's response to the civil-rights movement of the 1950s and early 1960s, he dramatized the farm worker's plight by presenting the grape strike as a broad movement for social justice.

Chávez carefully developed the strike movement on two basic principles, nonviolence and the use of outside help. Realizing that outsiders were more able and ready to stand up against pressures than local people, he made full use of a wide range of civil-rights and religious groups. In September 1965, he visited Stanford University and the University of California at Berkeley and invited both individuals and organizations (such as the Congress of Racial Equality and the Student Non-

violent Coördinating Committee) to take part in the struggle.
As a result of these visits, a steady stream of students, ministers,
nuns, priests, and civil-rights workers came to Delano; many
went back to spread the Delano story on the campuses and in
the cities.

Religion played and continues to play an important role in
Chávez' struggle. The symbolic invocation of the Virgin of
Guadalupe attracted Mexican Americans to the NFWA and also
had the effect, when coupled with the prestige of the California
bishops of the Catholic Church, of making the usual accusations
of Communism seem ridiculous. In March 1966, Bishop Hugh
Donohoe of Stockton, testifying before the Senate Subcommittee on Migratory Labor in Delano, read a position paper signed
by all seven California bishops. This statement upheld the farm
workers' right to organize and strike and called for legislation
to bring farm labor under the National Labor Relations Act as
a first step in settling farm labor conflicts.

State and national political leaders, notably Governor Ed-
mund G. "Pat" Brown and Robert Kennedy, played an important part in the strike movement from its inception. Support
also came from various labor leaders, union organizations, and
prominent Americans like Mrs. Martin Luther King, Jr. Most
important, however, was Chávez' strategy of always viewing
and presenting the strike as a moral issue, thereby appealing
to the American conscience.

When the 1965 grape strike began, Chávez sent registered
letters and then telegrams to thirty-seven growers in the Delano
area with the following NFWA demands: a pay raise from $1.20
per hour plus 10 cents per lug to $1.40 per hour plus 25 cents
per lug; enforcement of the standard working conditions prescribed by state law; and recognition of the NFWA as bargaining agent. In response, some growers raised hourly rates to
$1.40; but in most cases reaction to these union demands was

strongly emotional and included the cry of "Communism." The growers assumed and asserted that they knew their workers better than Chávez did and that the workers did not want a union. The townspeople of Delano were even more strongly opposed to Chávez and the NFWA and organized a Citizens for Facts from Delano, which viewed the strike as a revolutionary threat to their community. Later a group called Mothers Against Chávez was formed.

Initially the strike was successful in greatly reducing the vineyard work force. The NFWA claimed that 5,000 workers walked off the job; growers alleged that only a few hundred were on strike, but they refused to allow their records to be checked. In immediate response to the strike a Kern-Tulare Independent Farm Workers Union was organized, with two of its five directors being labor contractors for grape growers. Naturally growers showed a preference for it over the NFWA. However, from the beginning growers brought in strikebreakers from Bakersfield, Fresno, and Los Angeles who were often unaware that a strike even existed. Later in 1965, other strikebreakers ("scabs") were imported from Texas and Mexico; many greencarders were also included, although their employment as strikebreakers is prohibited.

The strike received wide support from various labor organizations and other groups. The San Francisco Labor Council began sending monthly motorcades of food and clothing to Delano; and in December, after an appearance and talk in Delano, labor leader Walter Reuther began sending $5,000 a month to support the strike. In San Antonio, Archbishop Robert Lucey, a veteran champion of Mexican American rights, came out in support of Chávez; in El Paso, Bishop Sidney Metzger urged Texas workers not to take jobs in Delano. In California, the Migrant Ministry gave active support to the strike from its beginning, and MAPA strongly backed the strike and its objectives.

However, many difficulties arose in carrying out the strike. Picketing thirty-five ranches in an area of 400 square miles presented an organizational problem of staggering proportions; another immense problem was that, throughout the strike, local officials were clearly on the side of the growers. Violence developed—mostly, but not entirely, on the growers' side. Chávez' insistence on nonviolence kept the strike remarkably free from serious outbreaks. However, strikers often found their tires deflated; and trucks, dusting machines, tractors, and spray equipment became weapons in the growers' fight against the NFWA. Local police feigned difficulty in discerning grower violence but moved quickly to arrest strikers for being "ready to violate the law," as Kern County Sheriff Roy Galyen testified before the Senate Subcommittee on Migrant Labor. Futhermore, when arrested, union pickets found their bail high, while growers usually were released on their own recognizance.

By the end of 1965, the three-month-old strike had had little result, and Chávez decided on the strategy of pitting Schenley Industries' national interests against its Kern County interests by organizing a nationwide boycott of Schenley. With this Alinsky-type strategy helping to focus national attention on the strike, sixteen NFWA organizers were sent to principal cities throughout the United States to set up boycott programs. From the standpoint of publicity, the most successful of these was in Boston, where a Boston Grape Party was staged, complete with lugs of grapes being dumped into Boston harbor.

Early in 1966, Chávez decided to march on the state capital at Sacramento, a move planned to involve state politicians in the Schenley boycott and to dramatize the grape strike. With about sixty NFWA members and supporters, on March 17 he began the 300-mile, 25-day walk which brought them to Sacramento on Easter Sunday. As they neared the capital, news reached the marchers that Schenley had agreed to accept the NFWA as the bargaining agent for its 450 vineyard workers, to use the NFWA instead of labor contractors, and to pay $1.75 per hour. Following this success, Christian Brothers, which earlier had suggested to other growers that collective bargaining had arrived in the vineyards, also signed an agreement with the NFWA. The giant DiGiorgio Fruit Corporation became the next obvious target of union activity.

In April 1966, negotiations were begun between DiGiorgio and the NFWA and continued into May. At this critical point, the NFWA suffered a setback, when the Teamsters Union announced that it would begin organizing farm workers in the San Joaquin Valley. Many growers, especially DiGiorgio, openly supported the Teamsters in preference to the NFWA. While discussions continued between the NFWA and representatives of DiGiorgio, the latter suddenly announced that a vote on union representation would be held within two days. Charging DiGiorgio with bad faith, Chávez had the NFWA removed from the ballot and DiGiorgio gave the teamsters a "sweetheart" contract. Political pressure from various organizations, especially MAPA, soon forced Governor Brown to send a labor relations expert, Ronald W. Haughton, to investigate Chávez' charges. The result was a recommendation for a new election. Both sides accepted this solution, and elections were rescheduled for August 30.

Teamsters Union organizers now opened a high-powered, full-scale recruitment campaign among DiGiorgio workers. Faced with this formidable opposition, César Chávez countered by merging NFWA with AWOC, thereby forming a new AFL-CIO organization, the United Farm Workers Organizing Committee (UFWOC). The ensuing campaign was bitterly fought, and the election resulted in a draw. The new UFWOC won the field workers by a vote of 530 to 331 but lost the shed workers by 43 to 94. Of approximately 1,800 persons eligible to vote, 1,017 voted; only 19 voted for no union, indicating the workers' interest in union representation, contrary to the growers' assertions. This victory in the field-worker election was merely the beginning of seven months of negotiation with DiGiorgio, finally concluded by a contract specifying a wage of $1.65 per hour, plus paid vacations and other benefits. This success was short-lived, since both Schenley and DiGiorgio subsequently sold their table-grape properties to other growers, and the contracts, which had applied only to grapes grown for the production of wine, did not transfer.

These first UFWOC successes affected agricultural areas outside California as well as within the state. In Texas, where wages of 40 cents per hour still persisted, between July and September 1966, more than 1,500 Mexican Americans marched from Rio Grande City on the southeastern border to the state capital at Austin (some 400 miles in the summer heat) to dramatize their demand that a special session of the state legislature be called to enact a $1.25-per-hour minimum-wage law. Although unsuccessful, this march took a first important step toward organization and unity in the socially backward Texas area.

Meanwhile, in California the struggle between UFWOC and the Teamsters continued. By mid-1967, the two groups compromised by dividing their spheres of activity; UFWOC had the right to organize field workers, while the Teamsters Union would organize warehousemen and cannery workers. This agreement persuaded other growers to allow union elections; and by the end of the year, UFWOC had eleven contracts, largely with wine-grape growers, including Gallo and Paul Masson.

In August, 1967, Giumarra Vineyards, Inc., one of California's largest table-grape growers, became the new target of UFWOC. Giumarra insisted that its workers were happy without a union; however, it increased its use of greencarders to work in the fields. As the Delano grape strike continued, with Giumarra as its principal focus, Chávez became concerned about a loss of spirit and a rising mood of violence among his followers. In February 1968, Chávez began to fast as a symbolic act of re-dedication to the principles of nonviolence. After twenty-five days his fast ended, but the struggle with Giumarra continued. The union now charged that scab greencarders formed a large percentage of Giumarra's work force and that the company habitually shipped grapes under other growers' labels. Giumarra's subsequent admission of using both greencarders and labels other than its own led to a table-grape boycott which spread all across the country and even abroad.

Meanwhile, in reaction to UFWOC pressures, the growers established the California Table Grape Commission in mid-1968 to promote their viewpoint; they also helped to organize a competitive (company union) labor group, the Agricultural Workers Freedom-to-Work Association. This organization, headed by Mexican Americans, was an unsuccessful ploy to combat the grape strike, the boycott, UFWOC, and César Chávez. More serious for the movement was the effect of the assassination of Senator Robert Kennedy and Chávez' fast-induced illness, which hospitalized him and limited his charismatic leadership role. In 1968, the strike and boycott inevitably became political issues; however, the election outcome in California indicated that voting patterns had scarcely been affected by the strike.

During the following year, boycott activities continued to spread in both the United States and Europe, but increased purchases of table grapes by the United States armed forces in part offset the boycott's effectiveness. In May 1969, some eighty

Coachella Valley grape growers were struck, and in June the strike was extended into Arizona, where UFWOC had been organizing workers for some time. In that same month, ten prominent Coachella growers began negotiations with UFWOC; these negotiations, however, broke down. Nearly a year later, though, in April 1970, three of the ten growers signed contracts with UFWOC, primarily through the mediation of the Bishops' Committee on Farm Labor Disputes, and in June, UFWOC won its most important victory up to that time, when it signed up Roberts Farms, one of the largest California citrus and nut growers, employing some 5,000 workers. The Roberts Farms victory led to a noticeably increased willingness on the part of growers to deal with UFWOC.

On July 29, 1970, the five-year struggle came to an "end" when Giumarra and twenty-five other Delano grape growers, producing about 50 percent of California table grapes, signed a three-year contract with UFWOC. This agreement, again mediated by the Bishops' Committee on Farm Labor Disputes, was hailed by both sides as the beginning of a new era in labor relations in California agriculture. During the ensuing victory celebration, Chávez announced that UFWOC's next target would be the Salinas Valley lettuce growers.

Whatever the outcome in the Salinas Valley, Chávez' efforts brought to an end the growers' assumptions that agricultural workers are a happy, contented lot who do not want the benefits of union organization. Furthermore, farm labor organization has changed the social and economic structure of California agriculture, and it can never return to its old patterns. (The farm workers may have won a Pyrrhic victory, however. One consequence of the union efforts is that farm laborers are being replaced by machines; between 1960 and 1969, the number of migrant farm workers in the United States decreased from 400,000 to 250,000. This decline in farm labor is, in part, a result of a trend toward mechanization that will continue, but the pace of its acceleration will probably be geared to the degree that unionization of farm workers is successful.)

While César Chávez was busy organizing farm workers in California, another Chicano activist named Reies López Tijerina attacked Anglo usurpation of lands in northern New Mexico, insisting that they be returned to their rightful owners. Born in Texas to a migrant family with eight children, Tijerina had little formal schooling. As a young man he was converted to a fundamentalist Protestant sect and, after a brief training period in a Texas bible school, went to California, where he began preaching. After 1951, he spent some time in Mexico, researching Spanish and Mexican land grants; later he moved to New Mexico, where he began to organize the separatist and millennial Alianza Federal de Mercedes (Federal Alliance of Land Grants) in 1963.

The basic tenet of the Alianza is that all problems of Chicanos derive from the loss of their lands to Anglo intruders. Tijerina had as his original primary objective the recovery of village common lands and creation of a Confederation of Free City-States in a socioeconomic atmosphere of rural utopian simplicity. However, other objectives such as ethnic identity have received increased stress in recent years. Tijerina believes that the United States government has failed to protect Spanish-speaking people from discrimination and insists that all public school teachers in New Mexico be fluent in Spanish as well as English, as required by the state constitution. Like Chávez' UFWOC, the Alianza is the product of intense personal leadership. Its uniqueness lies in its strong emotional religious flavor and a deep feeling of millennial purpose.

Within three years of its founding in 1963, the Alianza claimed 20,000 members, with its strongest support coming from New Mexico's northwestern Rio Arriba region. The charismatic and fiery Tijerina appeals most strongly to the more vocal elements in the Chicano community, especially youthful militants, and has on various occasions also solicited support for the Chicano cause from other minority groups.

Supported by his local following, Tijerina laid claim to millions of acres originally owned by Hispanic-Mexican communities and proposed to make this land the basis of a secessionist movement. This secessionism led directly to a military confrontation in the little northwestern New Mexican town of Tierra Amarilla. On June 5, 1967, a group of Tijerina's supporters burst into the courthouse in the town, looking for District Attorney Alfonso Sánchez and seeking to release fellow Alianza members who had been arrested earlier. During the onslaught, Tijerina's men released a barrage that wounded two deputies. Several hours later, having released eleven aliancistas from jail, Tijerina and his men abandoned the courthouse and left town with two hostages. There followed a massive manhunt with helicopters, two tanks, 200 state troopers and about 400 members of the National Guard. Eventually captured, Tijerina and other Alianza members were charged with attempted murder, kidnapping, and other crimes.

This dramatic occurrence in mid-1967 was the culmination of events that had been occurring since 1963, when Tijerina founded the Alianza. By the following year the Alianza claimed as members some 6,000 land-grant heirs in New Mexico, Colorado, Utah, Texas, and California, and it expounded a program which emphasized litigation and government action. The eventual failure of this approach led to frustration and violence. Some of Tijerina's followers, having little expectation of help from the United States, began posting "No Trespassing" signs on former village grant lands in a revival of the Mano Negra scare of the late 1800s.

In 1966 came a sharp change in the Alianza and particularly in Tijerina's leadership role. Returning from a trip to Spain and claiming to have researched early Spanish land grants in Seville archives, he began to develop both a cadre of leaders and a more aggressive, action-oriented program. To dramatize his goal of regaining the land and to create a feeling of group identity, Tijerina organized a sixty-two mile march from Albuquerque to the state capitol at Santa Fe over the July 4 weekend. Upon arrival at Santa Fe this large group presented Governor Jack Campbell with a petition asking support for a bill to investigate the land-claims issue.

This dramatic appeal proved fruitless. Believing that only an act of civil disobedience could focus attention on their causes, in October aliancistas attempted to take over part of the Kit Carson National Forest, which they claimed as their own. Their declaration of the Republic of San Joaquín del Rio de Chama was ignored by Forest Service rangers, who eventually tried to force them to leave the campground. In the process the rangers were seized by Alianza members. This chain of events led to the arrest of Tijerina and four aliancistas.

It was at this juncture that the courthouse raid took place. It resulted in the first national awareness of the Alianza movement and, more important, in its recognition by other Chicano groups. "Corky" Gonzales praised the course pursued by the Alianza, and both Bert Corona of MAPA and César Chávez made trips to Albuquerque—Chávez declaring that if he lived in New Mexico he would be a member of the Alianza.

While awaiting trial on indictments stemming from the courthouse raid, Tijerina and four other members of the Alianza were tried on the earlier charges of assaulting the rangers. In November, Tijerina was found guilty and given a two-year prison sentence, which he appealed to a higher court, leaving him free on bail. Soon thereafter a period of violence ensued, climaxing in the murder of the chief prosecution witness against Tijerina in the courthouse raid, jailer Eulogio Salazar.

Early in 1968, Tijerina was invited to participate in the Poor People's March on Washington by Dr. Martin Luther King, Jr. Although he and his aliancistas took part in the march, Tijerina quarreled with the black leaders, charging them with failure to consult Chicanos regarding overall policies of the Poor People's demonstration. This conflict was reconciled by giving Chicanos a role in the march, but it nevertheless left an aftertaste of bitterness.

While in Washington Tijerina used the occasion to lecture State Department officials on his interpretation of the Treaty of Guadalupe Hidalgo, especially as it related to land-grant guarantees. Returning to New Mexico, he laid plans to run for governor but was ruled ineligible because of his conviction the previous November. Meanwhile, his trial on kidnapping and lesser charges arising from the courthouse raid was held. Tijerina, conducting his own defense, won acquittal in December of 1968. Following his exoneration, the Alianza came under extensive attack from many quarters; in one instance shots were fired into Alianza headquarters in what was possibly an attempt on Tijerina's life. Nevertheless, his courtroom victory led to renewed and expanded support for his organization which had earlier appeared to be on the decline.

In February 1969, however, Tijerina and the Alianza suffered a setback when the Circuit Court of Appeals upheld his two-year prison sentence, and in October the United States Supreme Court turned down his subsequent appeal of this decision. A further blow came in January 1970, when he was given a one-to-five- and a two-to-ten-year jail sentence to run concurrently on charges arising out of the 1967 courthouse raid.

Shortly after entering prison, Tijerina resigned the Alianza presidency, and Santiago Tapia y Anaya was elected to take his place.

A split developed in the Alianza in 1970, and the organization, never tightly structured and now lacking Tijerina's leadership, suffered some deterioration. From prison Tijerina attempted to provide direction for the Alianza, and he wrote a lengthy prison letter in which he restated his belief in the righteousness of "la causa."

In July 1971, Tijerina was released from prison after serving two years; parole was granted on condition that he hold no official position in the Alianza. Bereft of his leadership, the Alianza continues its demand that millions of acres of grant lands be returned by the federal government; however, now its activities are largely limited to pamphleteering, filing law suits, and issuing statements to the press.

Meanwhile, to the north of Tierra Amarilla, "Corky" Gonzales, a strong proponent of Chicano nationalism, was busily organizing another civil-rights group. In 1965, he founded the Crusade for Justice in Denver, with headquarters in an old church building. A former well-known boxer, Democratic political leader, and official of the antipoverty program in the Southwest, he abandoned these roles to lead a movement to create a Chicano society based on humanism rather than materialism. He established the Crusade as a vehicle by which the objectives and priorities of the Chicano movement could be articulated and carried out. Basically a civil-rights organization, its demands are similar to those of other militant groups and include reformation of the police and courts, better housing, relevant education for Chicanos, greater and more diverse employment opportunities, and land reform.

Gonzales, well known as the author of the epic poem "Yo

Soy Joaquín," appeals strongly to Chicano youth and teaches that attainment of the Crusade's goals can be achieved only through an adequate power base. The Crusade for Justice builds Chicano identity by providing to its members a wide variety of social services with a Chicano perspective—educational, legal, medical, and financial. The slogan of the movement, "Venceremos" (We shall overcome) reflects its commitment and cultural awareness.

The poem "Yo Soy Joaquín" dramatizes the liberation of Chicanos from the usual goals of Anglo society and is indicative of the author's intellectual vision of a new cultural future for la raza. Dedicated to creating this new reality for Chicanos, the Crusade has begun to implement his ideas in a small way by establishing in Denver a school, with classes on all levels from kindergarten through college. Associated with it are such facilities as an art gallery, a library, a gym, a nursery, a community center, and a community cafeteria—all offering Chicanos a variety of social services. Gonzales has proposed forming a Congress of Aztlán to extend the idea of community programs in health, education, and legal services to Mexican Americans in the entire Southwest. The Crusade is a strongly nationalistic movement, as is indicated by his proposal to appeal to the United Nations for a plebescite to be held in the Southwest to determine whether la raza might not prefer independence from the United States.

In 1968, Gonzales joined with Reies Tijerina in leading a Chicano contingent in the Poor People's March on Washington. While there, he issued his "Plan of the Barrio," calling for housing that would meet Chicano cultural needs; for education, basically in Spanish, that would be based on the same concept of community; for barrio businesses that would be owned within the community; and for reforms in landholding, with emphasis on restitution of pueblo lands.

However, undoubtedly the most important contribution of "Corky" Gonzales has been the instituting of an annual Chicano Youth Liberation Conference. Initiated in March 1969, in Denver, the Chicano Youth Liberation Conference has brought together about 2,000 representatives of more than one hundred different Chicano youth groups each year since then. At that first meeting the assembled delegates voted overwhelmingly to adopt El Plan Espiritual de Aztlán, calling for Chicanos to work together in order to achieve their common goals by a revival of the legendary Aztec homeland of Aztlán. The Plan calls for a rebirth of Chicano nationalism, for a revival of cultural values, for implementation of the objectives of the Plan of the Barrio, and for the creation of a new political party. The Crusade, with its Plan of Aztlán, appeals strongly to Chicano youth and is the best example in the movement of the desire for self-determination based on a philosophy of nationalism.

Far to the southeast, in Crystal City, Texas, the site of an earlier stalemate in the development of Chicano aspirations, the politically astute José Angel Gutiérrez, youngest of these four leaders, was about to play a determining role to the Plan's objective of creating a new political party. Gutiérrez, founder and former state chairman of the Mexican American Youth Organization and a strong political realist, became convinced that Chicanos could never achieve power to control their own destinies by being part of either of the traditional political parties. Following Saul Alinsky's idea that equality can exist only when both sides have power and transforming his beliefs into action early in 1970, he established a new party, La Raza Unida. La Raza Unida has as its initial goal complete Chicano control—politically, economically, and socially—of some twenty counties in south Texas in which Chicanos have a large majority.

La Raza Unida took the position that Chicanos needed their

own separate political organization in order to achieve this and other goals. The preamble to the Raza Unida program states the decision of "The People of La Raza . . . to reject the existing political parties of our oppressor and take it upon ourselves form La Raza Unida Party which will serve as a unifying force in our struggle for self-determination."

Although basically a political party, La Raza Unida is also something more, as indicated by the last part of the above quotation. Its leaders envision it as an ethnic institution that will break the cycle of Chicano repression by organizing community classes as well as political groups, by launching massive registration drives, by providing draft counseling, and by supplying economic expertise and support to Chicano chambers of commerce. They see La Raza Unida not as means of achieving power in order to enter the mainstream of American society but as a way of safeguarding their bicultural and bilingual uniqueness. With the creation of La Raza Unida, the Chicano impetus toward greater self-determination reached a new intensity.

Acting on the basis of Raza Unida ideology, in April 1970, Gutiérrez and two other Chicanos ran as Raza Unida candidates in school-board elections at Crystal City and won handily, thereby creating for the first time a Mexican American majority on the school board. One of the first acts of the new board was to elect Gutiérrez board president. Under Gutiérrez' leadership, the board established a bilingual education curriculum, initiated a federal free-lunch program, and indicated clearly that discrimination against or neglect of Mexican American students would not be tolerated. These and other innovations of the board led to considerable Anglo reaction and resistance, ranging from calling Gutiérrez an outside agitator and a Communist to a movement of withholding payment of school taxes. Undaunted by these attacks, La Raza Unida in the spring of

1971 ran two more candidates for the school board, this time not against Anglos but against vendidos (Mexican American "sell-outs"), and once again it was victorious, thereby guaranteeing Raza Unida control of the board for several years to come.

Following this second school board victory, Raza Unida candidates also swept city council elections in Carrizo Springs and Cotulla, towns near Crystal City. These victories gave clear proof to Chicanos that the ballot box is a feasible route to power; they also caused conservative Texas Congressmen Henry Gonzales and Eligio de la Garza to attack La Raza Unida as reverse racist and un-American.

La Raza Unida has impressed veteran Chicano leaders like Bert Corona of MAPA, who on one occasion described it as the only route for the Mexican American, and "Corky" Gonzales, whose organization sponsored many candidates in the Colorado elections of 1970 under the banner of La Raza Unida. Development of La Raza Unida has progressed furthest in Texas, where it has been successful in winning school board and city council elections in several south Texas counties.

As a result of Raza Unida's vitality and commitment to political action, Crystal City has become a symbol to Chicanos of strength through unity. Through the capable leadership of Gutiérrez, Chicanos from varied backgrounds and from many communities of the Southwest and throughout the United States have come to Crystal City and worked to further Raza Unida goals. The political apathy that formerly was noted throughout the lower Rio Grande region is disappearing. In Crystal City itself there is a new dynamism, with dozens of projects related to housing, education, community organization, migrant workers, legal aid, sewage and water service, street paving, library improvements, medical clinics, mutual-aid societies, urban renewal, credit unions—even a Mexican Chamber of Commerce—all developing at once.

From Crystal City, the spirit of La Raza Unida has already spread over the Southwest, and branches are being organized not only in many Texas counties with Chicano majorities but also in Colorado, New Mexico, Arizona, and especially in California, where a massive drive to get the party on the 1972 ballot is under way. José Angel Gutiérrez sees La Raza Unida as becoming a serious threat to local and state Democratic and Republican candidates throughout the Southwest, especially as it gains members and momentum. La Raza Unida, Gutiérrez believes, will provide solutions to a century-old problem—the acceptance by Anglos of Mexican Americans and their culture.

Thus, during the decade of the 1960s, these four organizations—UFWOC, the Alianza, the Crusade for Justice, and La Raza Unida—have attracted support and have received national exposure as a result of successful activist programs. Differing somewhat in their approaches to ultimate objectives, they nevertheless all have the same goal—self-determination for Chicanos through equality based on economic and political power. Another common characteristic is their strong appeal to Mexican nationalism, as indicated by Chávez' use of the Virgin of Guadalupe, the patron saint of Mexico, and "Corky" Gonzales' proposal of an independent nation of Aztlán. In similar fashion, Gutiérrez has used Chicano nationalism as a basis for forming La Raza Unida Party in Texas, and the aliancistas of Reies Tijerina have proclaimed La República de San Joaquín del Río de Chama as a separatist approach to self-determination.

Today Mexican Americans are still segmented into many groups, each with its own interpretation of what the Mexican American is and where he is going. The Chicano community continues divided, with unifying elements of ethnicity and cultural heritage frequently being sidetracked by such mundane issues as economic position, social status, and professional attainment. Differences of opinion concerning means to the achievement of civil and political rights continue to plague the Chicano movement; however, conflicts within its leadership usually concern tactics, not goals. A broad consensus exists among Mexican Americans that they want many specific sociopolitical and economic benefits that other Americans enjoy.

Mexican American citizens today still face many problems. Health conditions within their communities are still poor, and health services continue to be inadequate; in housing, the picture is similar, although there has been some improvement. In education, Chicanos are still treated as second class in too many areas, and public schools continue to be unsuccessful in furthering the acculturation of Mexicans. Of all minorities, only American Indians have a lower median income than Mexican Americans. Economically, Chicanos in California enjoy the most favorable position, while those in Texas are least well off. But in whatever state, they continue to earn less in all occupational categories than do Anglo-Americans, by between 20 to 40 percent; there has been considerable improvement since World War II, but much more progress needs to be made.

Of critical concern, however, is the rate of change in ameliorating the conditions of Chicanos. To rectify the tremendous inequalities experienced by Mexican Americans in our society and to satisfy vociferous demands being made today by Mexican Americans for a greater share in American political, economic, and social benefits, the process of change must be greatly accelerated. This can be accomplished only if Mexican American leaders successfully articulate the common aspirations of la raza and if they and Anglo-American leaders organize and mobilize the resources, human and material, needed to achieve these aspirations.

# Bibliographic Essay

Although materials resulting from research into the experience of Mexicans and Mexican Americans in the Southwest exist to some degree, there are relatively few published accounts of the history of the Chicano since 1848. Widespread interest in Mexican American history is only a decade old, and virtually nonexistent are historical publications written from a Chicano perspective.

In the past, students and scholars concerned with Mexicans in the United States have concentrated their efforts in areas of sociology and education, frequently with a lamentable lack of objectivity. Historians, for the most part, have neglected

Mexican Americans both in broad historical coverage and in monographic detail; when they have been mentioned in general United States histories, typically the viewpoint has been negative.

This bibliographic essay does not purport to offer an exhaustive list of historical works on Mexican Americans but rather to make available to the reader a useful, selective, and critical list of major works, ranging from the scholarly to those of general interest. Selection has been made on the basis of availability, area of coverage, and scholarly worth. These selections will provide persons interested in pursuing the study of Mexican Americans in greater depth with additional sources.

Up to this time, the scant handful of general histories of the Mexican American have been of two varieties. In the first category are brief works aimed at grade school or junior high school level, usually with heavy emphasis on Mexican background, followed by a short history of la raza. The best of this genre is that of Rudy Acuña, *A Mexican American Chronicle* (New York: American Book Co., 1971). The other works are mostly of pamphlet size, largely descriptive, sociological, and educational, but including some history; a good example is Ernesto Galarza et al, *Mexican-Americans in the Southwest* (Santa Barbara, Calif.: McNally & Loftin, 1969). Carey McWilliams' pioneering work, *North from Mexico* (New York: J. B. Lippincott Co., 1949), today more than thirty years after its first publication remains a valuable (although journalistic and episodic) history of the Mexican in the United States to the end of World War II. An important work complementing McWilliams, that of Donald W. Meinig, *Southwest: Three Peoples in Geographical Change, 1600–1970* (New York: Oxford University Press, 1971) is an outstanding study of the historical interrelationship of man and geography as it affected the Indian, Mexican, and Anglo in the Southwest. Another recent publication of considerable value to historians is that of Joan W. Moore and Alfredo Cuéllar, *Mexican Americans* (Englewood Cliffs, N.J.: Prentice-Hall, 1970), which contains a great deal of history, especially in areas of education, politics, and community, but which basically looks at Mexican Americans in the United States from a sociological viewpoint.

A recent important addition to the field of Mexican American studies is that of Leo Grebler, Joan W. Moore, and Ralph C. Guzmán, *The Mexican-American People* (New York: The Free Press, 1970). This outstanding interdisciplinary resource book is the product of the Mexican-American Study Project, begun in 1963 at the University of California at Los Angeles under a Ford Foundation grant. Preceded by eleven published book-length Advance Reports on various topics, also of great value to students of Mexican American history, the final published distillation of this study includes an excellent bibliography of books, pamphlets, government publications, and periodical articles.

Interest in the history of the Mexican American has led to the publication in the past five years of a number of source books. The first of these, that of Julian Samora, *La Raza: Forgotten Americans* (Notre Dame: University of Notre Dame Press, 1966) is a collection of seven articles by authorities in various fields. A work by Feliciano Rivera, *A Mexican American Source Book* (Menlo Park, Calif.: Educational Consulting Associates, 1970) is designed to aid social studies teachers with an historical outline and supplementary materials. Manuel Servín's, *The Mexican Americans: An Awakening Minority* (Beverly Hills, Calif.: Glencoe Press, 1970), although criticized by some activists, remains an important collection of academically oriented historical articles. *A Documentary History of the Mexican Americans,* edited by Wayne Moquin (New York: Praeger, 1971) is an extensive collection of contemporary historical materials dating from the sixteenth century to the present.

The foregoing suggestions cover general works in Mexican American history; specific titles related to the five broad historical periods defined in the introduction of this work follow. The first period is subdivided into two general categories: the Amerindian background and the colonial Hispanic-Mexican experience. There exists a wealth of material dealing with the Aztec and Maya civilizations. Ignacio Bernal, *Mexico Before Cortez: Art, History and Legend* (Garden City, N.Y.: Doubleday & Co., 1963) is a concise history of Aztec and Toltec civilizations by a well-known Mexican anthropologist. C. A. Burland, *The Gods of Mexico* (New York: Capricorn Books, 1968) deals with the religions and philosophies of pre-Columbian meso-American peoples. Alfonso Caso, *The Aztecs: People of the Sun* (Norman: University of Oklahoma Press, 1958) presents an interpretation of symbolism in Mexican religion and world view by an outstanding authority. Harold S. Gladwin, *A History of the Ancient Southwest* (Portland, Maine: Bond Wheelright Co., 1957) is an excellent account of early man in the Southwest by a leading archeologist. Miguel León-Portilla, *The Broken Spears* (Boston: Beacon Press, 1962) offers the only collection in English of Indian accounts of the Mexican conquest. Octavio Paz, *The Labyrinth of Solitude* (New York: Grove Press, 1961) presents a controversial series of reflections on themes relating to Mexican life and thought including that of machismo. Frederick A. Peterson, *Ancient Mexico* (New York: G. P. Putnam's Sons, 1959) is probably the best one-volume history and description of pre-Columbian civilizations in Mexico. Samuel Ramos, *Profile of Man and Culture in Mexico* (Austin: University of Texas Press, 1962) furnishes an analysis of Mexican culture and character through history by an outstanding Mexican phi-

losopher. George C. Vaillant, *The Aztecs of Mexico* (Garden
City, N.Y.: Doubleday & Co., 1962) is perhaps the best-known
anthropological work on Aztec civilization in English. Eric
Wolf, *Sons of the Shaking Earth* (Chicago: University of Chicago Press, 1959) affords an outstanding account of Middle
American and Mexican history, especially of early man, by a
leading contemporary anthropologist.

Among the many works dealing with the colonial period in
Mexico, the following have special pertinence for Mexican
American history. Herbert E. Bolton, *The Spanish Borderlands* (New Haven: Yale University Press, 1921) provides a
popular account of the expansion of the northern frontier of
Mexico by the outstanding scholar on the area. Jack Forbes,
*Apache, Navaho, and Spaniard* (Norman: University of Oklahoma Press, 1960) puts forward a more recent interpretation
of Indian-Spanish relationships, finding the Spanish-Mexican
settlement a disruptive force. Cleve Hallenbeck, *Land of the
Conquistadores* (Caldwell, Idaho: Caxton Printers, 1950)
gives a complete picture of the history of colonial New Mexico.
Herbert E. Bolton, *Rim of Christendom* (New York: Macmillan Co., 1936) excels as a study of the Spanish-Mexican occupation of Arizona. Cleve Hallenbeck, *Spanish Missions of
the Old Southwest* (New York: Doubleday & Co., 1926) has
good material on the missions of the Southwest and on mission
life. Paul Horgan, *Conquistadores in North American History*
(New York: Farrar, Straus & Giroux, 1963) presents a vigorously written popular history of early Spanish exploration
northward from Mexico. Philip W. Powell, *Soldiers, Indians,
and Silver* (Berkeley: University of California Press, 1952)
affords a scholarly account of the advance of frontier settlement in northern Mexico up to 1600. Lesley B. Simpson, *Many
Mexicos* (Berkeley: University of California Press, 1967) contains an excellent synthesis of the Mexican colonial period by

an outstanding and witty author. Edward H. Spicer, *Cycles of Conquest* (Tucson: University of Arizona Press, 1961) contributes a well-documented and outstanding history of interrelations and conflict among the three major peoples who met in the Southwest: the Indian, Mexican, and Anglo. Marc Simmons, *Spanish Government in New Mexico* (Albuquerque: University of New Mexico Press, 1968) describes governmental institutions and practices in the Spanish period. Irving B. Richman, *California under Spain and Mexico, 1535–1857* (Boston: Houghton Mifflin Co., 1911), despite its age, is still of great value to the serious student. John A. Berger, *The Franciscan Missions of California* (Garden City, N.Y.: Doubleday & Co., 1948), although somewhat summary, is perhaps the most readable account of the founding of the California missions and life in them; there is a chapter on each of the twenty-one missions. Felix Riesenberg, Jr., *The Golden Road: The Story of California's Mission Trail* (New York: McGraw-Hill Book Co., 1962) supplies a highly readable popular history of the California missions.

Except for works on the Texas independence movement and the Mexican War, relatively little has been written on the northern frontier during the Mexican period. Eugene C. Barker, *Mexico and Texas, 1821–1835* (New York: Russell and Russell, 1965) is a reissue of a basic work by the leading authority on Anglo colonization in Texas. Hodding Carter, *Doomed Road of Empire* (New York: McGraw-Hill Book Co., 1971) offers a popular account of Texas history from the 1500s to the Mexican War and is valuable for information on José Bernardo Gutiérrez. Robert G. Clelland, *The Cattle on a Thousand Hills* (San Marino, Calif.: Huntington Library, 1941) gives a picture of social and economic development in southern California. Odie B. Faulk, *The Land of Many Frontiers* (New York: Oxford University Press, 1968) has two chapters on the Mexican period. George P. Hammond, *The Treaty of Guadalupe Hidalgo, 1848* (Berkeley: University of California Press, 1949) offers a thorough account of the treaty from an Anglo viewpoint. Paul Horgan, *Great River: The Rio Grande in North American History* (New York: Holt, Rinehart & Winston, 1954) is a two-volume Pulitzer Prize-winning history of the Southwest, with special emphasis on the Texas area. Samuel H. Lowrie, *Culture Conflict in Texas, 1821–1835* (New York: Columbia University Press, 1932) explains the cultural bases of conflict; especially the slavery issue, between Anglo colonists and Mexicans. Lynn Perrigo, *The American Southwest* (New York: Holt, Rinehart & Winston, 1971) surveys in panorama the peoples and cultures which make up the Southwest. Carlos E. Castaneda, translator, *The Mexican Side of the Texan Revolution* (Dallas: P. L. Turner Co., 1928) incorporates various contemporary accounts of that struggle including Santa Anna's. José M. Barcena, *Recuerdos de la invasión norteamericana, 1841–1848* (Mexico City, 1947) is an outstanding and complete history of the Mexican War as viewed from Mexico. Ralph E. Twitchell, *The Conquest of Santa Fe* (Truchas, N.M.: Tate Gallery, 1967; reissue) furnishes details of the American occupation of New Mexico.

As a result of the scarcity of monographic historical materials on the period of cultural conflict from 1848 to 1900, a number of state histories which have good chapters dealing with this period have been included in the following list. Warren A. Beck, *New Mexico: A History of Four Centuries* (Norman: University of Oklahoma Press, 1962) provides a broad survey and is especially valuable for its examination of cultural impact in this period. Louise A. Clappe, *The Shirley Letters from the California Mines* (New York: Alfred A. Knopf, 1949) imparts an excellent contemporary picture of Mexicans during the California gold rush. Clarence C. Clendening, *Blood on the Border* (New York: MacMillan Co., 1969) covers the entire period from 1848 to 1920 and includes material on Juan Cortina. Harvey Fergusson, *Rio Grande* (New York: Alfred A. Knopf, 1933) is a good journalistic history of the New Mexican area from the time of its colonization to about 1900. Erna Fergusson, *New Mexico: A Pageant of Three Peoples* (New York: Alfred A. Knopf, 1951) provides an excellent popular history of the New Mexican area, with historical information on sheep-raising. Robert F. Heizer and Alan J. Almquist, *The Other Californians* (Berkeley: University of California Press, 1971) describes racial and other prejudices under Spain, Mexico, and the United States up to the end of World War I. William E. Hollon, *The Southwest: Old and New* (New York: Alfred A. Knopf, 1961) contributes a good general coverage of southwestern history from its beginning until today. Joseph H. Jackson, *Bad Company* (New York: Harcourt, Brace & Co., 1949) has special interest for its detailed account of the Murieta story. Howard R. Lamar has written an excellent political history of the Southwest in *Far Southwest, 1846–1912: A Territorial History* (New York: W. W. Norton & Co., 1970), which includes material on the Santa Fe ring. Tom Lea, *The King Ranch* (Boston: Little, Brown & Co., 1957; two volumes) describes Mexican influence on the Anglo in the Southwest; volume 2 contains material on Cortina. Leonard Pitt, *The Decline of the Californios: A Social History of the Spanish-Speaking Californians, 1846–1890* (Berkeley: University of California Press, 1966) is an excellent pioneering monograph, one of the few written from a Mexican American viewpoint. While not a piece of historical writing, Cecil Robinson, *With the Ears of Strangers: The Mexican in American Literature* (Tucson: University of Arizona Press, 1963) furnishes invaluable insights into the history of Anglo attitudes and the development of stereotypes. Walter P. Webb, *The Texas Rangers* (Austin: University of Texas Press, 1965), in addition to describing the history of an agency intimately connected with Mexican American history, also supplies material on Cortina.

Immigration and organizational efforts dominate the fourth period, a time of resurgence from 1900 to 1940. *Mexicans in California, Report of Governor C. Young's Mexican Fact-Finding Committee* (originally published in 1930; San Francisco: R & E Research Associates, 1970; reissue) is an invaluable source of information on Mexican Americans in California during the 1920s. Clark A. Chambers, *California Farm Organizations* (Berkeley: University of California Press, 1952) covers the period from 1929 to 1940 and offers excellent material on agricultural labor unrest. James D. Cockcroft, *Intellectual Precursors of the Mexican Revolution* (Austin: University of Texas Press, 1969) includes information on the interaction of Mexican Americans and Mexican revolutionaries in the first decade of this century. Manuel Gamio, an outstanding Mexican social anthropologist, in his *Mexican Immigration to the United States* (Chicago: University of Chicago Press, 1930) deals with the origins of Mexican immigrants and their treatment in the United States. Mary K. Rak, *Border Patrol* (Boston: Houghton Mifflin Co., 1938) discusses this government agency's role in controlling the Mexican border. George I. Sánchez, an early pioneer in Mexican American studies, documents the results of the clash of two cultures in his *Forgotten People: A Study of New Mexicans* (Albuquerque: University of New Mexico Press, 1940), which reports the plight of the nuevo mexicano. Paul S. Taylor's works on Mexican immigration are outstanding; his *An American-Mexican Frontier: Nueces County, Texas* (Chapel Hill: University of North Carolina Press, 1934) describes cultural interaction in southern Texas, including border clashes at the turn of the present century. His *Mexican Labor in the United States* (Berkeley: University of California Press, 1928–1934; six volumes) covers the problems of Mexican labor in areas of Colorado, California, Texas, Illinois, and Pennsylvania.

Although lacking any general survey works, the contemporary period of Chicano history abounds in monographs on various aspects. Thomas P. Carter, *Mexican Americans in School* (New York: College Entrance Examinations Board, 1970), describes the problems and neglect of Chicano students in American education. Raul Morin, *Among the Valiant* (Los Angeles: Borden Publishing Co., 1963) recounts Mexican American military experiences during World War II and the resulting rise in levels of expectations. Pauline R. Kibbe, *Latin Americans in Texas* (Albuquerque: University of New Mexico Press, 1946) describes problems of discrimination against Mexican Americans in Texas based on the author's observation and involvement. Truman E. Moore, *The Slaves We Rent* (New York: Random House, 1965) includes materials on the migratory labor system and attempts to improve conditions of migrant laborers. Ernesto Galarza, *Merchants of Labor: The Mexican Bracero Story* (San José, Calif.: The Rosicrucian Press, 1965) deals with the bracero in California, emphasizing the period from 1950 to the end of the program. There are a number of works on César Chávez and the Delano grape strike. Mark Day, *Forty Acres: Cesar Chavez and the Farm Workers* (New York: Praeger, 1971) gives an insider's personal view of the strike. It includes a valuable chapter on the often forgotten role of Filipino workers in the Delano affair. John G. Dunne, *Delano: The Story of the California Grape Strike* (New York: Farrar, Straus & Giroux, 1967; revised 1971) reports an eyewitness account of the strike and its background by a liberal journalist. Peter Matthiessen, *Sal Si Puedes: Cesar Chavez and the New American Revolution* (New York: Random House, 1969) puts a heavy emphasis on Chávez and his role in the Delano strike. Eugene Nelson, *Huelga* (Delano Calif.: Farm Workers Press, 1966) presents the strikers' side of the first 100 days of the Delano strike. On Reies Tijerina the best work available is that of Richard Gardner, *Grito* (Indianapolis: Bobbs-Merrill, 1970), which probes all aspects of the events in Rio Arriba County. Peter Nabokov, *Tijerina and the Courthouse Raid* (Albuquerque: University of New Mexico Press, 1969) is more inclusive than the title indicates and contributes material on the loss of village lands in New Mexico to agencies of the federal government. Stan Steiner, *La Raza: The Mexican American* (New York: Harper & Row, 1969) imparts an impressionistic view of la raza today, with special emphasis on Chávez, Tijerina, and "Corky" Gonzales.

In recent years, a number of bibliographies related to Mexican Americans have appeared. These fall into two broad categories: those listing materials in particular libraries and those of a more general nature. Among the first group are *Chicano Bibliography* (University of Utah Libraries, 1971) and *Bibliografía de Materiales Tocante el Chicano* (San José State College Library in coöperation with the Mexican American Graduate Studies Program, 1971). Included in the second category are Ralph Guzmán, *Revised Bibliography: With a Bibliographical Essay*, Advance Report No. 3, Mexican American Study Project (Los Angeles: University of California, 1967); *A Guide to Materials Relating to Persons of Mexican Heritage in the United States* (Washington: Inter-Agency Committee on Mexican American Affairs, 1969); Luis Nogales, ed., *The Mexican American: A Selected and Annotated Bibliography* (Stanford: Stanford University Press, 1971; second edition); Ernie Barrios, *Bibliografía de Aztlán: An Annotated*

*Chicano Bibliography* (San Diego: California State College, 1971); and Matt S. Meier and Feliciano Rivera, *A Selective Bibliography for the Study of Mexican American History* (San José: San José State College, 1971).

# Index

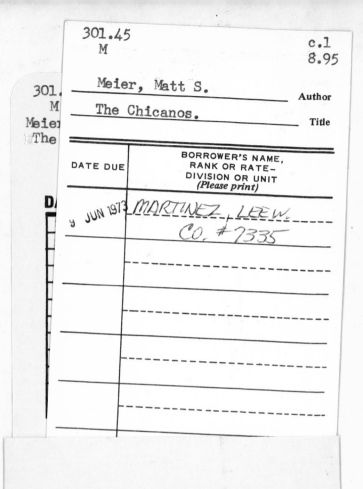